Rethinking Security in Post-Cold War Europe

edited by William Park and G. Wyn Rees

LONGMAN
ıdon and New York

Addison Wesley Lo
Edinburgh Gate
Harlow
Essex CM20 2JE
United Kingdom
and Associated Companies throughout the world

Published in the United States of America
by Addison Wesley Longman, New York

© Addison Wesley Longman Limited 1998

First published 1998

ISBN 0 582 30376 1

British Library Cataloguing-in-Publication Data

A catalogue record for this book is available from the British Library

Library of Congress Cataloging-in-Publication Data
Rethinking security in post-Cold War Europe / edited by William Park
and G. Wyn Rees.
    p.   cm.
  Includes bibliographical references and index.
  ISBN 0-582-30376-1 (pbk.)
  1. Europe—Politics and government—1989–   2. National security-
-Europe. 3. Europe—Defenses. I. Park, William, 1951–
II. Rees, G. Wyn, 1963–
D2009.R48   1998
320.94—dc21   97–39093
                                                              CIP

Set by 7 in 10/11 Times
Produced through Longman Malaysia, TCP

CONTENTS

LIST OF CONTRIBUTORS

Clive Archer is Research Professor in the Department of Politics and Philosophy at Manchester Metropolitan University. He has published extensively on security issues, particularly relating to northern Europe. He is the author, with Fiona Butler, of *The European Union Structure and Process* (second edition, Pinter 1996).

Andrew Cottey lectures in the Department of Peace Studies, University of Bradford. He has recently spent a year at the Institute for East–West Studies, Warsaw, and is the author of *East-Central Europe after the Cold War; Poland, the Czech Republic, Slovakia and Hungary in Search of Security* (Macmillan/St Martin's 1995).

Trine Flockhart is Senior Lecturer in Politics and International Relations at the University of Sunderland. She is the editor of a volume entitled *From Vision to Reality: Implementing Europe's New Security Order* (Westview forthcoming).

James Gow is Reader at the Department of War Studies, King's College, London. He is well known for his writing on Yugoslavia in particular, and his most recent book is *Triumph of the Lack of Will: International Diplomacy and the Yugoslav War* (Hurst Columbia University Press 1997).

Adrian Hyde-Price lectures at the Institute for German Studies at the University of Birmingham. He has published widely on European security issues, and his most recent book is *The International Politics of East Central Europe* (Manchester University Press 1996).

Paul Latawski is an Associate Fellow at the Royal United Services Institute and a lecturer at the School of Slavonic and East European Studies, London University. He has published widely on central European security issues, including *The Security Road to Europe: The Visegrad Four* (RUSI 1994).

William Park is Principal Lecturer at the Joint Services Command and Staff College, Bracknell. In addition to a book, *Defending the West; a*

History of NATO (Wheatsheaf 1986), he has published a number of chapters and articles on NATO. He has also just completed a chapter on NATO's role in implementing Europe's new security order, for publication in a volume edited by Trine Flockhart.

G. Wyn Rees lectures in International Relations at the University of Leicester. He researches in the field of European security and recently held a NATO Research Fellowship. His most recent book is *Anglo-American Approaches to Alliance Security* (Macmillan 1996) and he has a forthcoming book on the Western European Union with Westview Press.

Claire Spencer is Deputy Director of the Centre for Defence Studies, King's College, London. She has published widely on Mediterranean security and the Maghreb, including an Adelphi Paper in 1993, and she has recently written a piece on confidence-building measures in the Mediterranean region for *Mediterranean Politics* (forthcoming).

CHAPTER 1

Introduction: rethinking European security

WILLIAM PARK

The transformation of the European security order associated with the demise of the Cold War created the opportunity, and some argued the necessity, to develop a security architecture more specifically suited to the 'wider Europe's' circumstances (Miall 1994b). If a truly 'common European home' was to emerge, then common European institutions would be needed both to represent and to manage it. The most entrenched institutions, however, were the North Atlantic Treaty Organisation (NATO) and the European Union (EU).[1] The very fact that these bodies survived while not only the Warsaw Pact but also the Soviet Union itself disappeared did more than symbolise the West's Cold War victory, for their continued existence also seemed to imply, even threaten, the maintenance of a divided Europe. While the states of the western half of the continent remained anchored into secure, stable and even thriving structures, the former communist states of the East seemed to have been cut adrift. Unless more coherent and continent-wide arrangements were made which better reflected or even explicitly encouraged the unity of the 'new' Europe, the euphoria which greeted the collapse of the very visible dividing wall of the Cold War could be replaced by resentment at the emergence of a less tangible but hardly less real wall separating the rich and secure in the West from the poor and insecure in the East (Gogolewska, Dorina and Osolnik 1997).[2] In such a Europe, perhaps the main impact of the collapse of totalitarianism in the East would be that the region's inhabitants would now be afforded a clearer view of what it was they were being denied.

However, perhaps we should not be too surprised that the dominant trend in the post-Cold War restructuring of Europe's political landscape has been the opening of the West to incorporate the former East, rather than the dismantling of the West's institutional structures to create an entirely new architecture. In this light, the rather unceremonious absorption of the German Democratic Republic by the Federal Republic (Kelleher 1992) could be seen as just the first manifestation of a broader and more complex post-Cold War European phenomenon. This process of western 'expansion' is still in its very earliest stages, has many facets to it, and its ultimate outcome remains unclear and uncertain. Indeed, it is a process which might not only be of long duration, but which might never be quite completed. Something had to be done, hope had to be offered, and the West as it had been shaped during the Cold War era was in a position and was obliged to respond. But a reaction is not a plan, a response not the same thing as an objective, and quite where and how far the West might be prepared to go remains unresolved (Wallace 1997).

The legacy

As we ponder the reshaping of Europe, and particularly its security arrangements, we should remind ourselves how complex a phenomenon the Cold War was in reality (Gaddis 1989). It would be both simplistic and unhelpful if we were to remember it as an absolute division of Europe along East–West lines, with each bloc characterised by tight military, ideological and political unity, and driven by unremitting adversarial postures towards the opposing bloc (DePorte 1986). In fact, the reality was far fuzzier. For example, the security policies and military preparedness of NATO's two Balkan member states, Greece and Turkey, were arguably as much directed towards each other as they were towards the common Warsaw Pact threat (Brown 1991). Furthermore, of the Balkan region's Warsaw Pact members, Romania might best be regarded as having been semi-detached (Eyal 1989) while the region also contained two communist-led but non-Pact states in Albania and a Federal Republic of Yugoslavia which incorporated entities as divergent as, say, Slovenia and Kosovo province.

In the Baltic region and Scandinavia too, the lines were blurred (see Chapter 7). The regional balance hinged quite crucially on Finland's 'Finlandised' status as well as on an armed and active neutrality for Sweden which certainly ruled out NATO membership but which was additionally reinforced by non-membership of the EC. This was in spite of the essentially 'western' character of these two states. The region's two NATO members, Norway and Denmark, disassociated themselves from the nuclear dimension of the Alliance's strategy. Scandinavia's remaining NATO member, Iceland, made its territory available to its allies, but maintained no military capacity of its own. The three formerly independent states of Estonia, Latvia and Lithuania, annexed by the Soviet Union in 1940, retained their distinct 'Baltic' and 'European' consciousness throughout the Soviet era. Their incorporation into the Soviet Union was only ever recognised *de facto* rather than *de jure* by the major western states, offering them a status unavailable to other constituent republics of the Soviet Union (Hiden and Salmon 1991). Still on the Baltic's southern shores, intra-German relations too acquired a character all their own during the last decade or more of the Cold War as the two German governments strove to maintain their special *détente*, even during those periods when the atmosphere between their respective superpower protectors deteriorated (Hanrieder 1989). Indeed, the very fact of Germany's division served as a constant reminder that the strategic interests of the Cold War's eastern and western halves of the continent had not always been and were not immutably in conflict, that there was an artificiality inherent in Europe's division. There were other 'anomalies' that blurred the edges of Europe's Cold War division. Austria, formerly a constituent part of the Hitlerite Reich and initially also divided into eastern and western zones of postwar military occupation, had been able to re-emerge as a western, democratic, free market and unified state in return for accepting a neutral status which prohibited the country from joining either NATO or the EC so long as the East–West confrontation persisted. In Italy, up to one-third of the electorate of this NATO and EC member were prepared to vote for the country's communist party. The communist vote in France and elsewhere in the West was also substantial at times (Middlemas 1980). Spain's accession to NATO and the EC was not possible until the fall of the Franco regime there (Gil and Tulchin 1988), although the same restrictions were not applied to the equally undemocratic and authoritarian regime in neighbouring Portugal, which was a founder member of NATO. Another of NATO's founder members, France, developed a posture of self-exclusion from the Alliance's military structures (a position adopted by Spain too on its accession to NATO) and, if only intermittently and half-heartedly, pursued a dream of a Europe – possibly a Europe stretching from the Atlantic to the Urals – which might develop its own political and security identity and self-sufficiency free from American tutelage (Gordon 1993; Menon 1995). In the centre of Europe, the populations of Poland, Czechoslovakia and Hungary in particular periodically reminded the rest of Europe and beyond that they had had little say in the continent's postwar political arrangements, and were not necessarily impressed by them (Brown 1988; Lewis 1994). The Republic of Ireland, Switzerland, Malta and Cyprus also did not fit very neatly into the model of a Cold War Europe divided rigidly along East–West lines. Broadly speaking, the Cold War always had less resonance, less concreteness, in southern and south-eastern Europe (Chipman 1988), and arguably in the north too, than was the case at the continent's geographical heart.

The purpose of these reminders is to highlight the variegated nature of Europe's political, ideological and military arrangements even beneath the stifling 'overlay' (Buzan *et al.* 1990) of apparent superpower dominance of the continent. It should not surprise us that this richness and complexity should have become even more evident as this overlay has reduced. It is arguable that, during the Cold War, both the 'West' and the 'East' were over-categorised, and we have persisted with these images into the post-Cold War era. Neither was as uniform or as monolithic, or as absolutely separated and differentiated from the other, as is sometimes imagined. When central Europeans dream of returning to Europe, it is something like western Germany they conjure up in their mind's eye rather than, say, Greece or Portugal. West Europeans prefer to think of incorporating Prague rather than Tirana, let alone Yerevan.

Reminders such as these might enable us to better think our way through the alternative European futures which now potentially beckon. Furthermore, the Cold War disguised or hid many aspects of Europe's deeply rooted cultural, political and historical landscape, but it did not thereby necessarily eradicate them. Europe has not, in the wake of the momentous events of the recent past, moved into a new epoch shaped exclusively by its Cold War antecedents, influential though that period of history has surely been. Europe long predates the Cold War, and it is now living in the wake of the whole of that long and fluid history. In other words, the historical legacy with which today's Europe must grapple is in many respects centuries, not just decades or years, old (Davies 1996). Cold War overlay could not remove the distinct traditions, cultures, perspectives, experiences and habits of the various states and nations of Europe. French Gaullism, British Atlanticism and Swedish neutrality represented more than arid differences of opinion about the origins or nature of the Cold War. Germany's neighbours continue to perceive that country's behaviour and nature through the prism of its pre-Cold War impact on European history. Contemporary Polish foreign and security policy can only be appreciated in the light of the long and tragic struggle of the Polish people simply to have a state they can call their own (Davies 1992). The fierce ethnic conflicts which have torn apart not only the state but the peoples of the former Yugoslav Federation simultaneously represent repeat performances of similar clashes between the same communities in earlier historical epochs, as well as the consequences of the distorted ambitions of post-communist politicians in search of a new power base (Glenny 1992; Zametica 1992; Bennett 1995). The frameworks within which speculation about Russia's future direction is conducted sometimes draw on historical perceptions and legacies which go back centuries (Dukes 1990). The regions of Europe – the Baltic, the Balkans, the Mediterranean, central Europe – which have made such distinctive and separate contributions to the broader flood-tide of European evolution over the centuries, have not had their defining perceptions, security agendas and cultural uniqueness completely obliterated by a mere 40 years or so of division along East–West lines. Indeed, even Europe's current East–West divide, too simplistically characterised as wealth and stability in the West and poverty and instability in the East, might not exactly and in every respect be explicable in terms of contrasting Cold War fortunes. In a crude and inexact way, it is arguable that the Cold War division of Europe overlay a pre-existing fault-line in European history and evolution, so that earlier historical experiences might have explanatory value even here.

New contexts, new maps, new power balances

Additionally, the period corresponding to the Cold War was far from static. Processes were under way in Europe which, whether we explain them as integral components of the Cold War or not, have bequeathed to the 'new Europe' legacies which will be powerful determinants of the way in which Europe's future takes shape. The most significant of these processes have been the integrative trends in the western part of the continent, which have straddled the economic, social, cultural and political spheres (Wallace 1992). Already a debate has emerged about whether west European integration has been, is, or can be a self-generating, independent variable in the evolution of the continent, or whether it was made possible only by the mind-concentrating and geographically limiting contribution of the Cold War era. However, even those who believe that west European integration is essentially shallow and far from irreversible (Mearsheimer 1990) must surely concede that, at least for some time to come, its effects will have a major impact on the character of Europe's diplomacy, and therefore perhaps on the kind of security structure which eventually emerges in Europe as a whole (Caporaso 1992; Jopp 1994).

Then too there has been the rise and subsequent relative decline of the United States, as a world power and as a European power (Hunter 1988; Nye 1990). In the years after the end of the Second World War, American power in Europe was enormous, in military, political, ideological, cultural and economic terms. The contrast with its defeated, destroyed and demoralised European allies was very stark indeed. American economic assistance combined with its extension of a security umbrella might well have been the indispensable inspiration behind western Europe's positive post-war development. In any case, the outcome has been that continental western Europe's enjoyment of unprecedentedly high rates of economic growth for much of the post-war period has meant a substantial closing of the trans-Atlantic gap. A consequence of this phenomenon has been persisting tension between Washington and its European (and other) allies over the seemingly disproportionate share of the security burden which the United States continued to carry even as its partners – most notably Germany – grew wealthier. Indeed, some have argued that the United States's decline, relative to that of its allies and others, can be at least partly explained by an American global over-extension which provided a protective umbrella enabling others to concentrate on self-enrichment – that in the context of the Cold War, the very nature of Washington's superpower status contained the seeds of its own destruction, or at least of its erosion (Kennedy 1988). Growing domestic concern over both its economic performance and its social problems is now combining with the breathing space afforded by the removal of the Soviet menace to create intensified pressure within the United States for some degree of disengagement from global, including European, involvement, and for some more equitable sharing of the load (Gordon 1996). Whether we take American disgruntlement and relative weakness very seriously or not, to some degree or another it is a factor which alters the foundations on which Europe's security arrangements from now on will have to be built (Gebhard 1994).

Another historically quite unique feature of the post-Cold War European security landscape is the geographically truncated condition of the Russian state which has been left behind by the Soviet collapse (Dunlop 1993). The Soviet Union was, with modifications, the territorial successor to the Russian Tsarist Empire. The emergence of Russia as a European power was so coincident with Russia's incorporation of non-Russian territory that there is in effect no historical precedent for a more or less purely Russian national state playing an active role in European and world diplomacy. Russia has shifted further east, and direct Russian power has never before been so absent from the continent's heart in modern European diplomatic history (de Nevers 1994). The break-up of the Soviet Union has also bequeathed to the rest of Europe not merely a Russian state with a set of borders with which it has not had to contend before, but also newly independent European states – most especially the Ukraine (Larrabee 1996) and Belarus (Sanford 1996) – with little if any serious, recent or enduring historical experience of national autonomy. In this respect too, we are only in the first phase of Europe's post-Cold War history (Taylor 1994) and many would argue that some combination of Russian historical experience, the Russian mind-set, and the new state's geopolitical and geostrategic circumstances ensure the re-emergence of an imperial Russian policy, at minimum directed towards the states of the former Soviet Union (FSU) – the so-called 'Near Abroad' (Malcolm 1994; Arbatov 1997). Only time will tell how central an item on Europe's security agenda Russian 'expansionism' will be.

What should not be ignored is that the redrawing of Europe's geographical, political and strategic maps has been profound. With the unification of a rich and dynamic Germany, the dramatic lessening and withdrawal eastwards of Moscow's power, the (sometimes re-) emergence of new and generally weak states in the former communist areas, and the disappearance of the ideological divide which largely cut off the two halves of Europe from each other, Europe's transformation could hardly have been greater. To these more recent developments we must add the West's integration and the softened American presence. All these changes are bound to affect the way Europe as a whole evolves, and the way it impacts on other regions of the world. They will also influence the policies pursued by individual states, and the manner in which Europe's regions develop. The Cold War barriers to closer (or at least more intense) relationships between, say, the states of the Baltic Sea area, or central Europe, have reduced or been removed altogether. Europe's Mediterranean countries may feel freer to concentrate on security threats generated within their immediate neighbourhood (see Chapter 8). In south-eastern Europe, friendships and enmities might once again mirror pre-Cold War fault-lines rather than those imposed 'ahistorically' – and never very convincingly – by the requirements of Cold War Alliance structures (Carter and Norris 1996). German power and policies in particular will be cast in a new light. Whether to regard the unification of Germany as a 'new' development which a European security order needs to take into account, or simply the return of an old one, itself depends on other assumptions made. Either way, it is surely the case that Europe's overall agenda will increasingly be set by Germany (Janning 1996).

The idea of Europe

What, though, is Europe? What are its geographical limits, and how precisely can they be identified? Are notions of Europe and of European identity (Waever *et al.* 1993: 61–92) necessarily associated with a set of values and practices – typically, of liberal democracy, free markets, the rule of law and the like? Can or should Europe, or at least substantial parts of it, ever form a more or less unified and coherent entity manifesting many of the trappings we would otherwise associate with a sovereign state? Or is Europe too fragmented, not only into sovereign states but also into regions, perspectives born of divergent historical experiences and cultural values, and contrasting and conflicting interests (Smith 1992)? Where, on the spectrum between the two poles of 'Balkanisation' and genuine and all-embracing European unity and integration, is it reasonable to expect and hope that Europe might eventually come to settle? To what extent does it or can it ever make sense, certainly when discussing security issues and arrangements, to talk about North America (Holbrooke 1995) or the territories of the FSU as 'external to' Europe? This is one set of questions which must now be addressed, before we can turn to the continent's post-Cold War security issues.

Although the geographical definition of Europe is quite straightforward – from the Atlantic to the Ural mountains, and to the Mediterranean sea in the south – this does not prevent some vagueness and even disagreement about where Europe's edges are in more political terms. This stems from a number of factors. The territories of states such as Russia and Turkey straddle what are usually taken to be Europe's boundaries. Russia, whose non-European territories make up the bulk of the country's land mass, is one particularly difficult case. Turkey, which has played such a large role in European history and which throughout the twentieth century has sought to emphasise its European identity, but whose only geographically European region is the relatively small area of Turkish Thrace and whose population is almost entirely Islamic, is another. Measured by the impact of these two countries on the evolution of European history – not least where security issues have been concerned – and also on aspects of the continent's culture, it is hard to make sense of Europe without their inclusion. Yet excluded they both sometimes are. Some geographically European regions, such as the Caucasus and the Balkans, contain Muslim populations which sit uneasily with definitions of Europe which emphasise its Christian roots. Furthermore, regions such as these are so complex, so geographically, historically and culturally distant from what otherwise might be regarded as the European mainstream, that they can sometimes be excluded from European consciousness altogether (Santoro 1995). This inclination to question the truly European identity of some of its more peripheral – in all senses – states depends on what being European is taken to mean. Conceptualising what Europe is, however, is a rather subjective and fraught exercise. If geographical or cultural distance from some notion of the centre is brought to bear as a factor, then the implication could be that even areas indisputably within Europe but distant from its 'heartland' – wherever that is taken to be – become endowed with at best a rather watered-down European character. Turkey borders Greece and Bulgaria, for example, and Russia the Baltic states of the FSU, Norway and Finland. Are these countries to be regarded as in some way less 'European' than, say, Germany or Switzerland by virtue of their geographical proximity to non- or only peripherally European regions? Does a country become less European the greater the distance it is from core Europe and the closer it is to non-Europe?

It does indeed sometimes appear as if the 'real' Europe broadly coincides with a continental, west-central and largely Catholic Europe incorporating France, Germany, Austria, Switzerland, the Low Countries and at least northern Italy, perhaps with southern England, Denmark, and Spanish Catalonia thrown in (Hyde-Price 1993). West Germany's first post-war Chancellor, the Rhineländer Konrad Adenauer, was so Roman Catholic in his appreciation of what constituted the 'real' Europe that he claimed to feel more at home in Paris than in Berlin, and perhaps partly for this reason was relatively relaxed about the loss of the largely Protestant German east to the communist bloc. France's President de Gaulle vetoed British membership of the European Economic Community, as it then was, largely because he saw the country more as Anglo-Saxon and as part of the English-speaking world than as part of Europe. Some British people would sympathise with this characterisation, and Scandinavians too have generally been lukewarm in their 'Europeanism'. Although post-Francoist Spain has been quite enthusiastic about its belated inclusion in Europe – 'Europe' as defined by the EU, of course – Iberia's European identity nevertheless has to jostle with the peninsula's links to Latin America. During the Falklands conflict between the UK and Argentina, it was by no means clear that 'Europeanism' was stronger than 'Latinism' among the people of Iberia and Italy.

A number of points fall out of these observations, all of which might have serious implications for how Europe conducts its international relationships in the coming years and decades. Even within that geographical, historical and cultural conceptualisation of a Europe which seems unambiguously so, there still appears to be some centre-periphery structure, or even inside-and-outside perception, in the ways in which different Europeans perceive themselves or are perceived by other Europeans. Subjective European identity is not evenly distributed around the objectively European space. Multiple identities, especially where combined with a weak sense of a European identity, might be highly compatible not only with a 'Europe of nations' but also with a degree of 'regionalisation' within Europe (Hurrell 1995) in the way in which Europeans conduct their international politics and perceive their interests. Scandinavia, the Baltic region, north-west Europe, central Europe, the Slavic lands, the Balkans and the Mediterranean conceivably coincide with just some of the cognitive foundations around which Europeans of various kinds could organise elements of their international relationships. Any greater 'sub-regionalisation' of European politics could surely potentially undermine the construction of a more all-embracing European edifice as well as it could reinforce it. Multiple identities and cultural flows (de Witte 1990) might also prove compatible with diplomatic preferences which straddle Europe's borders with the non-European worlds, to create Atlanticism, Mediterraneanism, Latinism, or Islamism. Such fragmentation could render the creation of consensus within Europe more problematic; it could lead to the perception that security is not necessarily collective across Europe as a whole; and it could feed disagreement concerning the membership and functions of Europe's institutions.

A shared and strong European identity or evenly distributed awareness of and identification with Europe as a coherent region are not the only factors we need to take into account when considering what Europe is and what it could conceivably become. The integrative processes which have characterised post-war west European development are surely still more important. These processes have been based on the shared values associated with liberal democracy and free market economics: values which symbolise the 'Europe' to which the excluded peoples of the former communist bloc wish to 'return'. In creating interdependence and encouraging transnationalism, albeit more in the economic than the political sphere, western Europe's integration may have harmonised the interests of the west European states and peoples and created a habit and even a momentum of intergovernmental consultation and cooperation (Holland 1995). On the other hand, it is worth noting that this 'regionalisation' *of* western Europe is not entirely coincident with institutional membership. Countries such as Austria, Switzerland, Sweden and Norway, outside the EC throughout this period and, except in the latter case, outside NATO too, have been full participants in these integrative processes. Indeed, non-EC Austria surely became no less enmeshed, and probably more so than, say, Greece.

This in turn leads to the observation that much of western Europe's integration has been informal, and presumably would have happened even in the absence of the EC/EU. It also leads to the observation that informal integration within the EU might, as with 'European' identity although not necessarily coincident with it, be unevenly distributed, again pointing to the phenomenon – or spectre – of a tightly knit core surrounded by a more loosely associated outer core – here, even among existing EU members (de Schoutheete 1990). A third point to make is that, as the process of integration has in many respects been informal, it incorporates countries and regions beyond Europe's borders, however they might be defined – notably North America and Japan, but also increasingly the other dynamic economies of the Pacific rim. In other words, the 'regionalisation' *of* Europe has fuzzy edges, because it is part of a broader process of 'globalisation' which could ultimately serve to undermine any attempts at European union which hint at European exclusivity (Jacquet 1996–7). The EU's common policies may have encouraged (or perhaps discouraged, in some instances!) western Europe's integration, but they have not been its sole driver.

This line of argument suggests that what the former communist states of Europe need is not so much institutional membership *per se* – although this might well be useful to them, psychologically as well as in more material respects – but inclusion into the less formal integrative processes both of the European region and of the globe. The growth of a European identity in the western half of the continent, encouraged by integrative processes which have involved non-European regions but have largely excluded Europe's eastern half, paradoxically makes it possible to imagine the incorporation of central Europeans – and especially the Visegrad countries of Poland, the Czech and Slovak republics, and Hungary – into a 'Europe' in which they have hitherto paid little part. In sharing a rather selective version of Europe's pre-Cold War history, it is imagined that they can slot into its post-Cold War history – that they can indeed 'return to Europe'. Yet it can and has been argued that east and central Europe are closer to the 'neorealist' paradigm of competing states and international anarchy than western Europe – and the West more generally – now is and therefore the extension of the 'security community' to embrace the wider Europe may not be a foregone conclusion (Mayall and Miall, 1994; Miall 1994b; Hyde-Price 1996).

And what of Russia? It is impossible to think about European security without taking Russia – its presence, its interests, its policies, its capabilities – into account (Baranovsky 1997). Nor would any understanding of European culture – surely a significant foundation on which any European identity must be built – be complete without the incorporation of the contributions made by Russia's novelists, playwrights, poets, composers and the like. Furthermore, ethnically and linguistically Russians form the greater part of the Slavic world, and constitute the majority of Orthodox Christians. Russia, however, not least by contrast with central Europe in the way in which it is perceived, raises in rather stark form the different conceptualisations of 'regionalisation' or regional awareness which currently coexist in Europe. For many other Europeans, Russia is in some way the 'other' (Neumann 1996). Because of the way Russia is perceived by others and, increasingly perhaps, because of the way it perceives itself as 'Eurasian', the country appears to resist being slotted comfortably into a comprehensive and generally benign European collectivity. Geography, historical experience and Russian sensitivity reinforce the possibility, and even likelihood, that the other European areas of the FSU, perhaps excluding the Baltic states, will also continue to exist just beyond the horizon of some new conceptualisation of 'core' Europe. Russia appears to be simultaneously – as Konrad Adenauer expressed it – too big, too poor, and too Asiatic to be regarded as truly European.

The point here is to establish that the Russian case is uniquely difficult when we are considering what Europe is, and therefore what its future security and institutional arrangements might be. Russia might share security interests in common with core Europe, it might even in time adopt comparable economic and political systems. But any attempt to create some kind of European entity, rather than live with or return to a 'Europe of states' based on 'renationalised' even if cooperative security policies, seems likely to exclude Russia. Put crudely but not inaccurately, Russia's 'exclusion' from Europe will appear all the sharper the more that core Europe aspires to and succeeds in creating a degree of unification, and the more extensive core Europe is taken to be. Any expansion of NATO's membership also needs to be appreciated with this observation in mind (Zagorski 1997).

Security in the New Europe

During the Cold War, the concept of 'security' was generally understood in Europe as more or less exclusively concerned with militarily-related issues, and was dominated by the East–West confrontation. Security policies addressed themselves to matters such as defence, deterrence, alliance-management with allies and confidence-building with adversaries. The structure and functions of the continent's security institutions reflected these preoccupations. NATO and the Warsaw Pact were expected to deter military aggression and prepare to defend in the event of attack, while the Conference on Security and Co-operation in Europe (CSCE, now OSCE) represented a concession to the objective of increasing security by reducing military threat perceptions, military capabilities and the mistrust and suspicion which lay behind them. Environmental, economic and social issues were either accorded a low priority as security concerns, or were regarded as altogether inappropriate items for the continent's security agenda.

With the demise of the Cold War, security has come to be seen as a much more contested concept, and its relationship to the continent's institutional architecture as far more complex (Hyde-Price 1991: 189–236). The circumstances of the post-Cold War 'wider' Europe are rather different from those pertaining to western Europe in the aftermath of the Second World War. The threats today are rather diffuse and sometimes of a kind not susceptible to military solutions (Waever *et al.* 1993). Indeed, in the wake of the collapse of the Soviet system and the adversarial confrontation of the Cold War, what are Europe's security problems? How should traditional security items be distinguished from issues of a more political, economic or social nature, or has this distinction substantially eroded in contemporary circumstances? How should security 'threats' emanating from beyond Europe's shores be addressed, and how significant are they? Is Europe's security subjectively or objectively collective, or can and will security perspectives, policies and even institutional arrangements be disaggregated along regional, functional or conceptual lines? To what degree does post-Cold War Europe enjoy a 'blank page of infinite possibility' in its freedom and scope to design a new institutional structure, or is it more realistic to regard the security architecture which survived the end of the Cold War as having some kind of 'inert momentum' – that is, a capacity to persist beyond the circumstances from which it emanated? Is any institutional reform likely to be driven more by design or by unforeseen events? What kinds of institutional reform would best render Europe's existing structures more relevant to the continent's new security agenda (Jopp, Rummel and Schmidt 1991)? Should institutional reform and change be seen primarily as part of the solution to European security issues, or as part of the problem? What should be the relationship between the various security institutions in Europe, and how much functional and geographical overlap is either tolerable or desirable (Keohane 1989; Keohane 1994)?

Perhaps the first task in our exploration of the wider Europe's security agenda is to locate the continent into the fast-changing global context. The European continent, and especially its western half, for so long the centre of the world's power and the engine behind its development, will become increasingly less so in the decades to come (Jacquet 1992). The world is undergoing a profound shift in its structure, as new centres of economic, political, military and cultural power and influence emerge to not merely catch up with but even surpass the old world. There can be no guarantee that any new power centres will pursue policies respectful of Europe's economic well-being, physical security, or internal social and political values. Demographically, too, Caucasians are becoming an ever-smaller minority of the world's population as, broadly, birth rates explode precisely where people are poor and decline where they are rich. Phenomena associated with these shifts will combine with the growing interdependence of the global political and economic systems to create new economic, political and security agendas for Europe as a whole – but perhaps more particularly for its western half. Indeed, Europe might increasingly find itself in the unfamiliar and uncomfortable role of victim of the outside world's developments rather than instigator of them (Snow 1993)!

These trends in the regional and global economic, political and social systems have contributed to and combined with the emergence of a security agenda for Europe in which 'societal security' issues can seem as or more pressing than more traditional military threats (Waever *et al.*

1993: 1–58, 185–99). Thus, the materially comfortable but ageing populations in western Europe could find their social environment increasingly under pressure from relatively poor and young migrants both from Europe's east and from the African continent and elsewhere, as people seek not only to improve their personal economic prospects but also to escape the political and social turmoil and oppression that might be attendant on failed economic and political systems. Weak and corrupt administrative practices to the east and south might add to western Europe's indigenous environmental headaches, as well as to its susceptibility to organised crime syndicates trading in drugs, people, armaments and the stealing and laundering of money. Violent political and ethnic conflicts both within and outwith Europe might force their way on to Europe's security agenda because their political, social and economic consequences threaten to spill over and disrupt the continent's tranquillity. Such disputes could also serve to intensify the terrorist threat to Europe's people, cities and communications infrastructure (Snow 1993). The impact of any of these developments could be worsened by the rise of ideologies and cultural movements with militant anti-European – or in the case of post-communist Europe, anti-democratic (Schopflin 1994; Smith 1994) – biases. Thus the successful transition to political democracy and the proper functioning of free markets forms part of the security agenda not simply for the former communist states themselves, but for the continent as a whole (Miall 1994b). Something similar might be said of the non-European states of the southern shores of the Mediterranean (Spencer 1993).

Shifts in the global balance of power are also likely to pose more traditional, military, security problems to Europe. The proliferation around the world of the technologies of mass destruction, their delivery systems, as well as of substantial and worrying conventional military arsenals, might also feature highly on the 'new' Europe's security agenda. The emergence of unfriendly regional powers, of regional arms races, and of military threats to European markets, sources of raw materials and energy, and to Europe's allies, might paradoxically be fed both by eastern Europe's arms industries in search of new markets, hard currency and private gain, and by the West's armaments companies in search of substitutes for the loss of domestic customers. The historical evidence to date does not offer a sound basis on which to assume that there is or will be a ready consensus even in the West, let alone the wider Europe, about how threats such as these should be ranked, and what might be done to combat them. The scope for state-by-state and region-by-region differences in how to prioritise and respond to so variegated a security agenda, especially where it stems largely from developments beyond Europe's boundaries, is already evident (Stuart and Tow 1990) and might become more so.

The European continent itself may also still be capable of generating a security agenda of the traditional kind, and this too has to be addressed. As we have seen, there are those who argue that the post-

Soviet Russian state continues to be a potential source of threat to the security of its European neighbours. Certainly there are some disturbing political trends within Russia, but military expansionism on the part of Russia – or any of Europe's other major states and alliances – is surely off the continent's security agenda for the foreseeable future, except perhaps where Moscow's relations with some states and problems within former Soviet territory are concerned. On the other hand, Europe's history of inflicting on itself major and destructive wars has created an awareness that the continent's security arrangements must indeed make it possible to assert confidently that any repetition of such events is unthinkable in any reasonable time-span. Any such arrangements should also aim at minimising the likelihood of minor conflicts such as those seen on the territory of the former Yugoslavia from breaking out, spreading or being left unattended.

The construction of just such a security environment requires a number of elements. First, confidence-building measures have to be taken, and indeed are being taken, which undermine the 'security dilemma' caused by the tendency to regard a neighbouring state's armed forces as threatening. These might include negotiated arms control and reduction agreements, unilateral defence cuts, and transparency. Second, the practice and habit of consultation and of cooperative and open diplomacy has to be established, especially between the major actors and where major issues are involved, but also between local parties to a dispute. Preventive diplomacy surely has a role to play here. This is partially related to a third requirement of a benign security order: that the major powers especially must not be left with the sensation that their interests are being ignored. Here, the record is rather patchy. Russia could become a 'dissatisfied power' in the years to come, and such powers have notoriously emerged in the past as threats to European, and indeed global, good order.

Architecture and the creation of Europe

This is partly because it is, fourth, important that major powers should not be excluded from membership of the major international organisations or, if excluded, should in some way be reassured and compensated, and Russians are generally far from convinced that this has so far been the case or will be in the future. It is hard to envisage how the country could ever be fully embraced by NATO or by the EU, or how Russia's marginalisation can be convincingly avoided the more these institutions experience membership growth. Moscow's preference for an upgraded OSCE precisely so as to limit its own isolation has met with an almost universally unenthusiastic response. It should also be noted that, if Russian blandishments mean anything at all, Moscow's interest in establishing sway over its FSU neighbours could rise with the growth in NATO's membership eastwards. The security architecture might as easily contribute to as help resolve European tensions.

Trans-Atlantic relations are also potentially threatened by greater European institutional unity, especially on defence and security issues. Although there is an awareness of the risks of this on both sides of the Atlantic, and policies and initiatives are being taken in the more traditional security area which should minimise the dangers, an EU that inclined towards a 'Fortress Europe' in its economic relationships with the outside world could also threaten trans-Atlantic security relations – as could any trend towards American protectionism. Those who regard the West's 'pluralistic security community' as little more than a by-product of the shared perception of the Soviet threat, and the economic and social integrationism and transnationalism of the trans-Atlantic area as superficial, reversible, or as a potential source of conflict as well as of cohesion, would not be surprised if the post-Cold War era comes to witness a profound rupture in US–European relationships. Again, there is a risk here that the institutional arrangements which Europe arrives at might become part of the problem as well as part of any solution, in so far as the United States might be made to feel aggrieved in some profound way (Jopp 1994; Peterson 1996).

note
Kosovo
problem
US vs EU

It should also go without saying that a European region which is economically integrated but not politically so, is unlikely to acquire the capacity to act effectively as a diplomatic entity in non-economic spheres. Indeed, one could go further. Member states of the EU are obliged to consult and, in effect, cooperate wherever possible in the foreign and security policy area. However, it has thus far proved difficult for the EU states to obtain swift and far-reaching agreement in the sphere of security policy, especially where military action might be involved (Van Ham 1995). The history so far of the EC/EU's involvement in the conflicts in the former Yugoslavia suggests disagreement, disarray, inaction and inadequate action. Differential involvement on the part of EU member states is a more likely outcome of the obligation to consult than are firm, decisive, timely, unified and far-reaching policy decisions (Brenner 1993; Gow 1997). It might even be worth considering whether 'Europe' might not be better – or at least more active – at policing its own internal affairs if its constituent states were freer to act unilaterally or, if multilaterally, only with those states – inside or outside the EU or any other security institution – among whom some reasonable degree of consensus readily emerges. Hence all the talk about the requirement to establish multilateral 'coalitions of the willing' – or the grudging, perhaps – on an *ad hoc* and case-by-case basis, with institutional membership serving as neither an inclusive nor exclusive factor in determining who participates. The point here is certainly not to propose what is widely referred to – and feared – as the 'renationalisation' of European (and especially German) security policies (Wolf 1996), but to note that the alternatives to it might be either little in the way of unified and effective common European security policies, or continued dependence on American leadership and activism.

This is an important point when we are considering the process of

European integration. The undoubted, and undoubtedly significant, integration of EU and non-EU societies, economies, and political values that has so characterised west European development in the post-Second World War period, may indeed have intensified 'European' identity and may even have broadened and deepened the range of common interests. But the identification of common interests is a subjective as well as an objective exercise. It does not necessarily lead to agreement either on how best to pursue those interests or on how to prioritise them, and common interests and perspectives cannot be guaranteed to be tighter within Europe's (or the EU's) borders than across them. Indeed, any expansion in the membership of any of Europe's security institutions, or any attempt on the part of any of them to develop more far-reaching common policies, would surely test both the processes by which common decisions are arrived at and the softer, consensus-building activities on which they can be based. This indeed constitutes one of the major arguments against widening and enlarging.

Extensive cooperation on military or non-military security policy will not emerge in Europe simply because it is in itself desirable. Nor will it result *per se* from the construction of security institutions. In the circumstances of the post-Cold War, there is a widespread recognition across the whole of the European security area, including Russia, that multilateral cooperation is in principle a better means of achieving security both for each and for all. This throws up a historically unprecedented opportunity for continent-wide security cooperation to take root and to achieve some genuine degree of lasting success. If the integrative processes which have so bound west European states and societies together can be extended eastwards to embrace most or all of the rest of the continent, then both interests and perspectives might perhaps become more widely – if not universally – shared than ever before in European history. There are, in short, many good reasons to suppose that the end of the Cold War need not return European diplomacy to conflictual, confrontational, competitive inter-state rivalry in keeping with neorealism's conceptualisation of the true nature of international relations. To repeat, the Cold War was not the only thing that happened in Europe during the Cold War era, and nor is it the only historical epoch the continent is now in the wake of. The historical record contains a great deal that Europeans would not wish to repeat, and developments in the post-1945 period offer a sound base to build on. A 'spirit of cooperation' might help build more effective security institutions, which in turn might make it easier both to arrive at common policies and to facilitate their implementation. But there is no guarantee, and unrealistic expectations might lead to exaggerated perceptions of failure.

For central and south-eastern Europe, much of the security focus is on the prospect of being caught in a pincer between apparent western indifference on the one hand, and revitalised Russian power at some unspecifiable future date on the other. The countries of this region seek assurance (and this rather than *re*assurance) that a past which has too frequently left them at the mercy of their larger neighbours will not repeat itself. They also sometimes have problems with each other – over disputed borders, minorities, and the like – although the extent of this is at times exaggerated in the West. The post-communist states of central Europe do – or should – appreciate, however, that their enhanced security cannot be obtained simply by joining the right institutions. In essence, then, they simply wish to become part of an expanded 'West' and then, presumably, to acquire similar, diffuse, security concerns as their partners – and perhaps exercise their freedom to prioritise and respond to them as they each see fit. In today's Europe, there is scope for different degrees and types of security, different degrees and types of unity and cooperation, and different degrees and types of institutional involvement. And the variety of assessments of what the best mix might be stem not necessarily from deficiencies in the processes of abstract reasoning, nor from insufficient commitment either to 'Europe' or to 'peace and security', but more often from genuinely different perspectives and identities deriving from differing historical experiences, geographical locations, domestic circumstances and the like. One indispensable key to a more secure and even more 'unified' Europe might be a more universal recognition of the inherent legitimacy of many of these differences.

Notes

1. Where the period of time under consideration straddles the redesignation of the European Community as the European Union, 'EU' will be used.
2. As this chapter is offered as a broad overview, the referencing is indicative rather than comprehensive or definitive. In addition to specific citations, works are generally referenced because they are either representative, recent or particularly authoritative.

References

Arbatov, A. (1997) 'Russian foreign policy thinking in transition', in Baranovsky, V. (ed.) (1997) 135–59.

Baranovsky, V. (ed.) (1997) *Russia and Europe: The Emerging Security Agenda*, Oxford: SIPRI/Oxford University Press.

Bennett, C. (1995) *Yugoslavia's Bloody Collapse: Causes, Course and Consequence*, London: Hurst.

Brenner, J. M. (1993) 'EC; confidence lost', *Foreign Policy* 91 (Winter): 24–43.

Brown, J. (1991) *Delicately Poised Allies: Greece and Turkey,* London: Brassey's.

Brown, J. F. (1988) *Eastern Europe and Communist Rule*, Durham: Duke University Press.

Buzan, B., Kelstrup, M., Lemaitre, P., Tromer, E. and Waever, O. (1990) *The*

18   *Rethinking Security in Post-Cold War Europe*

European Security Order Recast: Scenarios for the Post-Cold War Era, London: Pinter/RIIA.

Caporaso, J. A. (1992) 'Has Europe changed? Neorealism, institutions, and domestic politics in the new Europe', in Jackson, R. J. (ed.) *Europe in Transition: The Management of Security After the Cold War*, London: Adamantine Press.

Carter, F. W. and Norris, H. T. (eds) (1996) T*he Changing Shape of the Balkans*, London: University College London Press.

Chipman, J. (ed.) (1988) *NATO's Southern Allies: Internal and External Challenges*, New York and London: Routledge.

Davies, N. (1992) *God's Playground: A History of Poland, 2nd Volume*, New York, Columbia University Press.

Davies, N. (1996) *Europe: A History*, Oxford: Oxford University Press.

de Nevers, R. (1994) 'Russia's Strategic Renovation', *Adelphi Papers,* 289, London: IISS.

de Schoutheete, P. (1990) 'The European community and its sub-systems' in Wallace, W. (ed.) (1990): 106–24.

de Witte, B. (1990) 'Cultural linkages', in Wallace, W. (ed.) (1992): 192–210.

DePorte, A. (1986) *Europe Between the Superpowers: The Enduring Balance*, New Haven, Conn: Yale University Press.

Dukes, P. (1990) *A History of Russia: Medieval, Modern, Contemporary*, Durham, N.C: Duke University Press.

Dunlop, John B. (1993) *The Rise of Russia and the Fall of the Soviet Empire*, Princeton, NJ: Princeton University Press.

Eyal, J. (1989) *The Warsaw Pact and the Balkans: Moscow's Southern Flank*, London: Macmillan.

Gaddis, J. L. (1989) *The Long Peace: Inquiries into the History of the Cold War*, Oxford: Oxford University Press.

Gebhard, P. S. (1994) 'The United States and European Security', *Adelphi Papers,* 286, London: IISS.

Gil, F. and Tulchin, J. (eds) (1988) *Spain's Entry into NATO: Conflicting Political and Strategic Perspectives*, London: Lynne Rienner.

Glenny, M. (1992) *The Fall of Yugoslavia*, Harmondsworth: Penguin.

Gogolewska, A., Dorina, N. and Osolnik, M. (1997) 'The 'other Europe' seeks a welcome', *The World Today*, 53(5): 122–4.

Gordon, P. (1993) *A Certain Idea of France: French Security Policy and the Gaullist Legacy*, Princeton, NJ: Princeton University Press.

Gordon, P. (1996) 'Recasting the Atlantic Alliance', *Survival*, 38 (1): 32–57.

Gow, J. (1997) *Triumph of the Lack of Will: International Diplomacy and the Yugoslav War*, London: Hurst.

Hanrieder, W. F. (1989) *Germany, America, Europe*, Yale: Yale University Press.

Hiden, J. and Salmon, P. (1991) *The Baltic Nations and Europe: Estonia, Latvia and Lithuania in the Twentieth Century*, London: Longman.

Holbrooke, R. (1995) 'America: a European power', *Foreign Affairs*, 74 (March/April): 38–51.

Holland, M. (1995) *European Integration: From Community to Union*, London: Pinter.

Hunter, R. (1988) 'Will the United States remain a European Power?', *Survival*, 30(3), May–June: 210–31.

Hurrell, A. (1995) 'Explaining the resurgence of regionalism in world politics', *Review of International Studies*, 21(4): 331–58.

Hyde-Price, A. (1991) *European Security Beyond the Cold War: Four Scenarios for the Year 2010*, London: Sage Publications/RIIA.

Hyde-Price, A. (1993) 'The system level: the changing topology of Europe', in Rees, G. W. (ed.) *International Politics in Europe: The New Agenda*, London and New York: Routledge.

Hyde-Price, A. (1996) *The International Politics of East-Central Europe*, Manchester: Manchester University Press.

Jacquet, P. (1992) 'From coexistence to interdependence', *Survival*, 34 (1): 89–108.

Jacquet, P. (1996/7) 'European integration at the crossroads', *Survival*, 38 (4): 84–100.

Janning, J. (1996) 'A German Europe – a European Germany? On the debate over Germany's foreign policy', *International Affairs*, 72(1): 33–41.

Jopp, M. (1994) 'The strategic implications of European integration', *Adelphi Papers*, 290, London: IISS.

Jopp, M., Rummel, R. and Schmidt, P. (eds) (1991) *Integration and Security in Western Europe: Inside the European Pillar*, Boulder, Colorado: Westview.

Kelleher, C. M. (1992) 'The new Germany: an overview', in Stares, P. (ed.) (1992): 11–54.

Kennedy, P. (1988) *The Rise and Fall of the Great Powers: Economic Change and Military Conflict*, London: Unwin Hyman.

Keohane, R. (1989) *International Institutions and State Power*, Boulder, Colorado: Westview.

Keohane, R. (1994) 'Redefining Europe: implications for international relations', in Miall, H. (ed.) (1994a): 229–40.

Larrabee, F. S. (1996) 'Ukraine's balancing act', *Survival*, 38 (2).

Lewis, P. (1994) *Central Europe Since 1945*, London: Longman.

Malcolm, N. (1994) 'The new Russian foreign policy', *The World Today*, February: 28–32.

Mayall, J. and Miall, H. (1994) 'Towards a redefinition of European order', in Miall, (ed.) (1994a): 262–77.

Mearsheimer, J. (1990) 'Back to the future: instability in Europe after the Cold War', *International Security*, 12 (1): 5–56.

Menon, A. (1995) 'NATO the French way: France, NATO and European security', *International Affairs*, 71(1): 19–34.

Miall, H. (ed.) (1994a) *Redefining Europe: New Patterns of Conflict and Cooperation*, London: Pinter/RIIA.

Miall, H. (1994b) 'Wider Europe, fortress Europe, fragmented Europe', in Miall, H. (ed.) (1994a): 1–15.

Middlemas, K. (1980) *Power and the Party: Changing Faces of Communism in Western Europe*, London: Deutsch.

Neumann, I. (1996) *Russia and the Idea of Europe*, London and New York: Routledge.

Nye, J. (1990) *Bound to Lead: The Changing Nature of American Power*, New York: Basic Books.

Peterson, J. (1996) *Europe and America: The Prospects for Partnership*, London and New York: Routledge.

Sanford, G. (1996) 'Belarus on the road to nationhood', *Survival*, 38 (1), Spring: 131–53.

Santoro, C. M. (1995) 'Ethnopolitics and the frontiers of Europe', *European Security*, 4 (3): 383–92.

Schopflin, G. (1994) 'The rise of anti-democratic movements in post-communist societies', in Miall, H. (ed.) (1994a): 129–46.

Smith, A. (1992) 'National identity and the idea of Europe', *International Affairs*, 68 (1): 55–76.

Smith, G. (1994) 'Can liberal democracy span the European divide?', in Miall, H. (ed.) (1994a): 113–28.

Snow, D. (1993) *Distant Thunder: Third World Conflict and the International Order*, New York: St Martin's Press.

Spencer, C. (1993) 'The Maghreb in the 1990s', *Adelphi Papers*, 274, London: IISS.

Stares, P. (ed.) (1992) *The New Germany and the New Europe*, Washington DC: Brookings Institution.

Stuart, D. and Tow, W. (1990) *The Limits of Alliance: NATO Out-of-Area Disputes since 1949*, Baltimore: Johns Hopkins University Press.

Taylor, T. (1994) *European Security and the Former Soviet Union: Dangers, Opportunities, and Gambles*, London: RIIA.

Van Ham, P. (1995) 'The prospects for a European security and defence identity', *European Security*, 4 (4): 523–45.

Waever, O., Buzan, B., Kelstrup, M. and Lemaitre, P. (1993) *Identity, Migration and the New Security Agenda in Europe*, London: Pinter.

Wallace, W. (ed.) (1992) *The Dynamics of European Integration*, London: Pinter/RIIA.

Wallace, W. (1997) 'On the move – destination unknown', *The World Today*, 53 (4): 99–102.

Wolf, R. (1996) 'Renationalisation of western defence and security policies: a German view on a hesitant spectre', in Trifonuvska, S. (ed.) *The Transatlantic Alliance on the Eve of the New Millennium*, The Hague: Kluwer Law International: 129–41.

Zagorski, A. (1997) 'Russia and European institutions', in Baranovsky, V. (ed.) (1997).

Zametica, J. (1992) 'The Yugoslav conflict', *Adelphi Papers* 270, London: IISS.

PART ONE

Institutions

CHAPTER 2

The OSCE and European security

ADRIAN HYDE-PRICE

The Organisation for Security and Co-operation in Europe (OSCE), formerly the Conference on Security and Co-operation in Europe (CSCE), is one of the great unsung success stories of modern European diplomacy. From its inauspicious beginnings in the early 1970s and through the heightened East–West tensions of the 'Second Cold War', the OSCE has emerged as one of the central pillars of the post-Cold War European security system. For this reason alone, it merits more serious attention than it usually receives.

The OSCE is also of tremendous significance because its existence and operation illustrates the extent to which the nature of security and international relations have changed in late twentieth century Europe. The OSCE reflects – and to some extent embodies – the key features of post-Cold War European order: of a Europe beyond bipolarity, but also of a Europe beyond the multipolar balance of power arrangements of Metternich and Bismarck, Churchill and Stalin. On the eve of the twenty-first century, Europe is not returning 'Back to the Future' as some would have us believe (Mearsheimer 1990). On the contrary, it is developing distinctly new forms of international and transnational inter-action, as globalisation, institutional integration, democratisation, deepening interdependence and multilateral cooperation transform the structural dynamics of European politics. These changes to the very nature of European international politics are generating a new security agenda in Europe, and require us to develop a new paradigm for the study of contemporary international security (Hyde-Price 1991: 13–16). Studying the OSCE can shed light on some of the key features of the new pattern of international politics and security in Europe, thereby helping us to rethink the nature of European security.

Understanding the OSCE

When assessing the contribution of the OSCE to Europe's evolving security architecture, it is essential to realise that the OSCE is in a number of respects very different from other international organisations and institutions. Four features in particular distinguish it from other elements in Europe's security architecture, and give the OSCE its unique function, character and identity.

First, the OSCE is the only pan-European body in Europe, and its definition of 'Europe' is very broad and inclusive. Comprising 35 states at its inception in 1975, the OSCE today embraces 54 participating states from Vladivostok to Vancouver, including the USA and Canada; the Central Asian Republics and the Caucasian states (members of the OSCE by virtue of being Soviet successor states[1]); Mediterranean states such as Turkey and Malta; and micro-states such as Lichtenstein and the Vatican.

Second, it is comprehensive in scope, embracing three 'baskets' of issues: security concerns; economic, scientific, technological and environmental cooperation; and the humanitarian dimension, which includes human rights. Its brief is therefore much more comprehensive than either NATO or the EU. Like these organisations, however, its policy agenda has broadened since the end of the Cold War, and now includes democratisation, minority rights, conflict prevention and post-conflict rehabilitation.

Third, the OSCE is not a treaty-based organisation like the EU or NATO involving elements of political integration or supranationalism. The OSCE actually began life as a diplomatic process, and only acquired some permanent institutional structures from 1990 onwards. Consequently the OSCE is not grounded on legally binding commitments having the full force of international law, but on political agreements which are only binding to the extent that the participating states have stated their determination to fully implement them. The OSCE today has been described as 'more than a regime but not quite an international organisation' (Peters 1996: 104), although this is changing as it acquires more of the characteristics of an international organisation such as an institutional apparatus.

Finally, the OSCE reaches its politically binding decisions on the basis of the consensus of all participating states.[2] This has been partially modified in order to allow 'consensus minus one' in 'cases of clear, gross and uncorrected violation of CSCE commitments',[3] and 'consensus minus two' in the context of the directed conciliation procedure. The OSCE also possesses some 'mechanisms' for consultation and investigation which do not rely on the consensus principle.[4] Nonetheless, the organisation still operates primarily on the basis of political consensus for all major decisions and – in contrast to the UN for example – lacks mechanisms to enforce compliance.

Given that the OSCE embraces an exotic *mélange* of different states who meet periodically to discuss a comprehensive range of issues, and who take decisions on the basis of unanimity, it may seem surprising that anything valuable has ever emerged from its deliberations. However, these four features are its strengths as well as its weaknesses, and account for the many and diverse achievements of the organisation since its inception.

From bipolarity to the *Paris Charter for a New Europe* (1975–92)

The initial impetus for the CSCE came from the Soviet's desire to consolidate their hold in central and eastern Europe and the West's desire, coupled with West German *Ostpolitik*, for a stable basis for East–West *détente* (Acimovic 1981: Marescu 1985). Nearly two years after it started, on 1 August 1975, the Helsinki Final Act of the Conference on Security and Co-operation in Europe (CSCE) was signed amid much pomp and ceremony (Volle and Wagner 1976). The Helsinki Final Act comprised four 'baskets'. The first basket dealt with security issues, and included an important ten-point 'Declaration on Principles Guiding Relations between Participating States', such as the inviolability of frontiers and the peaceful settlement of disputes. The second dealt with 'Cooperation in the fields of Economics, of Science and Technology, and of the Environment' but this never developed any substantive content. The third basket was concerned with cooperation in 'humanitarian and other fields' and particularly human rights (Bloed and van Dijk 1991). This proved to have profound long-term significance as it embodied a commonly agreed set of human rights principles that inspired a generation of dissidents in the East and undermined the already-thin political legitimacy of communist authoritarianism.

The final basket provided the key to the subsequent development of the CSCE as a *process*. It provided for a series of further meetings among participating states to consider progress in implementing the provisions of the Final Act. Follow-up meetings were held in Belgrade (October 1977 – March 1978), Madrid (November 1980 – September 1983) and Vienna (November 1986 – January 1989). These meetings established patterns of procedure;[5] served to keep East and West dialogue alive despite the 'Second Cold War' (Halliday 1983)[6] and provided a forum for the agreement of useful Confidence and Security Building Measures (CSBMs) (Brauch 1986; Birnbaum and Huldt 1987).[7] By the time the Vienna follow-up meeting opened in November 1986, East–West relations were entering a period of unprecedented cooperation and understanding (Wrede 1990; Lehne 1991). The Vienna meeting was therefore the last in the history of the CSCE process which had begun in 1973. As communist regimes across Europe entered their *Götterdämmerung* in the autumn of 1989, the geopolitical premises on which the Helsinki process had developed also disintegrated. With the collapse of this bipolar structure, the CSCE found itself sorely in need of a new *raison d'être* and a refashioned *modus operandi*.

The demise of the Cold War and the emergence of new democracies in most of central and eastern Europe generated an exhilarating mood of optimism throughout Europe, a belief that at long last Europe really could become 'whole and free', as President George Bush declared. Many of these hopes and expectations, particularly among the new democratic elites of east central Europe, were focused on the CSCE because it was the only truly pan-European body on the continent. There was a desire for the CSCE to be developed into the central architectural structure of a 'common European home' that would render both of the military alliance structures redundant. The goal was to create a collective security system, in which an attack on any one state would be met by a collective response of all other states – in other words, 'one for all and all for one'.

Western responses to the plethora of ambitious and inventive plans for the shaping of a new CSCE collective security regime were, on the whole, polite but sceptical. With the notable exception of Hans-Dietrich Genscher, the majority of western political leaders had no desire to give up the proven advantages of an existing collective defence alliance (namely NATO) for the dubious promises of an untested collective security system. Nevertheless, western countries did agree that the CSCE could provide a key forum for broad-ranging cooperation in a Europe no longer divided into hostile blocs. The goal, in other words, was to be *cooperative* – not collective – security.

The result was a convergence between western and eastern Europe around the more limited goal of *institutionalising* the CSCE. A broad consensus emerged in favour of transforming the CSCE into a more permanent institution which could play an important role in Europe's post-Cold War security architecture as part of a system of interlocking and overlapping structures – the other key institutions being NATO and the EC.

Thus the CSCE Heads of State and Government meeting in Paris, in November 1990, was a watershed. It heralded the transformation of the CSCE from a means of mitigating the worst effects of the Cold War into one of the institutional pillars of the post-Cold War European order. The rebirth and institutionalisation of the CSCE was trumpeted in a grandly titled document reflecting the new-found confidence which pervaded Europe at the time – *The Paris Charter for a New Europe*. The *Paris Charter* created three new bodies for institutionalised political consultation and dialogue: regular Summits of Heads of State and Government; a Council of Ministers (involving foreign ministers) – subsequently renamed the Ministerial Council); and the Committee of Senior Officials (one of the key bodies in the organisation – subsequently renamed the Permanent Council). It also established three standing institutions: the Secretariat (based initially in Prague, although most of its staff and functions have since been transferred to Vienna); the Office for Democratic Institutions and Human Rights (in Warsaw); and the Conflict Prevention Centre (in Vienna – subsequently renamed the Forum for Security Cooperation). Finally, it decided to establish a CSCE Parliamentary Assembly, whose inaugural was held in Budapest in July 1992.

On the basis of the *Paris Charter* therefore, the CSCE reconfigured its role in order to provide a framework for the evolution of a new system of international relations in Europe, based on fostering cooperation among states committed to the common values of democracy, market economies and the rule of law (Weidenfeld and Janning 1992: 83). To this end, a major concern of the CSCE in the post-wall environment was to consolidate democracy as the only system of government of participating states. This was evident from two specialist meetings organised by the CSCE: one, in Geneva in July 1991, emphasised that the rights of national minorities could best be guaranteed within democratic political systems; while the other, in Oslo in November, provided a forum for an exchange of information on constitutional law, electoral mechanisms, party systems and the rule of law. By providing the young democracies in the former communist states with information, advice and assistance, it was hoped that the CSCE could help strengthen democratisation and thereby usher in a new, less confrontational approach to European security.[8]

The OSCE and conflict prevention: *The Challenges of Change* (1992–94)

Despite the optimism of the *Paris Charter*, by early 1992 it was increasingly apparent that the 'new era of democracy, peace and unity' remained more of an aspiration than a reality. While the continent had been freed from the spectre of nuclear Armageddon, ancient animosities were reigniting and new conflicts flaring up in parts of eastern Europe, the Balkans and the Caucasus. With bitter fighting in former Yugoslavia and on the fringes of the former Soviet Union, the newly institutionalised CSCE found itself ill-equipped to manage, let alone resolve, these conflicts. Thus it soon became apparent that if the CSCE was to remain relevant to the new security challenges of post-Cold War Europe, it could not simply act as a forum for developing pan-European cooperation. Rather, the CSCE had to focus more on the new issues of preventive diplomacy, conflict prevention and crisis management (Bloed 1994).

The change of mood in Europe was apparent from the fourth CSCE follow-up meeting in Helsinki from 1–10 July 1992. While the Paris summit had agreed the positive-sounding *Paris Charter for a New Europe*, 'Helsinki II' (as this meeting was dubbed) issued the more sober-sounding document, *The Challenges of Change*. Prior to Helsinki II, the CSCE had already begun to develop its conflict-prevention and crisis-management capability. At the experts meeting on the peaceful settlement of disputes in Valetta (15 January – 8 February 1991), for example, a 'dispute settlement mechanism' within the CSCE was created. This involved a panel of qualified figures who could provide non-binding 'advice and comment' in cases of dispute between participating states (CSCE 1991). The Valetta report was endorsed by the Berlin meeting of the CSCE Ministerial Council, which also took the important step of creating a new CSCE 'emergency mechanism'. This mechanism allowed meetings of the Permanent Council (PC) to be called at short notice without consensus – which was subsequently done on a number of occasions as international concern mounted about the escalating violence in Yugoslavia.

The Challenges of Change declared that the CSCE's task was now 'managing change' and outlined several initiatives designed to strengthen the organisation's capability for conflict prevention and crisis management.[9] First, in terms of organisational structure, the Permanent Council (PC) was given a key role. The PC meets on a weekly basis in Vienna at ambassadorial level, and combines both political leadership and a decision-making capability with day-to-day operational supervision of CSCE organisations and functions. The PC thus provides the key institutional buckle between the political level of the OSCE and its functional agencies.

Second, the highly important post of High Commissioner on National Minorities (HCNM) was created. The problem of national minorities and their collective rights was now a major item on the post-Cold War security agenda and the role of the HCNM was to provide 'early warning' and, as appropriate, 'early action' in regard to national minority issues that had 'the potential to develop into ... conflict(s)' (CSCE 1992: 12). Max van der Stoel, a highly thought-of former Dutch foreign minister, was subsequently appointed to the post.

Third, the CSCE was provided with the capability to undertake peace-keeping operations. These were to conform to UN principles and resolutions, and no operation would be undertaken without an effective ceasefire, written agreement between the CSCE and the parties concerned, and guarantees for safety for CSCE personnel. Such operations would require unanimous approval by the council or Committee of Senior Officials (CSO) but would in future be able to draw on the experience and resources of organisations like the EC, NATO and the Western European Union (WEU).

Finally, Helsinki II established a new CSCE institution, the Forum for Security Cooperation (FSC). The FSC, which met for the first time on 22 September 1992 in Vienna, was given an ambitious 'programme for immediate action', with three priority tasks: negotiating new disarmament and confidence-building measures; harmonising existing obligations; and formulating 'codes of conduct' on civil–military relations.

Thus, *The Challenges of Change* sought to equip the CSCE with institutions and procedures designed for preventive diplomacy, conflict prevention and crisis management (Heraclides 1993) and represented a new departure for the organisation. Subsequent meetings in 1992 also served to bolster this aspect of the CSCE's work. On 12–23 October 1992, for example, a meeting on the peaceful settlement of disputes took place in Geneva. This created two new mechanisms – in addition to the Valletta Procedure for Peaceful Settlement of Disputes (PSD) agreed in January 1991. These were, first, 'directed conciliation', by which the Permanent Council could rule on disputes without the consent of the disputing parties ('consensus minus two'), and second, a

Court on Conciliation and Arbitration, to be based on a legally binding international convention. This Convention on Conciliation and Arbitration' entered into force on 5 December 1994 and by November 1995 had been signed by 34 states. However, none of the Peaceful Settlement of Disputes procedures have yet been used.

During the course of 1991–92, the CSCE soon found its embryonic structures for preventive diplomacy and conflict prevention tested to the limit by four international conflicts. The first was Yugoslavia, which descended into the nightmare tragedy of intercommunal conflict, ethnic cleansing and widespread atrocities. While the CSCE was quickly sidelined by the EC and the UN, it remained a convenient pan-European forum for discussing the deepening crisis. It also deployed monitoring teams in Yugoslavia and 'sanctions assistance teams' in countries bordering on Yugoslavia to ensure compliance with UN sanctions. Moreover, from September 1992 a CSCE mission was based in Belgrade with the task of reporting on the human rights situation in Kosovo, the Sanjak and Vojvodina, and promoting dialogue between the Serbian authorities and the ethnic communities. A mission was also sent to Macedonia (whose application for CSCE membership was deferred until 12 October 1995 in view of Greek objections to its name). The CSCE explicitly attributed responsibility for the Bosnia-Herzegovina conflict to Serbia/Montenegro, in which light rump Yugoslavia was excluded from participation in CSCE meetings from 8 July 1992.[10] Finally, the CSO published a report in November 1992 which recommended the creation of an international tribunal to try the perpetrators of war crimes alleged to have been committed in former Yugoslavia, thus providing further support for the creation of the International Tribunal for Former Yugoslavia in late 1993.

The other three conflicts were all in the former Soviet Union. In Nagorno-Karabakh, the CSCE created the 'Minsk Conference' on 24 March 1992 with a view to providing a framework to help diffuse deep-seated hatreds between Armenians and Azeris. The CSCE also declared a willingness to supply monitors and a CSCE peace-keeping force if a ceasefire and a peace settlement could be agreed, but unfortunately this has remained deadlocked.

In Georgia, where conflict over South Ossetia and Abkhazia had escalated, a six-person CSCE mission arrived in early December 1992 and agreed a division of labour with the UN, whereby the CSCE took responsibility for South Ossetia. Once again, the CSCE sought to encourage a viable peace process by establishing a visible presence; identifying sources of tension; liaising with local military commanders in support of the ceasefire; and assisting the creation of a framework to achieve a lasting political settlement between the Georgian authorities and disaffected groups in Ossetia. One complicating factor, however, was that the road to peace in Georgia inevitably went via Moscow, given Russia's dominant influence in the region.

The final conflict was Moldova, where a secessionist movement in the Transdniestr region was supported by the Russian Fourteenth Army, led by its charismatic leader, General Lebed. A CSCE mission arrived in Moldova in April 1993, but progress proved to be painfully slow. The CSCE mission and the Office for Democratic Institutions and Human Rights (ODIHR) have actively monitored the human rights situation, and the parliamentary elections of February 1994. The CSCE was involved in the negotiations between the Moldovan and Transdniestrian authorities and, in what represents a major step forward for the organisation, the OSCE Secretariat was subsequently designated as depository for the agreement on the non-use of military force and economic pressure signed by the two sides in July 1994 (OSCE ODIHR 1996: 26).

Given the embryonic nature of its conflict-prevention and crisis-management procedures, it is no surprise that the CSCE was unable to resolve any of the most intractable disputes. Nonetheless, this does not necessarily demonstrate the failure of the CSCE as an organisation. No other major international body – including the EC, NATO and the UN – were able to solve these complex problems. What is significant is that there has been wide agreement within Europe that the CSCE/OSCE offers – at least potentially – a valuable instrument for multilateral preventive diplomacy and conflict prevention. Moreover, since early 1992, the CSCE/OSCE has steadily built up greater expertise and experience, and now provides a more effective means for diffusing conflicts before they reach crisis dimensions.

The potential of the CSCE in the area of preventive diplomacy is perhaps best demonstrated by the work of its first HCNM, Max van der Stoel. His brief, from the beginning of 1993, was to investigate the grievances of ethnic minorities with a view to providing an early-warning mechanism capable of defusing potential conflicts. His early work focused on the Baltic Republics of Estonia and Latvia and, later in 1993, he moved on to Hungary and Slovakia. The following year he added Albania, Ukraine, Romania, Macedonia and Central Asia to his list. The results have been mixed, but few would dispute that his contribution to intercommunal understanding – and hence to European peace and security – has been a positive and significant one. The HCNM often operates confidentially, avoiding media attention – an approach which has proved successful in helping to promote dialogue and compromise between antagonistic communities.[11]

From CSCE to OSCE: reshaping the European Security System (1994–96)

By 1994, the issue of conflict prevention and crisis management had moved to the top of the European security agenda and the CSCE had become, in its own words, 'the primary instrument' for dealing with these problems in the region (CSCE 1994). Within a European changing security system, the primary role of the CSCE was to strengthen the normative consensus in Europe, particularly as regards human rights and democracy; to provide a forum for pan-European multilateral diplomacy; and to engage in early-warning, conflict prevention and crisis management. Given that many of the ethno-national conflicts wracking Europe were located in the former Soviet Union, many western diplomats privately expressed the hope that the CSCE could be used to restrain or guide Russian policy in its 'near abroad'.[12] Russia, on the other hand, wished to see the CSCE develop in ways which would institutionalise its Great Power role in European affairs and reduce the importance of the NATO alliance (Hurlburt 1995).

A major concern of the CSCE in 1994 was strengthening its cooperation with other relevant international organisations (OSCE 1995: 74–6). In February 1994, formal relations were established with the Commonwealth of Independent States (CIS). This was followed by the establishment of links with NATO's North Atlantic Cooperation Council (NACC) with a view to possible cooperation in peace-keeping operations (George 1996). The CSCE also deepened its relationship with the UN in 1994 (Kemp 1995). Cooperation had begun with the UN over Georgia (Abkhazia) in 1992–93, and similar forms of cooperation had developed in Tajikistan and Nagorno-Karabakh. In August 1994 this cooperation was extended to Bosnia by an agreement in which the UN Protection Force (UNPROFOR) was to supply logistical support to the CSCE mission to Sarajevo.

Elsewhere CSCE cooperation with the EU had already borne fruit, in the form of seven jointly run Sanctions Assistance Missions (SAMs) to enforce UN sanctions against Federal Yugoslavia.[13] The CSCE also sent a high-level delegation to the EU-sponsored Conference on Stability in Europe held in Paris in May 1994, which was designed to provide a framework for managing minority disputes and border questions. The CSCE/OSCE was made the repository for this 'Pact for Stability' and – more importantly – was entrusted with the task of expanding its aims. The Pact constituted a major exercise in preventive diplomacy, and demonstrated the potential for EU–OSCE cooperation (Hyde-Price 1996: 254).

During this period, the CSCE was developing its responsibility for election monitoring through its Warsaw-based Office of Democratic Institutions and Human Rights (OSCE ODIHR 1996). Monitoring took place in countries as diverse as Moldova, Macedonia, Hungary, Tajikistan, Latvia and Armenia – a total of 31 in all. In addition, a new area of CSCE activity which dated from 1993–94 was the integration of the newly participating states of Central Asia into the organisation. Once it became clear that the Central Asian republics were interested in developing some institutional links to the organisation, efforts were made to tailor OSCE activities to their concerns. Following the visit of the CSCE Secretary-General to the region in February–March 1994, a CSCE Liaison Office was established in Central Asia. This initiative was accompanied by a series of specialised regional seminars in Central

Asian locations on various themes germane to the purposes of the CSCE.[14] These activities helped to reinforce the existing work of the HCNM and the ODIHR in the region.

In December 1994, CSCE heads of state and government met in Budapest for another of their regular summit meetings. This was preceded by the Budapest Review Conference, which was designed to clarify future tasks and to develop the organisation's structures and decision-making procedures. Unfortunately the review conference and summit took place at a time of growing friction between Russia and the West – primarily over the issue of NATO enlargement. Yeltsin's ominous warnings about the rising danger of a 'cold peace' in Europe were accompanied by disputes over Bosnia and Russian peace-keeping operations in its 'near abroad'.

On a more positive note, the Budapest summit endorsed a document entitled *Towards a Genuine Partnership in a New Era*, which articulated common concerns about ethno-national conflict, terrorism and nuclear proliferation. Ukraine used the occasion to finally renounce nuclear weapons and sign the Nuclear Non-Proliferation Treaty and a 'Code of Conduct on Politico-Military Aspects of Security', drawn up by the CSCE Forum for Security Cooperation (FSC) was approved. Most significantly, it was agreed (subject to UN Security Council approval) to send 3000 CSCE peace-keeping troops to Nagorno-Karabakh once a formal cessation of armed conflict had been declared. Although a ceasefire was never achieved, the decision represented a willingness to endow the CSCE with a peace-keeping capacity.

Finally, the Budapest summit decided to underline the CSCE's permanent status by changing its name to the Organisation for Security and Cooperation in Europe (OSCE). While this was not accompanied by any substantial strengthening of the organisation's structures, it was designed to reflect its consolidation as an integral component of Europe's post-Cold War security architecture.

The OSCE 1995–96: from Budapest to Lisbon

Following its relaunch, the OSCE continued to build on its efforts in the area of preventive diplomacy and conflict prevention. Max van der Stoel had his appointment renewed for a further three years in December 1995. The ODIHR also organised a series of meetings and expert seminars on themes such as 'Building Blocs for Civic Society' (Warsaw, April 1995) and 'Tolerance' (Bucharest, May 1995). At the same time, however, it was becoming increasingly clear that the ODIHR – like other elements within the OSCE – was becoming a victim of its own success, given that the growing requests for its expertise from participating states and OSCE missions were stretching its resources to their limit.

The OSCE 'Missions of Long Duration' represent an increasingly significant aspect of the OSCE's work. These missions are distinct from short-term fact-finding or rapporteur missions which can be sent to investigate specific situations of a human rights or military nature.[15] They are designed to demonstrate the OSCE's long-term commitment to conflict prevention and crisis management on the ground in a particular country or region. By the end of 1996, ten missions had been deployed, each with a different mandate reflecting the specific needs of the individual countries. There were missions in Georgia, Tajikistan, Ukraine, Moldova, Latvia and Estonia. The remaining four missions were all to parts of former Yugoslavia. The mission to Skopje advised the Macedonian government on issues as diverse as education, minority rights and economic development, while the one in Sarajevo was concerned mainly with the protection of human rights. The OSCE mission to Kosovo, Sandzak and Vojvodina remained suspended by the Belgrade government, while in the case of Croatia, an OSCE fact-finding mission resulted in an invitation by the government to establish a long-term mission. This was mandated to facilitate the peaceful reintegration of formerly Serb-held territories and began work in Zagreb in July 1996 (OSCE Newsletter, July 1996: 1). Finally, an OSCE mission was sent to Bosnia-Hercegovina to work on post-conflict rehabilitation. This was quickly expanded to 250, becoming by far the largest of the ten missions.

Indeed, the signing of the Dayton peace accords (the General Framework Agreement for Peace in Bosnia-Hercegovina) led to the OSCE being allocated a central role in the process of post-conflict rehabilitation. The Dayton agreement gave the OSCE a key role in supervising the planned elections; monitoring human rights; and facilitating negotiations on localised CSBMs and sub-regional arms controls. The role of the OSCE mission was to monitor the elections and to 'assist in democracy building and be active in Human Rights promotion and monitoring, in particular to support the ombudspersons throughout Bosnia and Hercegovina'.

Dubbed 'Mission Impossible' by some, the OSCE faced enormous difficulties in Bosnia. Organising elections in such a country was a particularly arduous task, not least because nearly half of the three million voters were displaced or had fled abroad. In the light of this and other problems, the Swiss OSCE Chairman-in-Office, Flavio Cotti, told the OSCE Permanent Council on 25 June 1996 that the political conditions for 'free, fair and democratic elections' (as defined by the Dayton agreement) did not yet exist but he recommended that elections should proceed in September. The OSCE subsequently reported that these elections were conducted in a 'technically correct manner' and that 'the overall results gave well-founded cause for hope'. Nonetheless, municipal elections were postponed until 1997.

Elsewhere in former Yugoslavia, the OSCE found itself in the eye of the storm which broke after President Milosovic cancelled the results of the Serbian municipal elections in November 1996. A highly critical report by the ODIHR led Flavio Cotti to express the OSCE's 'extreme concern'. OSCE criticism was an important indication of the international community's disapproval of the increasingly authoritarian methods of Milosovic, and provided an important fillip for the antigovernment protesters.

Another important area of OSCE activity recently has been Chechnya. The eruption of bitter fighting at the end of the 1994 led to Istvan Gyarmati, the personal representative of the Chairman-in-Office, visiting the region three times in early 1995. The outcome was the creation of an 'assistance group' on 6 April which, despite becoming targeted in the fighting, played a quiet yet effective role as a facilitator between the Russian and Chechen sides. Its Head of Mission, Ambassador Tim Guldimann, was active as a neutral mediator and the OSCE gave official approval to the agreements reached after lengthy negotiations in Moscow, Nazran and Khasavyurt. The OSCE was the only international organisation present in Chechnya, demonstrating its growing significance in contemporary European diplomacy. By accepting OSCE involvement in a conflict Moscow regards as a domestic matter, Russia conceded that its actions were a matter of legitimate concern for all OSCE participating states (Cotti 1996: 9).

In December 1996, despite disputes over the future of European security, the Lisbon Summit of the OSCE reached several important decisions. It agreed a document on a 'Common and Comprehensive Security Model for Europe for the Twenty-first Century'. This was long on platitudes and short on concrete proposals, but it did nonetheless include a recognition 'of each and every participating states to be free to choose or change its security arrangements, including treaties of alliance, as they evolve' (OSCE 1996b: 7). More importantly, the Summit agreed to begin negotiations on adapting the Conventional Forces in Europe (CFE) Treaty, mainly because of Russia's insistence that it should be allowed to deploy more of its military forces on its exposed northern and southern flanks. Thus, two key documents were agreed upon: 'A Framework for Arms Control' and 'Development of the Agenda of the Forum for Security Cooperation'. Negotiations on the CFE Treaty are due to begin in Vienna in January 1997.

The five key functions of the OSCE in contemporary Europe

The OSCE has five main functions in the contemporary European security system. First, the OSCE provides a forum for pan-European multilateral diplomacy across a comprehensive range of issues within the broadly defined area of security and cooperation. It thus provides an established framework for institutionalised consultation and negotiation among all participating states. This is important in reducing the friction that inevitably accompanies international relations.

Second, it provides a means of promoting and codifying shared values and standards of behaviour among its participating states, particularly in the sphere of human rights and the non-use of force. In doing so, it provides an important normative framework for a cooperative security system within Europe's society of states. As one analyst has argued, 'contemporary international relations in Europe are characterised by an element which was largely absent from this arena until relatively recently. While norms constraining state behaviour have always been present to some degree in inter-state relations, never before have they been codified so clearly to represent the obligations and expectations of states, both in their dealings with other states and in the way they treat their domestic populations' (Hanson 1993: 29).[16]

Third, it offers a series of mechanisms for the continuous monitoring of human rights, both for individuals and for national minorities (Huber 1993). The institution of a series of review conferences after the Helsinki Final Act gave the CSCE a means to exert influence on states' respect for human rights. This has remained a key function of the organisation, as can be seen by the creation and subsequent operation of the ODIHR.

Fourth, it acts as a forum for promoting military transparency, arms controls, and CSBMs – including the CFE agreement and the Open Skies treaties (Croft 1996: 121–5). It also acts as guarantor for the Pact for Stability and acts to strengthen regional security by localised arms agreements in the context of the Dayton accords.

Finally, crucial to post-Cold War European security, the OSCE is developing instruments for early warning, preventive diplomacy and crisis management (Huber 1994; Höynick 1994). One of the key lessons of Bosnia, Pauline Neville-Jones has written, is that 'crisis prevention and management must be taken more seriously ... This means willingness to spend small sums of money in order to avoid greater costs later' (Neville-Jones 1996: 63).[17] The OSCE has only recently begun to develop this side of its activities, but has already chalked up some significant successes in central Europe, the Baltic states and even, perhaps, Moldova.

Problems facing the OSCE

While the OSCE has succeeded in carving out for itself a valuable and important role based on the five functions enunciated above, it still faces a number of significant problems.

First, OSCE is run on a shoe-string. It has a relatively small permanent staff and constant financial problems (Gießmann 1996: 58–60). Indeed, the paucity of its resources stands in glaring contrast to its almost millenarian aspirations – defined by Flavio Cotti as 'developing the concept of the shared responsibility of all states, in a common area of European civilisation', characterised by peace, cooperation, democracy and security for all. By 1996, the OSCE's constant shortage of finance and resources was becoming even more of a liability. This was embarrassingly apparent in the case of the mission to Bosnia-Hercegovina – one of the OSCE's most important responsibilities – which found it difficult to acquire sufficient financing and personnel (OSCE Newsletter, November 1996: 3).

Second, the OSCE has itself become a veritable 'alphabet soup' of institutions and offices. As the OSCE has grown as an organisation, it has begun to suffer the problems of institutional rivalry, bureaucratic infighting and lack of cohesion. This has particularly been the case with the HCNM, the ODIHR and the missions.[18] In future, the Permanent Council, the Secretary-General and the Chairman-in-Office need to play a more concerted role in coordinating the work of OSCE institutions.

Third, the OSCE's relationship with other European and international organisations needs clarifying. Since the end of the Cold War, the aim has been to forge a European security system based on 'interlocking' institutions: the danger, instead, is that they will be 'interblocking'. There is already evidence of continuing institutional 'turf-wars' between the OSCE and the Council of Europe. Similarly, the consultative work of the Forum for Security Cooperation duplicates the activities of the NACC. The relationship between the OSCE and NATO, the WEU, the Council of Europe and the UN thus needs further clarification. The OSCE has sought to improve relations with the UN, CIS and EU, but there is still much work to be done.

Conclusion: the OSCE and Europe's 'society of states'

In many ways it is easy to be cynical about the OSCE's role in European security – particularly when faced with the inflated expectations that have surrounded its development. Yet the OSCE does deserve serious consideration. Its achievements and influence on European affairs has been impressive given its limited personnel, resources and finance. Its shortcomings reflect not so much the failure of its institutions, but rather the lack of political will among its participating states. It has also fulfilled a particularly important function in oiling the wheels of European diplomacy, and in diffusing tensions before they erupt into open conflict – an achievement which never receives the publicity it deserves given the media's tendency to focus on crises and conflicts.

At the very least, the existence of the OSCE demonstrates the extent to which a 'society of states' has become firmly entrenched in European international politics. In the words of Hedley Bull '[a] *society of states* exists when a group of states, conscious of certain common interests and common values, form a society in the sense that they conceive themselves to be bound by a common set of rules in their relations with one another, and share in the working of common institutions' (1977: 13).

While the development of the OSCE clearly demonstrates that a society of states exists in Europe in the sense of being 'more than the sum of its members' (Bull 1977: 71), in some respects the organisation reflects the extent to which European international politics have evolved beyond the Westphalian model of international society. The Westphalian model is based on the principle of autonomous and sovereign states, yet the weakening of the principle VI of the Helsinki Final Act indicates that more complex forms of multilateral governance may be developing – at least in parts of Europe.[19] Principle VI codified the principle of non-interference in the domestic affairs of participating states (a defining feature of 'sovereignty'), yet it has always been in an uneasy tension with principle VII (respect for human rights and fundamental freedoms). Today, it is broadly accepted that 'violations of OSCE rules and values can no longer be legitimised by reference to non-interference in domestic affairs principle according to international law' (Peters 1996: 114). This is evident from the decisions at the Moscow and Copenhagen human rights conferences; the Geneva Report on National Minorities (Preece 1997: 88–92); the creation of the Berlin and Moscow Emergency Mechanisms; and the acceptance by Moscow of an OSCE presence in Chechnya.

The development of the OSCE demonstrates other ways in which the essential character of European order has changed. Hedley Bull argued that international order rests on the five main institutions of international society, namely: the balance of power; international law; diplomacy; the managerial system of the Great Powers; and war. In late twentieth century Europe, the relative significance of these institutions has fundamentally altered. To begin with, international law, political agreements and diplomacy have come to play an increasingly important part and there has been a growing normative consensus around fundamental values such as democracy, human rights and non-use of violence. In stark contrast, war and the balance of power have become much less significant. This is reflected in the security agenda of the OSCE, which is increasingly concerned with preventive diplomacy and crisis management. In most regions in Europe – with the notable exception of the Balkans and the Caucasus (both on the fringes of Europe) – there is broad agreement that war should no longer be regarded as a continuation of politics by other means. Military force will continue to play a role in maintaining European order, but the tasks of armed forces today are increasingly likely to be peace-keeping and humanitarian operations, rather than high-intensity conventional military campaigns.

The growing obsolescence of major war is linked to the second key change in the character of European order: the demise of traditional balance of power politics.[20] The decline of bipolarity has not resulted in the rebirth of the type of balance-of-power politics traditionally associated with multipolar systems. This is in part due to the emergence of a trans-Atlantic 'security community', but also reflects the impact of multilateral integration, economic interdependence and democratic government on much of Europe. It is also due to the emergence of an informal 'concert' of the Great Powers following the end of the Cold War, a development apparent from cooperation in such cases as German unification, the Gulf war and – despite some spats – policy towards Bosnia. Traditional *Realpolitik* conceptions still cloud the judgement of policy-makers in parts of eastern and south-eastern Europe, but the 'logic' of the balance-of-power no longer determines the functioning of European international society as a whole.

One final point to note is that the development of the OSCE also illustrates the changed nature of European security. European security is no longer focused on the military balance between antagonistic alliance systems, nor is it dominated by fears of inter-state conflict between European Great Powers. The days of Frederick the Great, Louis XIV or Stalin are well and truly over. While conflicts, rivalries and even hatreds are still a feature of the European landscape, they assume a very different form and significance today. In the Europe of the late 1990s, therefore, conflict prevention and crisis management will play an increasingly important role. This is clearly reflected in the contemporary concerns of the OSCE – from the preventive diplomacy of the HCNM, to the OSCE missions in Georgia, Estonia and Tajikistan. The OSCE has thus emerged as an integral part of the new European security system.

Notes

1. Not all commentators have welcomed the inclusion of the Central Asian states in the OSCE. Roland Dannreuther, for example, has written that '[t]he extension of the CSCE ... to the Central Asian states was an ill-conceived move which did little to alleviate the security concerns of Central Asia or its immediate neighbours' (1994: 68).

2. This principle was laid down in paragraph 69 of the Final Recommendations of the Helsinki Consultations in June 1973. This declared that: 'Decisions of the Conference shall be taken by consensus. Consensus shall be understood to mean the absence of any objection expressed by a Representative and submitted by him as constituting an obstacle to the taking of the decision in question' (Lehne 1991: 3–4).

3. This was done twice in 1992 in the case of the Federal Republic of Yugoslavia, resulting in its suspension from the organisation on 8 July 1992.

4. These are the Vienna mechanism for 'unusual military activity' (1990); the Moscow Mechanism for human rights (1991); and the Berlin mechanism for 'consultation and cooperation with regard to emergency situations' (1991). For an analysis of their significance, see Rotfeld (1995).

5. These procedural agreements were contained in the so-called 'Yellow Book' for Belgrade, and the 'Purple Book' for Madrid and Vienna.

6. During this 'Second Cold War', the CSCE became one of the few channels of communication, thereby 'helping to maintain communication during crisis situations' (Peters 1996: 96–7).

7. The Stockholm document was regarded as a major leap forward in the development of CSBMs, because it provided for mandatory on-site

inspections, which contributed to transparency. However, for a more sceptical assessment see Marie-France Desjardins (1996: 16–17).

8. On the link between democratisation and security in east central Europe, see Hyde-Price (1996: 274–9).

9. As John Major put it at the Helsinki summit, 'The CSCE ... must develop the means and the will to act before fighting begins' (Dalton 1994: 105).

10. At the time of writing (February 1997), the rump Yugoslav Federation remains suspended from participation in OSCE activities.

11. When asked by a TV company where it could film preventive diplomacy in action, Marrack Goulding, the UN Undersecretary-General, replied: 'If you can film it, it probably isn't working' (Mortimer 1997).

12. For example, at the Budapest CSCE Summit in December 1994, western proposals to subject Russian peace-keeping forces in Georgia, Moldova and Tajikistan to scrutiny were vetoed by Moscow.

13. The Sanctions Assistance Missions were established in Hungary, Romania, FYROM (Macedonia), Albania, Bulgaria, Croatia and Ukraine, following a decision of the London Conference in August 1992. A Sanctions Committee (SANCOMM) was set up in Brussels in October 1992 to facilitate communication and coordination. The work of the SAMs ended after sanctions against Federal Yugoslavia and Republika Srpska were terminated (OSCE Newsletter, October 1996: 4).

14. Since the winter of 1995/96, the ODIHR has also published a Newsletter on Central Asia and Transcaucasia ('C.A.&T. Newsletter').

15. While the OSCE usually takes decisions by consensus, short-term fact-finding or expert missions can be sent without the agreement of all. This is known as the 'Moscow mechanism' and the receiving OSCE participating state may not refuse the mission. Examples include missions to Croatia, Moldova and Chechnya.

16. For a more theoretical analysis of the impact of international norms on states' behaviour see Goertz (1994).

17. As Jonathan Eyal has written, '[i]n electoral terms, convincing politicians to invest in conflict prevention is like asking a teenager to start saving for a pension: the argument may be correct, but the advantages are too hypothetical to seem real at the time' (Mortimer 1997).

18. The need for the Chairman-in-Office and the Secretary-General to facilitate greater coordination between the HCNM and the missions was highlighted by the HCNM himself in his report to the Vienna Review Meeting (Van der Stoel 1996: 11).

19. Elsewhere I have suggested that in post-Cold War Europe an increasingly complex, multidimensional and multilayered system of international relations is emerging, characterised by a variety of actors, authorities, loyalties and identities. This may well resemble the 'new Medievalism' outlined by Hedley Bull, which he described as 'a system of overlapping authority and multiple loyalty' (1977: 254–5). See Hyde-Price (1977: 34) in Landau and Whitman (1977).

20. Robert Cooper, a senior British diplomat, (writing in a personal capacity) has noted that 'what happened in 1989 was not just the end of the Cold War, but also the end of the balance-of-power system in Europe' (1996: 7).

References

Acimovic, L. (1981) *Problems of Security and Cooperation in Europe*, Alphen aan den Rijn: Sijthoff & Noordhoff.

Birnbaum, K. and Huldt, B. (eds) (1987) *From Stockholm to Vienna: Building Confidence and Security in Europe*, Stockholm: Swedish Institute of International Affairs.

Bloed, A. (ed.) (1994) *The Challenges of Change: The Helsinki Summit of the CSCE and its Aftermath*, Dordrecht: Martinus Nijhoff.

Bloed, A. and van Dijk, P. (1991) *The Human Dimension of the Helsinki Process*, Dordrecht: Martinus Nijhoff.

Brauch, H. G. (ed.) (1986) *Vertrauensbildende Massnahmen und Europäische Abrüstungskonferenz*, Gerlingen: Bleicher Verlag.

Bull, H. (1977) *The Anarchical Society. A Study of Order in World Politics*, London: Macmillan.

Cooper, R. (1996) *The Post-Modern State and the World Order*, London: Demos.

Cotti, F. (1996) 'The OSCE's Increasing Responsibilities in European Security', *NATO Review*, November: 7–12.

Croft, S. (1996) *Strategies of Arms Control. A History and Typology*, Manchester: Manchester University Press.

CSCE (1991) *Report of the CSCE Meeting of Experts of Peaceful Settlement of Disputes*, Valletta: CSCE.

CSCE (1992) *Helsinki Document 1992. The Challenges of Change*, London: HMSO.

CSCE (1994) *Towards a Genuine Partnership in a New Era*, Budapest: CSCE Secretariat.

Dalton, R. (1994) 'The Role of the CSCE', in Miall, H., (1994): 99–111.

Dannreuther, R. (1994) *Creating New States in Central Asia*, Adelphi Paper 288, London: Brassey's for the IISS.

Desjardins, M-F. (1996) *Rethinking Confidence-Building Measures. Obstacles to Agreement and the Risks of Overselling the Process*, Adelphi Paper 307, London: Brassey's for the IISS.

George, B. (1996) 'Forging the NATO–OSCE Partnership', *OSCE ODIHR Bulletin*, 4(3): 45–7.

Gießmann, H-J. (1996) *Europäische Sicherheit am Scheidenweg – Chancen und Perspektiven der OSZE*, Hamburg, Hamburger Beiträge zur Friedensforschung und Sicherheitspolitik, Heft 97, March.

Goertz, G. (1994) *Contexts of International Politics*, Cambridge: Cambridge University Press.

Halliday, F. (1983) *The Making of the Second Cold War*, London: Verso.

Hanson, M. (1993) 'Democratisation and Norm Creation in Europe', European Security After the Cold War, Part 1, Adelphi Paper 284, London: Brassey's for the IISS: 28–41.

Heraclides, A. (1993) *Helsinki II and its Aftermath. The Making of the CSCE into an International Organisation*, London: Pinter.

Höynick, W. (1994) 'CSCE Works to Develop its Conflict Prevention Potential', *NATO Review*, 42(2): 16–22.

Huber, K. J. (1993) 'The CSCE and Ethnic Conflict in the East', *RFE/RL Research Reports*, 2(31): 30–6.

Huber, K. J. (1994) 'The CSCE's New Role in the East: Conflict Prevention', *RFE/RL Research Reports*, 3(31): 23–30.

Hurlburt, H. (1995) 'Russia, the OSCE and European Security Architecture', *Helsinki Monitor*, 6(2): 5–20.

Hyde-Price, A. (1991) *European Security Beyond the Cold War: Four Scenarios for the Year 2010*, London: Sage.

Hyde-Price, A. (1996) *The International Politics of East Central Europe*, Manchester: Manchester University Press.

Hyde-Price, A. (1997) 'The New Pattern of International Relations in Europe', in Landau and Whitman, (eds) (1997): 15–35.

Kemp, W. (1995) 'The OSCE and the UN: A Closer Relationship', *Helsinki Monitor*, 6(1): 24–31.

Landau, A. and Whitman, R. (eds) (1997) *Rethinking the European Union. Institutions, Interests and Identities*, London: Macmillan.

Lehne, S. (1991) *The Vienna Meeting of the Conference on Security and Cooperation in Europe, 1986–1989. A Turning Point in East–West Relations*, Oxford: Westview Press.

Marescu, J. J. (1985) *To Helsinki, The Conference on Security and Cooperation in Europe, 1973–1975*, Durham, N.C.: Duke University Press.

Mearsheimer, J. (1990) 'Back to the Future: Instability in Europe after the Cold War', *International Security*, 15(1): 5–56.

Melvin, N. (1995) *Russians Beyond Russia. The Politics of National Identity*, London: Pinter .

Miall, H. (ed.) (1994) *Minority Rights in Europe. The Scope for a Transnational Regime*, London: Pinter.

Mortimer, E. (1997) 'Action for Peace', *Financial Times*, London, 23 January 1997.

Neville-Jones, P. (1996) 'Dayton, IFOR and Alliance Relations in Bosnia', *Survival*, 38(4) (Winter 1996–97): 45–65.

OSCE (1995) *OSCE Handbook. 20 Years of the Helsinki Final Act 1975–1995*, Vienna: OSCE Secretariat.

OSCE (1996a) *OSCE Handbook 1996, Second Edition*, Vienna: OSCE Secretariat.

OSCE (1996b) *Lisbon Document 1996*, Lisbon: OSCE.

OSCE ODIHR (1996) *Annual Report for 1996*, Warsaw, Ref. RM/59/96 (25 October).

Peters, I. (1996) *New Security Challenges: The Adaptation of International Institutions. Reforming the UN, NATO, EU, and CSCE since 1989*, New York: St Martin's Press.

Preece, J. J. (1997) 'Minority Rights in Europe: from Westphalia to Helsinki', *Review of International Studies*, 23(1): 75–92.

Rotfeld, A. D. (1995) 'The Evolution of the Helsinki Process', *OSCE ODIHR Bulletin*, 3(3): 1–6.

Van der Stoel, M. (1996) *Report to the OSCE Review Meeting, Vienna, 4–21 November 1996*, Vienna, Ref. RM/71/96 (4 November).

Volle, H. and Wagner, W. (1976) *KSZE. Konferenz über Sicherheit und Zusammenarbeit in Europa in Beiträgen und Dokumenten aus dem Europa-Archiv*, Bonn: Verlag für Internationale Politik.

Weidenfeld, W. and Janning, J. (1992) 'European Integration after the Cold War – Perspectives of a New Order', *International Social Science Journal*, 131: 79–89.

Wrede, H.-H. (1990) *KSZE in Wien*, Köln: Verlag Wissenschaft und Politik.

Further reading

Clarke, M. (ed.) (1993) *New Perspectives on Security*, London: Brassey's.

Mastny, V. (1986) *Helsinki, Human Rights and European Security*, Durham, N.C.: Duke University Press.

Mastny, V. (1992) *The Helsinki Process and the Re-integration of Europe*, London: Pinter.

Vincent, R. J. (1986) *Human Rights and International Relations*, Cambridge: Cambridge University Press.

NATO transformed: the Atlantic Alliance in a new era

ANDREW COTTEY

Introduction

Since its establishment in 1949, the North Atlantic Treaty Organisation (NATO) has been the main institutional framework for the coordination of the foreign, security and defence policies of western Europe and North America. During the post-war period when NATO was focused on the threat from the Soviet Union, its members came to form what Karl Deutsch termed a 'security community' – a 'zone of peace' where war between them was largely inconceivable (Deutsch et al. 1957). Their economies, their foreign and security policies and their armed forces increasingly became 'integrated', both through formal institutions such as NATO and the European Union (EU) and through various forms of less institutionalised cooperation. This process of integration and security community building was not uniform or complete: the United States by virtue of its geographic separation from Europe was less integrated than most west European states and war between Greece and Turkey remained conceivable. Nevertheless, most observers would accept that the western countries were increasingly bound together. With the end of the Cold War, however, they faced a radically new security environment. What role NATO should play in that environment was an open question.

The members of the Atlantic Alliance now face new forms of 'instability' and 'uncertainty' not only to their east and south, but also globally. This includes both more 'traditional' security concerns (Russia's residual military potential, armed conflict on Europe's periphery and beyond, the proliferation of nuclear, chemical and biological weapons and their means of delivery) and 'new' security concerns (mass migration, environmental degradation, transnational crime). In this new strategic environment, the western security community faces a twofold challenge. First, that of maintaining, and many would argue further deepening, the integrative processes which have facilitated trans--Atlantic cooperation. Second, that of responding to the complex, multi-faceted security problems on Europe's periphery and beyond. The diverse character of these security problems, however, means that the security concerns of western states are increasingly differentiated. NATO's 'northern tier' members are more concerned by developments in central Europe, the western former Soviet Union and Russia. NATO's 'southern tier' members are more concerned by developments in the Mediterranean region. The United States, as a global power, is more concerned by developments in other regions (such as the Persian Gulf, East Asia). Without the unifying effect of the 'Soviet threat', the countries of western Europe and North America may find it increasingly difficult to develop concerted policies on security issues.

In this new strategic environment NATO faced an uncertain future. NATO's relevance to the new, post-Cold War security challenges – the problems of transition in post-communist Europe, 'instability' to Europe's south, 'small' conflicts on Europe's periphery, nuclear proliferation, non-military security concerns – was unclear. If NATO was to be relevant, fundamental changes in the Alliance's structures and policies would be necessary. Other institutions, however, might arguably be better suited to addressing the security problems of post-Cold War Europe such as the EU and the Organisation for Security and Cooperation in Europe (OSCE). Even if NATO remained intact, doubts remained about the willingness of the United States to maintain a long-term commitment to European security and the ability of the Alliance to maintain unity in the face of the increasingly differentiated security concerns and interests of its members. In short, the end of the Cold War posed fundamental questions not only about NATO's future direction but also about its very existence. As one observer put it, not only whither NATO but also whether NATO (Heisbourg 1992)?

NATO governments argued that the Alliance's traditional roles of balancing Soviet/Russian power, maintaining a US role in Europe and integrating Germany into western security structures remained relevant. The Soviet Union and, after its break-up, Russia remained the single largest military power in Europe and faced an uncertain political future. The experience of the twentieth century suggested that active US engagement would remain important for the prevention of large-scale conflict in Europe. Germany's growing political and economic power highlighted the importance of its integration into western security structures. At their July 1990 London summit, NATO leaders stated that 'the North Atlantic Alliance has been the most successful defensive alliance in history ... We need to keep standing together, to extend the long peace we have enjoyed these past four decades' (NATO 1990: 32). German unification played a particularly important role in consolidating the consensus that NATO should be maintained.

At the end of 1991, NATO leaders agreed on a new Strategic Concept endorsing an Alliance role in crisis management, the development of a European Security and Defence Identity (ESDI) within the Alliance and the creation of the North Atlantic Cooperation Council (NACC) to facilitate cooperation with the central/east European (CEE) states. Despite these steps, however, by the mid-1990s NATO faced a growing sense of crisis. The debate over the development of an ESDI had provoked serious rifts. The NACC had failed to satisfy the demands of the

CEE states who were seeking intensive cooperation with and membership of the Alliance. Above all, NATO's inability to respond effectively to the Yugoslav conflict was fundamentally threatening the Alliance's unity and credibility. Europe's worst conflict since the Second World War was occurring on NATO's doorstep, yet the Alliance could not bring a halt to the bloodshed. European members of the Alliance had deployed peace-keeping forces in a situation in which there was no peace to keep and faced criticism of appeasement from the United States. The US demanded more forceful action but was not itself willing to deploy ground forces. By 1993–94, the Alliance faced perhaps the worst dispute in its history, leading to a questioning of US willingness to remain centrally engaged in European security. One observer concluded that 'the Western alliance is dead ... if NATO's mission is not to contain military conflicts across borders, then what role *does* NATO have to play?' (Chace 1993: 89). In these circumstances, the ability of the Alliance to respond effectively to the new challenges of instability to Europe's east and south was open to serious doubt. As US Senator Richard Lugar argued, 'NATO will either develop the strategy and structure to go "out-of-area" or it will "go out of business" ' (Chilton *et al.* 1994: 5).

Against this background, led by the Clinton administration, NATO began to respond to the challenge of moving out-of-area and adapting to the new era. At their January 1994 Brussels summit, NATO leaders initiated the Partnership for Peace (PfP) Programme for enhanced cooperation with the CEE countries and the former Soviet Union, agreed in principle that the Alliance was open to new members, agreed to develop the Combined Joint Task Force (CJTF) concept for future NATO military operations and initiated discussions on an Alliance policy framework on the problem of the proliferation of nuclear, biological and chemical weapons (NATO 1994). Since then, the transformation of NATO has accelerated, with the development of a wide range of PfP cooperative activities, progress towards Alliance enlargement, the development of a new relationship with Russia, agreement on the CJTF concept and initiation of a major reform of NATO's command system providing for flexible 'coalitions of the willing'. Progress has also been made in developing a concerted approach towards proliferation and an outreach programme to the countries of the Mediterranean.

Bosnia, however, proved to be the central testing ground of NATO's transformation. By the spring and summer of 1995, the credibility of NATO and the UN was stretched to its limits. The Bosnian Serbs continued to shell UN designated 'safe areas', took UN peace-keepers hostage and overran the 'safe areas' of Srebrenica and Zepa (committing atrocities in the process), while limited NATO airstrikes had little impact. These developments, combined with the building-up of the Croatian and Bosnian armed forces enabling them to retake territory from the Bosnian Serbs, galvanised NATO. Vulnerable UN peace-keepers were withdrawn from Bosnian Serb-held territory, a UK–

French led Rapid Reaction Force was established within Bosnia and NATO threatened the wider use of airstrikes if the remaining 'safe areas' were attacked. At the end of August, the further shelling of Sarajevo by the Bosnian Serbs triggered *Operation Deliberate Force*. Over a period of two weeks, NATO proceeded to destroy the Bosnian Serb military infrastructure, thereby forcing them to the negotiating table. The Dayton peace agreement was signed in November 1995, mandating the deployment of a nearly 60 000 strong NATO-led peace implementation force (IFOR) (IISS 1996), including forces from the US and PfP countries. *Operation Deliberate Force* and the IFOR restored NATO's credibility and unity, indicated that NATO could indeed operate out-of-area, symbolised a renewed US willingness to play a leading role in European security, and showed that NATO could cooperate with its former enemies in complex peace support operations.

In combination, these developments have shifted the Alliance from an organisation focused on collective defence to one whose main activities relate to the new security challenges outside the NATO area. Nevertheless, NATO is likely to face continuing policy dilemmas in a range of areas, such as the Balkans, NATO enlargement and relations with Russia, which could generate new intra-Alliance tensions. Disputes are likely to continue between NATO's members over the balance of political power and leadership within the Alliance, command arrangements and possible future peace-keeping and enforcement operations. NATO's policies towards its southern neighbours in the Mediterranean, on proliferation and on wider global security issues are less developed than its new eastern policy but may pose equally serious dilemmas in the longer term: how to engage with the unstable situation to NATO's south, whether NATO should have a military role outside Europe, whether to develop missile defences, how far the Alliance can or should develop common positions on security issues in regions such as the Middle East or East Asia. Against this background, the rest of this chapter explores in detail the issues and policy dilemmas NATO has faced since the end of the Cold War and is likely to face in the future. It concludes with the prospects for NATO and trans-Atlantic relations.

NATO's new 'Ostpolitik'

Enlargement to include new CEE states has posed enormous dilemmas for the Alliance. Failing to enlarge the Alliance might leave the CEE countries in a dangerous security vacuum, creating an on-going source of instability in the region which had triggered two World Wars and the Cold War. Bringing new members into NATO might risk provoking a new confrontation with Russia and undermining the security of those states lying between an enlarged NATO and Russia. By the mid-1990s, NATO enlargement had become the most controversial issue in European security.

NATO's initial steps towards engagement with the East were cautious. In 1990, NATO offered 'the hand of friendship' through a declaration on non-adversarial relations, the expansion of diplomatic and military contacts and arms control agreements (NATO 1990). In December 1991, facing growing pressure for an institutionalised relationship, NATO established the NACC – a multilateral framework bringing together NATO's members with all the former adversaries. While the NACC facilitated increased dialogue on security issues, it failed to differentiate between the various CEE and former Soviet states and resulted in little substantive military cooperation. It was inflexible because decisions were made by consensus – giving each member a veto. Nor did it address the issue of opening NATO to new members in central/east Europe. Critics described it as 'a holding operation that provides only meagre psychological reassurance' (Asmus, Kugler and Larrabee 1993: 32).

In the light of continued pressure, in January 1994 NATO leaders announced in principle that the Alliance was open to new members and initiated the PfP (NATO 1994). Unlike NACC, PfP would be based on 'sixteen plus one' relations between NATO and individual eastern partner states, allowing each side to determine the extent and content of their relationship and facilitating greatly increased political and military cooperation. Initial responses to PfP, however, were sceptical. CEE states feared it was another holding operation, while Russia feared it was a first step towards enlarging NATO. The substance of PfP cooperation was unclear. Since then, however, PfP has developed into a substantive and successful outreach programme, contributing to security in a number of ways. Virtually all the CEE, former Soviet and European neutral states have become PfP partners. NATO has provided substantial political and military support to the reform of their security policies and armed forces. PfP prepares aspirant states by facilitating their adoption of NATO standards for defence planning, civilian control of the military and the inter-operability of armed forces. Multilateral exercises within the PfP framework act as a confidence-building measure, bringing together the militaries of former and potential adversaries in a cooperative framework.

PfP, however, failed to address the issue of expanding NATO's membership. By the mid-1990s, membership of NATO and the EU was the central foreign policy goal of the majority of CEE states. Russian political élites, in contrast, were increasingly opposed to NATO's enlargement, on the grounds that it would isolate them. Strong arguments could be advanced both for and against expanding NATO. Bringing CEE states into the Alliance would ensure their independence from Russia; provide stable security arrangements for the region; support democratic political forces, market economic reforms and foreign investment in these countries; and encourage cooperative relations with neighbouring states. Indeed, the desire for NATO membership had already encouraged countries such as Poland and Hungary to improve their relations with their neighbours and assert civilian control over their armed forces.

Critics countered that in the absence of a military threat NATO enlargement was unnecessary; that the EU could better provide the political and economic integration with the West; that NATO enlargement risked provoking confrontation with Russia and strengthening authoritarian forces; and that the security of states outside an enlarged NATO (such as the Baltic states and Ukraine) would be undermined. In essence, enlargement posed a classical security dilemma for NATO. Refusing to extend membership to the CEE states risked leaving them in a vulnerable security limbo, creating an on-going source of insecurity at the heart of Europe and undermining their stability and progress in democratisation. Expanding NATO risked new tensions with Russia and undermining the security of 'left out' states.

The most radical solution to NATO's dilemma was to turn the Alliance into a pan-European collective security system by enlarging it to include all states *including Russia* (or alternatively replacing NATO with a strengthened OSCE) – an argument advanced by Russia and some in the West. Theoretically, such a system could provide security for both the CEE states and Russia. In practice powerful arguments weighed against such an approach. While western states might be willing to extend NATO's mutual defence guarantee to some CEE states, they were unlikely to do so for Russia and the former Soviet states. The last thing the CEE states wanted was a similar guarantee from Russia. Looser security assurances would lack credibility. While a Security Council or an informal Great Power 'Concert' might underpin such a system, it would depend on cooperative relations between the major powers. Given the political uncertainty in Russia, both NATO's current members and the CEE states were unlikely to make their security dependent on a system in which Russia had an effective veto.

Against this background, NATO faced essentially three options for enlargement (Asmus, Kugler and Larrabee 1995). First, enlargement could be 'threat driven', occurring only if a direct Russian military threat to central/east Europe emerged. Second, NATO enlargement could be timed to follow that of the EU as part of a longer term strategy of integrating CEE states with the West. Third, enlargement could be undertaken earlier, by about the year 2000, as a way of providing stability for central/east Europe. While the first two of these approaches would have held open the option of enlargement, they would in all probability have amounted to an indefinite postponement. Such a strategy might have been viable at the beginning of the 1990s but after the January 1994 summit, the Clinton administration began to press for early enlargement. To have stepped back from enlargement at this stage – especially under Russian pressure – would have been viewed as a major betrayal. Thus, NATO's 1995 'Study on Enlargement' made clear that the Alliance would move ahead with enlargement and that this would take place as part of a strategy to promote security and stability in central/east Europe (NATO 1995).

Despite doubts within some member countries about the wisdom of enlargement, NATO moved ahead with its plans. During the 1996 US Presidential election campaign President Clinton stated that the first new members should join the Alliance in 1999 on the fiftieth anniversary of the signing of the North Atlantic Treaty. At the end of 1996, NATO agreed to a special summit at Madrid in July 1997 to issue invitations to the first new members and confirm other reforms of the Alliance. As the states which had made the most progress in democratic, economic and foreign and security policy reforms, Poland, the Czech Republic and Hungary were duly invited to join the Alliance. Slovenia and Romania, whose candidatures were pressed by several European NATO states, were not invited in the first wave of new members but were singled out for special mention at the summit as likely future members.

At the same time, Russian opposition to NATO's enlargement intensified, while those states likely to be left outside NATO became increasingly concerned. These multiple pressures led the Alliance towards a complex strategy designed to 'square the circle' of enlargement, maintaining cooperative relations with Russia and providing security for those states left outside. By early 1997, the components of this strategy were becoming clear: a limited enlargement involving only three-to-five states in the 'first wave'; a commitment that NATO remained open in principle to further new members; an enhanced PfP, involving intensified political and military cooperation for the 'left outs'; a politically (but not legally) binding NATO–Russia charter, involving a new NATO–Russian council and new forms of cooperation; a parallel NATO–Ukraine cooperation agreement; the combination of NACC and PfP to create a more high profile 'Atlantic Partnership Council'; a commitment not to deploy nuclear weapons on the territory of new NATO members and, from the US, to discuss further cuts in strategic nuclear forces; and the renegotiation of the Conventional Armed Forces in Europe (CFE) Treaty.

How far NATO could be 'successful' in squaring the circle was an open question. For the states remaining outside NATO – Ukraine, the Baltic states and Romania – their fear of Russia and commitment to integration with the West was likely to lead them to continue to seek close ties with NATO and the EU. A few states which were already less western oriented – most prominently Belarus, but also perhaps Slovakia – might turn further towards Russia. The greatest problem, however, was clearly Russia. As one Russian observer put it, Russia's opposition to NATO enlargement was 'a geo-psychological complex' (Clark and Freeland 1997). It was doubtful whether NATO would ever fully satisfy Russian concerns. Competition among Russian political forces to take a hard line over NATO enlargement was likely to force Russia's leadership to respond to NATO enlargement. The real issue appeared to be the content and extent of Russia's reaction to NATO enlargement. Russia might take a number of steps: refusing to ratify the START II nuclear arms reduction treaty; intensifying political and economic pressure on countries such as Ukraine and the Baltic states; increasing efforts to achieve reintegration in the former Soviet Union; redeploying conventional forces westwards. A number of factors, however, seemed likely to constrain Russia's reaction: its economic and military weakness; its need for economic aid from the West; more pressing domestic economic and social problems; the influence gained from such cooperation as the IFOR; the more immediate security problems of Russia's south in the Transcaucasus and central Asia; and longer term concerns about Chinese power. In these circumstances, the most likely outcome was that Russia would withdraw from some elements of cooperation with NATO in the short term, but gradually return to such cooperation – as it had done when it initially rejected PfP but later joined the programme.

NATO enlargement also faced a different but related obstacle. The accession of new signatories to the North Atlantic Treaty must be ratified by the parliaments of NATO's existing members. Given that extending NATO membership involves defence guarantees, such ratification was inevitably controversial. By the mid-1990s, doubts were raised about the willingness of NATO parliaments (particularly the US Senate, where a two-thirds majority was required) to ratify enlargement. Ratification of NATO enlargement might also be 'held hostage' by certain member states. Early in 1997, Turkey threatened to veto NATO enlargement unless it received a clear commitment to join the EU, while Greece raised the issue of early membership of the EU for Cyprus. A failure by one or more member state to ratify enlargement would provoke a very serious crisis within the Alliance – especially if that failure resulted from deep divisions among NATO members and/or 'backing down' in the face of Russian pressure. Indeed, it could be argued that, having moved so far towards enlargement, failure to ratify it at this stage would deal a mortal blow to the Alliance's credibility and unity and would be seen as an enormous betrayal in central/east Europe. Ironically, this very danger would probably enable advocates of enlargement (particularly the US government) to gain the domestic support and broker the intra-Alliance compromises necessary to achieve its ratification.

Even if a 'first wave' of NATO enlargement was successfully managed, eastern policy was likely to continue to pose dilemmas for the Alliance. Having stated in principle that the Alliance was open to further new members, NATO would have to address the issue of whether, when and how to undertake a 'second wave' of enlargement. Much would depend on the longer term evolution of Russia's relations with NATO. A gradual improvement in NATO–Russia relations and Russian recognition that the Alliance did not threaten it might create the circumstances in which further NATO enlargement to include most of central/east Europe, the Baltic states and perhaps even Ukraine would be acceptable to Russia. More radically still, a stable, democratic Russia with good relations with the West might perhaps one day join NATO.

In the interim, NATO seemed likely to face a difficult task in balancing its relations with Russia and the other former Soviet states. The Baltic states, Ukraine, Moldova and (to varying degrees) the Transcaucasian states were seeking closer ties with the West in general and NATO in particular (including through PfP) in order to strengthen themselves *vis-à-vis* Russia. Russia, seeking to maintain influence in the former Soviet Union and driven by historic fears of encirclement, opposed the expansion of western/NATO influence in the region. In the worst case, there was potential for serious confrontation between the West/NATO and Russia in the former Soviet Union.

New military roles: peace-keeping and peace-enforcement

During the Cold War, NATO had effectively no 'out-of-area' role. In the post-Cold War European security environment it became increasingly clear that NATO must develop policies towards conflicts outside the territory of its members if it was to remain relevant. In 1992, NATO foreign and defence ministers agreed to consider on a 'case-by-case' basis possible support for UN or OSCE authorised peace-keeping operations and began to discuss military planning for 'peace support operations' (Rader 1996: 143, 152–4). Whether and in what circumstances the Alliance should undertake peace-keeping or peace-enforcement operations, however, remained controversial.

The issue was posed, above all, by the on-going conflict in the former Yugoslavia. From 1992–93, NATO monitored compliance with and enforced UN sanctions against the former Yugoslav republics and the UN 'no-fly zone' over the former Yugoslavia. This resulted in the joint NATO–WEU (Western European Union) naval *Operation Sharp Guard* and extensive NATO air operations over the region. European NATO members also provided the majority of forces for the UN peacekeeping operation in the former Yugoslavia and NATO's Northern Army Group (NORTHAG) provided the initial core of the headquarters for the operation (Rader 1996: 146–8). Despite successfully enforcing the sanctions and the 'no-fly zone', the question of NATO intervention in the conflict became increasingly controversial. As was noted earlier, European efforts at peace-keeping when there was no peace to keep and the US reluctance to commit ground forces for any possible attempt to enforce a peace led to deep divisions within the Alliance. Only when the Bosnian government and Croatian armed forces were built up as a counter-weight to those of the Bosnian Serbs, vulnerable UN peacekeepers were withdrawn from Bosnian Serb territory and NATO was willing to undertake extensive airstrikes against the Bosnian Serbs, was NATO able to broker the Dayton peace settlement and the deployment of the IFOR.

NATO's experience in the conflict suggested several important lessons for the Alliance's future role in peace-keeping and peace-enforcement: that attempts at peace-keeping are unlikely to succeed (and may even be counterproductive) in circumstances where there is no peace to keep; that indirect forms of pressure, such as 'no-fly zones', have only limited effects in the absence of supporting ground forces; that the Europeans lack the military resources to undertake peace-enforcement operations without US support; that divisions can seriously undermine the Alliance's ability to respond effectively. The relative success of *Operation Deliberate Force* and the IFOR (and subsequent Stabilisation Force), however, also suggested that, when united behind a coherent approach, NATO has substantial potential to deal with conflicts.

In considering its future role in peace-keeping and peace-enforcement, NATO also faced some broader problems inherent in all such operations. The legitimacy, authorisation and control of such operations was one key issue. NATO's commitment to consider such operations was taken on the basis that they be under 'the responsibility of the CSCE' (NATO 1992a: 31) or 'the authority of the UN Security Council' (NATO 1992b: 29). Authorisation by the UN Security Council or the OSCE provides international legitimacy, which may be vital to gaining support for any action both within NATO and from other states. Depending on such authorisation, however, also constrains NATO's independence, since it gives the mandating organisations substantial influence over the execution of those operations. The issue of political and military control of operations may also be important, since it can determine what action is (or is not) taken. In the former Yugoslavia, under 'dual-key' NATO–UN arrangements for the authorisation of airstrikes, UN political leaders were seen to be thwarting US efforts to adopt a more robust approach. Against this background, a 1993 internal NATO discussion paper by the US mission to NATO, entitled 'With the UN Whenever Possible, Without When Necessary?', questioned 'the wisdom of having tied NATO so tightly to the UN's apron strings' (Chilton *et al.* 1994: 57). While one could not rule out circumstances where NATO would want to take military action alone, in most situations NATO seemed likely to seek broad UN or OSCE authority to act while attempting to maximise its operational independence and control.

NATO also faced the challenge of determining the most effective and appropriate military approach to intervening in complex, multi-faceted conflicts such as that in Bosnia. Although NATO was attempting to develop a common doctrine for peace-support operations, how such operations should be approached remained in practice a controversial question. In some circumstances – brief interventions to extract one's own citizens, traditional peace-keeping in situations where peace (or at least an effective ceasefire) had already been established – determining the most appropriate military response might be relatively easy. In on-going, complex conflicts, however, determining the right approach was always likely to be difficult and dependent on one's political objectives. The other extreme – massive intervention of the type undertaken in the 1990–91 Gulf War – appeared to be equally inappropriate. In between, however, lay a range of options: the use of force to deliver humanitarian aid; attempts to protect civilian populations in 'safe areas'; the use of airpower for coercive purposes; the use of ground and air forces to enforce a peace, which had uncertain prospects for success. The possible risks ranged from being dragged into a Vietnam-style conflict to appeasement of aggression because of a misplaced reluctance to use force. Learning from the Bosnian experience and developing a common NATO doctrine might help. The most appropriate form of military action, however, was always likely to be an intensely political and often controversial question.

Most fundamentally, NATO still faced the problem of how far and in what circumstances it could and should take on the tasks of peace-keeping and peace-enforcement. In the US, the Clinton administration supported the idea that NATO might take on a wider range of peace-keeping/enforcement tasks, including beyond Europe's periphery. In 1995, the Chairman of the US Joint Chiefs of Staff, General John Shalikashvili, had recommended considering the use of NATO forces in Rwanda. He argued that, in future, 'the NATO horizon would stretch beyond Europe. I can envisage the day when the member nations see it useful to deal with humanitarian and other operations in Africa or the Middle East, utilizing NATO command and control' (Walker 1996: 2). While a gradual expansion of NATO activities was perhaps likely, it also faced a number of problems. The European allies might fear US domination of such operations while non-NATO countries might fear the Alliance becoming a 'world policeman'. Perhaps most importantly, however, the expansion of NATO's out-of-area operations was likely to be limited by the willingness of member states to involve their armed forces in complex conflicts, where their immediate interests were limited and intervention might involve substantial risks.

NATO looks south: a clash of civilisations?

While much attention has focused on the controversial issues of NATO's eastern policies, the Alliance also faces equal security challenges to its south over the longer term. In North Africa, the Mediterranean and the Middle East, the Alliance faces a series of politically unstable and impoverished states; the risk of large-scale migration driven by economic factors or violent conflict; conflicts (in Algeria, Cyprus, the Middle East and the Persian Gulf); anti-western political movements, sometimes resorting to terrorism; the rise of Islam as a political force; and the possible proliferation of weapons of mass destruction. These problems are themselves part of the larger north–south political and economic divide. These have led to warnings of a coming 'clash of civilisations' between 'the West and the rest', with tensions between the largely Christian countries of western Europe and north America and their largely Islamic neighbours as one element of that clash (Huntington 1993). Indeed, some within NATO viewed a possible 'Islamic threat' as one of the main dangers facing the West. In 1994, then NATO Secretary-General, Willy Claes, argued that Islamic fundamentalism was 'at least as dangerous as communism used to be to the West' (Serfaty 1996–97: 153). The real danger, however, probably lies not in an inevitable 'clash of civilisations', but rather in the adoption of confrontational policies which could make such a clash a self-fulfilling prophecy.

Relations with the Alliance's Mediterranean neighbours has become one of the key concerns of NATO's 'southern tier' members. In 1994, NATO began to develop proposals for dialogue with Mediterranean countries. This was duly initiated with Egypt, Israel, Mauritania, Morocco, Tunisia and Jordan, aimed at promoting transparency, mutual understanding and stability in the region. However, as analysts noted, there was 'no clear consensus within NATO, or within the dialogue countries, on what the content or ultimate aim of this initiative should be' (Asmus, Larrabee and Lesser 1996b: 31). NATO's dialogue with its Mediterranean neighbours was far less developed than that with its PfP partners. Although such dialogue might help to build confidence, it was difficult to see what role NATO could play in addressing the central problems of political instability and economic underdevelopment in the region. While NATO was able to engage in dialogue with those states which broadly were pro-western, engaging in dialogue with more anti-western states would be far more difficult. Nevertheless, the development of a dialogue on security concerns and threat perceptions might help to reduce mutual 'enemy images' and eventually lead to practical military cooperation (Asmus, Larrabee and Lesser 1996b: 31).

The possible proliferation of nuclear, chemical and biological weapons and their means of delivery has also become a major NATO concern. Proliferation could pose new threats not only to NATO's members' territories but also to their armed forces operating outside the NATO area. At their January 1994 summit, NATO leaders initiated work on an 'overall policy framework' on proliferation (NATO 1994: 32). The policy framework, agreed in June 1994, recognised proliferation as a threat to NATO's members and their interests and stated the need for continuing diplomatic efforts to prevent proliferation and also for the Alliance to consider its defence capabilities in the light of possible proliferation. This was followed by an assessment of the risks posed by proliferation and the military capabilities NATO might require as a consequence of these risks (Joseph 1996: 119–25).

Even more controversial was the question of whether NATO's members should collectively develop defences against attack by ballistic missiles. Within the US, there was growing support for the development and deployment of missile defences for both forces deployed overseas and the US national territory. European allies, however, remained concerned about the costs of defences, their effectiveness, their impact on arms-control agreements and US control of the technology for such systems. How far to collectively pursue the development and deployment of missile defences seemed likely to remain a sensitive question within the Alliance (*Economist* 1997). In the context of growing concerns about proliferation, NATO's members also needed to consider a number of other controversial issues: whether the nuclear arsenals of the US, the United Kingdom and France should be further reduced as part of efforts to stem proliferation; whether the Alliance should adopt a policy of 'no first use' of nuclear weapons; and whether international (e.g. UN) control of nuclear weapons, the development of 'virtual' nuclear arsenals (dismantling nuclear weapons but retaining the capability to build them for deterrence purposes) or a nuclear weapon-free world should be considered as serious objectives for the Alliance.

More broadly still, NATO's members faced the question of how far the Alliance could and should be a forum for coordinating its members' policies towards parts of the world beyond Europe. With the end of the Cold War, some of the key security concerns of the Alliance's members (especially the US) lay beyond Europe: the growing power of China, prospects for stability in the Persian Gulf, East Asia and the Korea peninsula. Some US analysts suggested that unless the European allies were willing to actively support the US in developing policies towards such regions, the US would gradually withdraw from Europe, where its interests were less direct. They concluded that a new US–European grand bargain, perhaps incorporated into a revised NATO Treaty, should include a renewed US commitment to European security in return for a European commitment to support the US in other regions and a willingness on both sides to deploy forces to these ends (Asmus, Blackwill and Larrabee 1996; Gompert and Kugler 1995). Whether such a grand bargain was a realistic prospect, however, was open to doubt. While gradual progress in coordinating policies outside Europe might be possible, a more radical or rapid globalisation of NATO's role seemed unlikely. Even if such a step were possible it might create the image of NATO as a self-appointed 'world policeman', thereby intensifying north–south antagonisms and creating the 'clash of civilisations' some feared.

Adapting the Alliance

NATO's adoption of new roles and missions outside its traditional area required the adaptation of the Alliance's own political and military structures. As the Soviet bloc collapsed, it rapidly became clear that NATO's military strategy of forward defence and flexible response was no longer appropriate. At their July 1990 summit, NATO leaders announced the development of a new military strategy to be based on smaller, more mobile conventional forces with lower levels of force readiness and 'making nuclear forces truly weapons of last resort' (NATO 1990: 33). Within this context and facing domestic pressures to reduce defence spending, NATO's members cut their forces substantially, while developing more flexible, mobile forces with a greater degree of professionalisation. Most of NATO's forward deployed tactical nuclear weapons were withdrawn from Europe, and the US, under the START I and II agreements with Russia, significantly reducing its strategic nuclear forces.

Relatively quickly, it became clear that NATO's most likely future missions would involve 'coalitions of the willing' undertaking humanitarian, peace-keeping or peace-enforcement actions outside the NATO area. As a consequence, NATO took steps to develop more flexible force structures and command arrangements to allow differing groups of states and differing types of forces to undertake a wide variety of missions. In 1991, agreement was reached on a new NATO force structure, including a new Allied Command Europe Rapid Reaction Corps (ARRC) capable of being 'used for operations across the full spectrum of military activity' (Chilton *et al.* 1994: 7). At their January 1994 summit, NATO leaders endorsed the concept of Combined Joint Task Forces (CJTFs), command arrangements and force packages designed to provide 'separable but not separate military capabilities that could be employed by NATO or the WEU' (NATO 1994: 31). In June 1996 agreement was reached on the implementation of CJTF, based on a 'single multinational command structure' and 'separable but not separate' capabilities, assets, headquarters and command positions (NATO 1996: 3, 5). These reforms also allowed non-NATO states to participate in NATO or WEU-led operations.

One of the most significant consequences of these reforms was to facilitate the 'Europeanisation' of NATO, giving the European allies greater influence within NATO's command structure and the possibility of undertaking operations using NATO command structures and assets without US involvement. The adoption of the CJTF concept was a significant compromise, involving practical US endorsement of the development of an ESDI in return for European acceptance that this be within the overall NATO framework. Against this background, member states which had traditionally been wary of US domination of NATO moved closer to the Alliance: Spain agreed to join NATO's integrated military command and France rejoined NATO's Military Committee (though not yet the integrated military command). Nevertheless, there remained significant tensions – particularly between the US and France – over the allocation of positions within NATO's new military command structure. These tensions reflected underlying political and military problems which could not be easily overcome. The US, while agreeing in principle that it might make its national resources available to its allies for military operations in which it was not involved, could not realistically be expected to sign a 'blank cheque' for the provision of its assets to its allies in unknown future circumstances, while the Europeans remained dependent on the US. While European governments might wish to reduce their dependence on the US, developing independent European military capabilities for power projection would be an expensive and long-term task and it was not clear that European governments and publics were willing to commit the necessary resources.

The changed security environment, the reform of the Alliance's structures and its enlargement also raised important longer term questions about decision-making and the implementation of policies within NATO. With the security concerns of NATO's members increasingly differentiated, groups of states were likely to wish to be more (or less) active in differing areas of NATO policy. Those members geographically close to or having historical ties with particular central/east European states have taken a leading role in designing and implementing PfP activities. Similarly, NATO's 'southern tier' members have taken a lead in shaping NATO's Mediterranean policy. The Bosnian experience indicates that differing coalitions of NATO's members will want to be involved to differing degrees in future military operations. The reform of NATO's military structures is clearly designed to facilitate this. The reform of NATO's command structures will also result in greater regionalisation within the Alliance, with members from respective regions playing a greater role (for example, in the planning of military operations or in relevant PfP activities). In this context, NATO appears to be moving towards a situation where broad policies are agreed by all its members but where different groups within the Alliance take part in their implementation. This will give NATO greater flexibility. At the same time, if taken too far, such steps could weaken the solidarity of the Alliance, thereby undermining much of its value and influence. While smaller groups of allies may be able to take the lead in limited military operations and some PfP/outreach activities, active US leadership is likely to remain vital for large operations and strategic decisions, such as on enlargement (Bailes 1996: 31–3). Finally, while a limited enlargement involving only three or four central European states may not require fundamental changes in NATO's structures, a 'second wave' of enlargement (giving the Alliance perhaps 20 or more members) might raise difficult questions about how far the Alliance could maintain consensus decision-making.

Conclusion

The 1990s has seen the transformation of NATO from an organisation focused on collective defence of its members to one focused on new security challenges beyond its borders. The Article V commitment to collective defence remains an important symbol of mutual solidarity and is one of the key factors behind the CEE countries desire to join the Alliance. Nevertheless, NATO's intervention in Bosnia, its progress towards enlargement, its engagement with its PfP partners, its outreach towards the Mediterranean, the development of the Alliance framework on proliferation and the internal adaptation of the Alliance are all shaping NATO in ways which shift its focus away from collective defence and towards new security concerns beyond its borders. This process is logical: in a situation where most of NATO's members face few immediate threats to their security, NATO will only be relevant to their security needs if it can address the more diffuse security problems that they face. The many challenges facing NATO as it moves beyond its traditional focus are, however, likely to raise difficult policy dilemmas and generate new tensions among its members.

The preceding analysis also suggests a number of other broad conclusions. First, NATO's transformation has been driven not by the rhetoric of its new Strategic Concept and other political declarations but rather by its ability to respond to real security issues. Second, US leadership has been vital to the transformation of NATO. On the Alliance's most central issues, particularly intervention in Bosnia and enlargement, only the US has had the power and influence to initiate and drive through major policies. While the EU is gradually developing its Common Foreign and Security Policy, the reality remains that European states views often diverge and rarely is any single European state powerful enough to provide strong policy leadership alone. Militarily, the European allies also lack the capability to undertake large-scale military operations, particularly peace-enforcement actions, without the involvement of the US. Third, while NATO has been substantially transformed, it remains an essentially political-military security instrument – even as NATO moves 'out-of-area' the new security problems it is addressing are largely political and military in character. While NATO may be able to address many new issues, broader 'soft' security problems (migration, environmental degradation, economic causes of instability, transnational crime) are likely to remain beyond its remit (see Chapter 4).

Against this background, it is also worth considering the longer term future of NATO and trans-Atlantic relations. NATO's longevity has been underpinned by a combination of common values and shared interests. Despite the changes wrought by the end of the Cold War, a strong case can be made that the common values and shared interests of NATO's members are deep enough to sustain the Alliance in the longer term. NATO's members retain a strong interest in sustaining the security community – the 'zone of peace' – which exists among them, in managing their relations with Russia, in promoting stability on Europe's periphery, in managing conflicts like that in Bosnia, and in addressing the problem of proliferation. While the extent to which particular issues affect each NATO member may differ, these are strategic issues which affect western Europe and north America as a whole. NATO may not always be the vehicle its members choose to use to address such issues. There may not always be sufficient unity for NATO to act. Nevertheless, NATO remains one of the central institutional pillars binding the western security community and on many of the key security issues facing its members, the Alliance remains a key vehicle for the development of concerted trans-Atlantic policies.

Some have argued that more fundamental reforms of trans-Atlantic security relations are necessary if the US–European partnership is to be maintained in the longer term: merging NATO and the EU to create a new Atlantic Union binding the countries of North America and Europe together both politically and economically (Kupchan 1996); a new trans-Atlantic bargain involving a European commitment to support the US militarily beyond Europe in return for a renewed US commitment to Europe (Asmus, Blackwill and Larrabee 1996); an economic partnership in the form of a Trans-Atlantic Free Trade Area (TAFTA); NATO replacement by a new US–EU Treaty, covering political, security and economic areas of cooperation. These ideas, however, fail to recognise that the future of US–European security relations and trans-Atlantic cooperation will be determined not primarily by institutional arrangements but rather by the extent to which the countries of western Europe and north America share common values and interests and are willing and able to forge common policies. NATO's post-Cold War transformation suggests both that the values and interests binding the countries of western Europe and North America together remain substantial and that the Alliance will remain at the core of trans-Atlantic efforts to develop concerted security policies.

References

Asmus, R. D., Blackwill, R. D. and Larrabee, F. S. (1996) 'Can NATO Survive?', *The Washington Quarterly* 19 (2): 79–101.

Asmus, R. D., Kugler, R. L. and Larrabee, F. S. (1993) 'Building a New NATO', *Foreign Affairs* 72 (4): 28–40.

Asmus, R. D., Kugler, R. L. and Larrabee, F. S. (1995) 'NATO Expansion: The Next Steps', *Survival* 37 (1): 7–33.

Asmus, R. D., Larrabee, F. S. and Lesser I. O. (1996b) 'Mediterranean Security: New Challenges, New Tasks', *NATO Review* 44 (3): 25–31.

Bailes, A. J. K. (1996) 'NATO: Towards a New Synthesis', *Survival* 38 (3): 27–40.

Chace, J. (1993) 'Present at the Destruction', *World Policy Journal* X (2): 89–90.

Chilton, P., Nassauer, O., Plesch, D. and Patten, J. (1994) *NATO, Peacekeeping and the United Nations*, London/Washington, DC/Berlin: British American Security Information Council/Berlin Information Centre for Transatlantic Security.

Clark, B. and Freeland, C. (1997) 'Reinvention of the Weal', *The Financial Times*, 22/23 February.

Deutsch, K. W., Burrell, S., Kann, R., Lee, M., Lichterman, M., Lindgren, R. (1957) *Political Community and the North Atlantic Area: International Organisation in the Light of Historical Experience*, New Jersey: Princeton University Press.

Economist (1997) 'Circles of Fear', 4 January: 49–55.

Gompert, D. and Kugler, R. (1995) 'Free-Rider Redux', *Foreign Affairs* 74 (1): 7–12.

Heisbourg, F. (1992) 'The Future of the Atlantic Alliance: Whither NATO, Whether NATO?', *The Washington Quarterly* 15 (2): 127–39.

Huntington, S. P. (1993) 'The Clash of Civilizations?', *Foreign Affairs* 72 (3): 22–49.

IISS (International Institute for Strategic Studies) (1996) 'A Fragile Peace for Bosnia', in *Strategic Survey 1995–1996*, London: Oxford University Press for IISS: 126–38.

Joseph, R. (1996) 'Proliferation, Counter-Proliferation and NATO', *Survival* 38 (1): 111–30.

Kupchan, C. A. (1996) 'Reviving the West', *Foreign Affairs* 75 (3): 92–104.

NATO (1990) 'London Declaration on a Transformed North Atlantic Alliance: Issued by the Heads of State and Government participating in the meeting of the North Atlantic Council in London on 5th–6th July 1990', *NATO Review* 38 (4): 32–3.

NATO (1992a) 'Communiqué of the Ministerial meeting of the North Atlantic Council in Oslo, 4th June 1992', *NATO Review* 40 (3): 30–2.

NATO (1992b) 'Communiqué Issued by the Ministerial meeting of the North Atlantic Council, Brussels, 17 December 1992', *NATO Review* 40 (6): 28–31.

NATO (1994) 'Declaration of the Heads of State and Government participating in the meeting of the North Atlantic Council held at NATO Headquarters, Brussels, on 10–11 January 1994', *NATO Review* 42 (1): 30–3.

NATO (1995) *Study on NATO Enlargement*, Brussels: NATO.

NATO (1996) 'Ministerial Meeting of the North Atlantic Council in Berlin, 3 June 1996, Final Communiqué', Press Communiqué M-NAC-1 (96) 63, NATO: Brussels.

Rader, S. R. (1996) 'NATO', in T. Findlay (ed.) *Challenges for the New Peacekeepers,* SIPRI Research Report No. 12, Oxford: Oxford University Press: 142–58.

Serfaty, S. (1996-97) 'Algeria unhinged: What next? Who cares? Who leads?' *Survival* 38 (4): 137–53.

Walker, M. (29 December 1996) 'It's Still the Economy, Stupid', *The Guardian Weekly* 155 (26): 1–2.

Further reading

NATO (1991a) 'Rome Declaration on Peace and Cooperation: Issued by the Heads of State and Government participating in the meeting of the North Atlantic Council in Rome on 7–8 November 1991', *NATO Review* 39 (6): 19–22.

NATO (1991b) 'The Alliance's New Strategic Concept: Agreed by the Heads of State and Government participating in the meeting of the North Atlantic Council in Rome on 7–8 November 1991', *NATO Review* 39 (6): 25–32.

CHAPTER 4

A core Europe? The EU and the WEU

TRINE FLOCKHART AND G. WYN REES

Introduction

It is paradoxical that the end of the Cold War and the resultant decrease in the importance of military issues has intensified the revival of the defence-oriented Western European Union (WEU) and deepened the debate about giving the European Union (EU) a foreign policy and perhaps even a defence dimension. Throughout the period of the Cold War, the European Community (EC) was one of the two dominant institutions in western Europe along with the North Atlantic Treaty Organisation (NATO), but it was a civilian power with only very limited powers in security matters and no competence in the field of defence. Because of the all-pervasive nature of the defence issue during the Cold War, it had been left in the hands of NATO since the failure to ratify the European Defence Community in 1954. The primacy of NATO satisfied the interests of many of the European countries as it served to guarantee the involvement of the United States. The WEU was an institution with competence in defence, but it possessed limited capabilities and was acknowledged to be subordinate to NATO (WEU Council of Ministers 1987).

With the end of the East–West confrontation, both the newly created EU and the WEU had to reconsider their roles within the European security architecture. Indeed, they had been reassessing their roles even before 1989 (Buzan et al. 1990). With the Cold War over, the two organisations were confronted with the issues of whether they should unify into a single structure and whether defence matters should come within the purview of the EU. In varying degrees they had to reappraise their definition of security as well as their approach towards the new agenda of security issues facing the continent. It was apparent that security now included a range of non-military factors, such as economic and environmental matters, and therefore needed to be approached from a broader perspective (Buzan 1991; Waever 1994). This strengthened the position of the EU as its concept of security has always been broader than simply the military dimension. While other institutions such as NATO had to undergo a substantial reorientation in their thinking, in the case of the EU the reappraisal of security was more modest.

Another paradox brought about by the end of the Cold War was that it became commonly accepted[1] that the way towards increased security was through a form of strengthened integration. Whether integration was to occur through a process of either 'deepening' the cooperation between the existing members, or 'widening' the circle to bring in states from the East, was a contested issue. But there was widespread agreement that further integration would provide more, rather than less, security. The practical question of to whom to offer membership of the WEU and the EU remained open to debate.

The aim of this chapter is to consider the on-going debate in the EU and the WEU in relation to these institutions' reconceptualisation of security and their processes of adaptation. The analysis will be couched within the framework of the debate over widening and deepening, and whether these processes were necessarily incompatible.

Adapting to the new environment

When instability reigned in Europe in 1989, both the then EC[2] and the WEU were engaged in their own challenging processes of political change. The EC was in a period of vigorous integration following the approval of the Single European Act (SEA) in 1987. It was seeking to implement the legislation that would create a Single Market by the target date of 1992 and was taking steps towards the Intergovernmental Conference on Economic Union. It was ironic that the EC had called for so long for change in the East, yet when it came, it found the EC unprepared and preoccupied with its own internal development.

The WEU, under the leadership of its Dutch Secretary-General Willem Van Eeklen, was busily defining its own role as the Cold War ended. Historically, the organisation had fulfilled a modest function as a forum for European views on defence but by the 1970s it had become virtually moribund. The organisation was revived in 1984, partly as a result of French pressure, in order to marshal more effectively European views on defence. This was perceived to be necessary because of the US administration's increasingly erratic behaviour as demonstrated, for example, at the Reykjavik meeting of November 1986 when the US came close to abandoning its reliance on a policy of nuclear deterrence in Europe. The WEU even assumed a limited operational role in the 1987 Gulf War where it coordinated the naval contribution of its members. Its strength lay in its flexibility and the fact that its membership was cohesive and that its legal base, the modified Brussels Treaty, did not confine the WEU to activities within a specified geographical area.

However, the enormity of the changes in the East demanded immediate institutional responses from the West. Within weeks of the collapse of the Berlin Wall, it was apparent that the prior preoccupations of the EC and the WEU were swamped by a new range of challenges. There were the tasks of coping with instability and economic reorganisation in the East, while simultaneously providing a framework for the process of

German reunification. The EC appeared as a potential model for the continent's future, demonstrating the way in which long-standing antagonisms between states could be put aside within a multilateral institution. The EC represented an island of stability to the turbulent states of the East and an organisation which they might aspire to join. The opportunity for enhancing the integration process within the EC was also recognised by some of its supporters. In April 1990, Germany and France were quick to press for political union to be added to economic and monetary union.

Within the prevailing consensus that integration was the key to future European stability, the debate concentrated on how security could best be assured. One view was that the EC should speed up its process of internal integration in order to ensure its position as the stabilising influence on the continent. According to this perspective, the competencies of the EC should be enlarged into all areas, including those hitherto regarded as taboo, namely foreign and defence policy. The last time that this had been attempted, in the Genscher-Colombo proposals of the early 1980s, the initiative had ended in failure and the Solemn Declaration of Stuttgart had effectively endorsed the *status quo* (Cahen 1989: 12).

In the 1992 Treaty on European Union (TEU), the decision was taken to move beyond European Political Cooperation and create a Common Foreign and Security Policy (CFSP). It was a compromise between those states that advocated a fully fledged role for the EU in foreign policy and those that sought to constrain the remit of the Union. The CFSP was established as an intergovernmental pillar which ensured that policy could only be decided by unanimity and excluded the influence of bodies such as the European Parliament and the Court of Justice. The Union was allowed to deal with 'soft' security issues such as arms control, nuclear proliferation and relations with the Conference on Security and Cooperation in Europe (CSCE – later renamed the OSCE). It was denied responsibility for matters where the use of military forces was concerned.

A second element within the TEU was the possibility of merging the WEU into the EU. This would have meant finding a way for the modified Brussels Treaty of 1954 to be absorbed into the Union and ending the autonomy of the WEU. Germany and France were favourably disposed to this idea, envisaging it as providing the basis for a commitment to a common defence within the EU. Yet countries such as Britain, The Netherlands and Portugal were firmly opposed and they were successful in ensuring that the WEU was preserved as a separate organisation. It was agreed that the WEU could only be 'requested', rather than 'instructed', to undertake defence tasks by the European Council (Treaty on European Union 1992). Nevertheless, in order to achieve a compromise with the more ambitious French designs, Article J4.1 of the TEU specified that the EU might seek in the future to establish a common defence policy, which might in time lead to a common defence.

This left open an important question to the subsequent political will of the member states.

This whole approach was built on the fear that the post-war integration of the western half of the continent reflected the external pressure of the Cold War rather than a benign political will within western Europe for closer union. The logic of this position dictated that, with the Cold War over, the process was in danger of unravelling, leading to wholesale fragmentation. Thus, it was argued that the West should concentrate on furthering integration and moving towards majority decision-making. Only when the process of western integration had reached completion, should the EU seek to export stability to the east and south, lest its own inner strength be undermined. In that sense the events of 1989 were seen as in danger of derailing the process of European integration. This has been characterised as a 'Fortress Europe' viewpoint.

A contrary perspective was that European institutions had to be prepared to bring in new members quickly in order to overcome the legacy of the past. The argument for this was that a window of opportunity to unite the continent had been presented by the end of the Cold War, but that a cautious response would allow the opportunity to slip away. Absorbing states such as Sweden, Finland and Austria presented few problems as these countries were pro-western in orientation, were economically prosperous and politically stable. The only tension in welcoming them to western institutions was their historically neutral status. Yet these states recognised that their neutrality was of less relevance after the Cold War and they acknowledged that their exclusion from the key organisations would marginalise their influence and leave them on the periphery of a unified core of states. Hence, they welcomed the opportunity to join the EU (January 1995) and to become Observers in the WEU, while the existing members were confident that these new adherents would be net contributors to the organisations.

States from central and eastern Europe (CEE) fell into a different category. Their value to their western neighbours was founded on the historic opportunity to overcome the division of the continent, rather than their inherent attractiveness. There were a host of CEE states that had cast off their former Soviet embrace and were seeking to benefit from inclusion into the West, but they were economically backward and lacking in democratic maturity. Both the EU and the WEU were faced with demands for membership from such states who quickly identified membership of the west European organisations as their main foreign policy objective (Flockhart 1996). Their supporters in the West advocated a rapid enlargement of both the EU and WEU, in addition to other organisations such as NATO, on the grounds that the transformations might not prove to be irreversible. There was a danger of these states collapsing into chaos or returning to an authoritarian style of government.

The EU acted as a magnet to the CEE countries, because of its economic strength and the fact that it represented a cohesive community of European states. The attraction of membership of the EU was that it offered access to western markets, direct investment and it bolstered the legitimacy of newly independent states. These factors accorded the EU a strong influence and a disciplining power over the CEE countries. The promise of certain rewards and ultimate membership granted the EU an important foreign policy tool for inducing the sort of behaviour that it desired. However, what would happen once membership was granted to some, but not all, countries remained a different question. There would no longer be an incentive for states to act in a responsible manner. Therefore, some argued that the strategy of the EU should be to hold out the prospect of membership for as long as possible, while others called for the rapid inclusion of aspirant states.

Two factors needed to be borne in mind in treating the process of integration as a means to increase European security. First, as suggested by Waever, the fact that it is a *process* is important, meaning that it can neither stop nor have an end (Waever 1994: 3). Second, integration is seen as a means to enhance security by the élite, but the view is not shared by the European publics, who treasure their national identity. Hence the 'Catch 22' position is that speeding up integration in order to halt the spread of nationalism in eastern Europe has the unintended side-effect of promoting neo-nationalism in western Europe (Waever 1994: 22). A fine balancing act is required, which must provide enough core integration to prevent the major European powers from returning to unilateralism, but not so much as to cause west European publics to demand a halt to progress. It must also provide enough promise of eastern enlargement to maintain the desired level of influence, but not so much that it causes the core integration process to stop.

Deepening versus widening: incompatible processes?

The two perspectives for increasing European security are usually presented as mutually incompatible. Either the West must concentrate on deepening integration, or it must widen so as to include new members and export some of its own stability, most probably at the cost of its own inner strength. However, the argument that there is a contradiction between the two goals is questionable, and may hinge on old geographical and conceptual perspectives of security. It may well be that as a result of a broader concept of post-Cold War security, a perception that new issues have achieved greater salience and a reinterpretation of the geographical extent of Europe, that there simply is no choice but that both goals must be pursued either simultaneously or in close procession. Indeed, it has come to be recognised that only by deepening the EU, through the extension of majority voting, can any widening be made viable because with 20 or 25 members there would be a danger of paralysis. Therefore, the key becomes not so much which goal the EU and WEU will work towards, but rather a question of timing.

Such thinking was reflected in Jacques Delors' concept of 'concentric circles'. This view prescribed a process of expansion that would be based upon successive phases. First, the twelve members of the EU would seek to fulfil the 1992 objectives and adapt their institutions to prepare for a wider membership. Second, they would enlarge to the 'unproblematic' European Free Trade Area (EFTA) group, and finally to take in the CEE countries in stages (Laurent 1990: 155). Similar conceptual thinking has been in evidence on the part of the major European institutions who, despite serving different functions, have recognised that their enlargements must be synchronised. The North Atlantic Council in its communiqué of December 1994 stated that EU and NATO expansion should be conducted in parallel and should be complementary (Rühle and Williams 1995: 84).

Creating a core Europe _- Aften 2 Cos vs Chaos_

According to the advocates of a Fortress Europe, one of the primary functions of the EU/WEU is to ensure that the core remains intact. This is important in order to prevent a return to the nightmare scenario of Great Power rivalry in Europe, particularly between France and Germany. Economic and political integration provided a mechanism for controlling Germany's new-found strength within a wider policy framework. This has allayed the fears of Germany's neighbours, both in the West as well as the East. The alternative might be a renationalisation of policy, regarded as particularly dangerous in the defence field. Chancellor Kohl has warned consistently that the slowing down of the 'European construction' project could lead ultimately to renewed fear of war, based on the assumption that the process either keeps moving forward or faces the possibility of going into reverse (*Economist* 1996a: 15). Hence, according to proponents of this view, it remains important that Europe has one power centre rather than several.

The Treaty on European Union went some way towards rationalising a structure for a European core. By linking the WEU to the European Union, the enlargement of the former institution was made contingent on the latter. The issue of overlapping memberships of the two organisations was also resolved by creating levels of membership within the WEU. For example, the status of 'Observers' was created for the Republic of Ireland and Denmark who were members of the EU but not a part of the WEU. This status was extended subsequently to Austria, Finland and Sweden. Those states who were members of NATO but not the EU, such as Turkey, Norway and Iceland, were granted 'Associate' membership of the WEU. Although this complicated the structure of the WEU, it ensured that there was less cause for friction between this organisation and the EU.

The WEU also provided a linkage or bridge between the EU and the Atlantic Alliance. In the Declaration which accompanied the Maastricht Treaty, the WEU was stated to represent the European pillar within

NATO (*Declaration on the Western European Union* 1992). This was designed to reassure the United States about the compatibility of a greater European identity in security and defence with the existing trans-Atlantic structures. This was a vital factor in that it assured a strong relationship between the EU and the United States. The US continued to act as an important stabilising influence on the continent; its reduced, yet still significant, military presence served to offer confidence to Russia as well as to the neighbours of Germany. The US was also the ultimate guarantor of security through the Article V commitment in the NATO Treaty. It was recognised that more effort by the Europeans in this field presupposed a continued American role.

Preserving a European core amid the variety of pressures on the EU has figured prominently in the 1996–97 Intergovernmental Conference (IGC), designed to review and amend the TEU. One important viewpoint in the negotiations has been that the EU must maintain the momentum of its integration. Regarding the CFSP there have been proposals to reform the decision-making procedure, such as through the introduction of majority voting. This was aimed at improving the efficiency of the organisation but there was not unanimous support for this step at the European Council Summit in Amsterdam in June 1997. There were also demands for a joint analysis mechanism and for a senior figure to be appointed to represent the Union in foreign policy. Article J8 of the new Treaty stated that the Secretary-General of the Council of Ministers would be given the title of 'High Representative' for foreign policy (Amsterdam European Council Summit 1997).

It was clear from the meetings that led up to the Amsterdam summit that there was a good deal of opposition among some EU members to further integration. They argued that diversity of interests remained in Europe and therefore common views should not be manufactured artificially where they do not exist. Such views, vigorously championed by the UK, insisted that further integration could only be permitted to proceed by consensus. In the face of such obstacles, countries such as France and Germany have looked for mechanisms by which they would be able to press forward without the participation of all states. The concept of 'flexibility' was launched as a way to allow smaller groups of like-minded states to create multiple cores on different issues.

In the defence sphere there were demands among a majority of WEU members to integrate the organisation into the EU. Only one state, the United Kingdom, dissented from this view at the WEU Ministerial Council in Madrid in 1995. The British Labour government chose to reaffirm the position of its Conservative predecessor by insisting on the institutional autonomy of the WEU (Foreign and Commonwealth Office 1996). It was duly successful in preventing steps being taken at the Amsterdam summit to merge the WEU into the EU. The UK argued that the cohesiveness of the WEU would be undermined by allowing states who are currently not full members, such as Ireland, a *droit de regard* over future military operations. It has insisted that it would be unacceptable to give either the European Commission or the Parliament greater powers over defence matters, in which they lack experience. Another argument has been that it would render cooperation with the US harder to achieve where the Europeans would be seeking to borrow military assets for the conduct of independent operations.

Projecting stability — *Cos us Chaos Chp 3*

Threat Response

Assessments have differed over the potential military threat to the CEE countries from the territories of the former USSR but there has been little debate over their internal problems: weak economies, border disagreements and tensions over ethnic minorities. The EU and the WEU have attempted to export stability to these states and prevent the sorts of tensions that could result in violence in the future (Rummel 1997). Although in 1990 the EC refused to entertain the prospect of CEE membership for the immediate future, the European Commission responded to the changed situation in the East with a variety of economic instruments available in the first pillar. One was the Poland and Hungary: Assistance for Restructuring Economies (PHARE) programme, aimed at providing technical assistance, which was offered first to Poland and Hungary and then extended to five other CEE countries (van Ham 1993: 173). However, as it became obvious that such programmes were insufficient, the EC entered into Association or 'Europe' Agreements with selected eastern neighbours. The focus of this effort was to eradicate trading barriers between the EC and these countries over a period of time. Thus far, Association Agreements have been signed with ten CEE states but this has yet to lead to an offer of membership.

The 1994 Stability Pact was an additional initiative undertaken by the EU to signal its desire to help CEE states. Originally pioneered by the Balladur government in France, and later adopted by the EU as a whole, the Stability Pact was designed to increase the eligibility of states and was made a precondition of granting them accession. It focused on the same states with whom the EU held Association Agreements, expecting them to adhere to the aims and principles of the Pact, namely the maintenance of good neighbourly relations, the settlement of border disputes and the respect for minority rights (Europe Documents 1994). One notable success was the conclusion of the border disagreement between Hungary and Slovakia. The EU could justify setting such criteria for aspirant countries because it had succeeded in resolving tensions between its existing members. Through the mechanism of the Stability Pact, the EU was skilfully employing its magnetism towards the CEE countries without going so far as to guarantee future membership.

The WEU complemented the EC's signing of Association Agreements by instituting its own process of interaction with states to the east. Concentrating on the same countries as the EC, the WEU created a

'Forum of Consultation' in June 1992 which provided the Visegrad and Baltic states, Romania and Bulgaria with a dialogue on security matters. With the signing of the Kirchberg Declaration in May 1994, the WEU raised the status of the CEE states to that of 'Associate Partners' which accorded them the right to participate in Council meetings, play an active part in working groups and deploy forces in support of low-level military tasks. By drawing states into its inner decision-making structures, the WEU demonstrated a willingness to surpass what organisations such as NATO had offered to central and east European countries at that time.

Yet neither the WEU nor the EU have offered an explicit timetable for admitting aspirant states. The WEU stopped at the level of Associate Partners and indicated that its further enlargement would have to depend on NATO and the EU. The WEU was incapable of carrying out Article V guarantees to new members because it lacked the resources and the ability to project military power over long distances. The WEU was dependent on the extension of NATO assurances to CEE states and the US was determined that the Atlantic Alliance should not be drawn into territorial guarantees through the backdoor of the WEU. In addition, the raising of the three Baltic states to Associate Partner status had been controversial as it had increased the prospect of friction between the WEU and Russia.

As for the EU, at the June 1993 Copenhagen meeting, agreement was reached on the entry criteria for CEE states. In December of the following year at Essen, a pre-accession strategy was hammered out, which could be interpreted as the agenda for the development of the EU prior to eastern enlargement. Apart from the two separate pillars of the CFSP and Justice and Home Affairs, the Essen Council Meeting envisaged developments in such areas as the internal market, agriculture, environment, and education and cultural affairs (Udenrigsministeriet 1995: 64).

At the Amsterdam summit in June 1997, it was reaffirmed that the EU would begin negotiations with the next round of aspirant members in the following six months. The difficulty of enlarging the EU, with its complex body of Community law, its bloated agricultural policy and its cohesion funds, had grown to be appreciated by its 15 members. As a consequence, the EU came over time to accept that NATO enlargement, scheduled to begin in 1999 (United States Information Service, 1996), would precede that of the EU. This was in spite of the fact that the process of institutional enlargement had hitherto been anticipated to occur in parallel. Even if agreement with the first wave of aspirants is reached relatively quickly, the process of ratification will ensure that it will be well into the next millennium before the EU increases in size.

Nevertheless, the expansion of the EU to nearly triple its original number is likely to cause increased stress on its complicated and overstretched institutional structure. Hence the thorny question of institutional reform accompanies the issue of enlargement. A persistent fear in the IGC was that failure to overhaul such mechanisms as Qualified Majority Voting (QMV) would seriously handicap the EU once enlargement took place. At the Amsterdam summit, the 15 failed to agree on a formula for reweighting voting majorities and deferred the issue until the next accession (Amsterdam European Council Summit 1997). Prospective new members from central and eastern Europe will undoubtedly bring with them their own interests and diverse agendas. The implication is that the EU's capability to continue to project stability eastwards might be imperilled.

Towards a common defence? – Ch.4

In the years immediately after the end of the Cold War, there was tension between the EU–WEU and NATO over the question of whether efforts to build up a European defence identity would be at the expense of the Atlantic Alliance. Countries such as France and Spain were committed to the goal of enhancing the status of Europe in the defence sphere and limiting the role of NATO to the territorial defence of the continent. Yet it became apparent that the EU was not going to become a major defence actor in the short-term future. There was an absence of will among some of its members to move towards a common defence policy and the military capabilities of its defence arm, the WEU, remained circumscribed. West European countries had taken steps to reduce their defence expenditures after the Cold War, Britain and Germany had done this immediately, while France followed in 1995. There was no evidence that they would reverse this process; rather there was every indication that the process would continue and the military power of the European states would diminish.

Nevertheless, it was the debate about military capabilities that was most often in the public eye, and it was this that was used to judge the efficacy of EU–WEU structures and institutions. The ability of each organisation to act in crises and conflicts was the standard on which they were assessed and determined their level of public approval. Little account was taken of the fact that both of these institutions were starting from a modest base. The European Union, for example, only established its CFSP in the Maastricht Treaty and it was to be the end of 1993 before all member states had ratified its provisions. Similarly, the WEU was in the early stages of establishing a Planning Cell (small in size compared to that of NATO) and creating a mechanism by which its member states could make forces available to the organisation in a time of conflict. Only in June 1992, at its Petersberg meeting, was it agreed that the WEU could undertake humanitarian missions, peace-keeping and crisis-management tasks (*Petersberg Declaration* 1992).

As a consequence, it was less than fair to deride the EU and the WEU for their poor performances in dealing with the conflict in former Yugoslavia. The use of traditional instruments in the crisis, such as economic sanctions, proved to be ineffective in the face of parties that were determined to use force. The weakness of the CFSP and the lack of political will to task the WEU did indeed demonstrate the hollowness of the European capability in defence matters, but this was hardly surprising at this early stage of development. The Yugoslav crisis was the wrong kind of crisis at the wrong time. Institutional change of the kind encountered in the EU–WEU's transition to a security and defence role was complicated and time-consuming and it needed to go through several stages before an operational capability was in place. These stages required that the necessary structures and expertise were built up within the organisations, and then that the member states possessed the political will to utilise them effectively.

Only limited missions at the low-intensity end of the conflict spectrum have been assigned to the WEU. It has concentrated on building up operational capabilities under the concept of Forces Answerable to WEU (FAWEU). The framework in which the WEU's missions were conceived was focused on specifically European contingencies, based on the assumption that the US would not want to be involved. Despite being low-intensity operations, it was recognised that these were likely to be more prevalent in the future than inter-state conflicts. For instance, the 1997 internal conflict in the state of Albania presented the kind of emergency in which the WEU could be called on to assist in the evacuation of west European nationals and the distribution of humanitarian assistance (Europe Documents 1997).

At the 1994 NATO Brussels summit, the United States agreed that NATO assets could be made available to European operations, under the mantle of the WEU. Although it was to be two years before the practicalities of this arrangement were worked out, because of French obstructionism, it resolved the underlying tension between the WEU and the Alliance. The Combined Joint Task Forces (CJTF) project was approved at the NATO meeting in Berlin in June 1996. The WEU was saved from the prospect of having to duplicate the provision of military capabilities, such as military headquarters and long-range transportation systems, that would have necessitated considerable new spending. In return, the US was granted an effective veto over European operations. The CJTF arrangement has, on the one hand, made small-scale European-only military operations more credible, while at the same time symbolised the subordination of the WEU to NATO.

Broadening the concept of security

The European security debate has tended to focus on military-security issues such as the difficulties in establishing a common defence policy. This has meant that the importance of the EU and the WEU in broader security issues has been neglected. This is despite the many references, not only in the academic debate (Buzan 1991), but also in policy statements, that security also includes economic, political, environmental and societal factors.[3] The EU in particular has come to be perceived as an influential actor in non-military issues and Serfaty suggests that it has developed into a collective security organisation, while NATO (regardless of its *Rome Declaration*) has remained wedded to collective defence (Serfaty 1996: 41).

(margin note: Chp 3 Threat)

The new 'agenda' of security issues, such as economic instability in CEE states, the danger of political and economic collapse and large-scale migration, are regarded as issues of pressing concern to the states of western Europe since they directly impinge on their members' interests (Rees 1993). Similarly, issues such as environmental degradation, the safety of neighbouring nuclear reactors and the preservation of the human rights of ethnic minorities, have come to be regarded as relevant to the security debate. The reason why these issues have now been included in the security agenda is that the collapse of an east European economy, the outbreak of civil war, or the meltdown of a nuclear reactor, are bound to have major implications for all states on such a highly interdependent continent.

(margin note: Response)

Such issues are particularly appropriate for the EU to address as they call for principally economic and technical, rather than military, responses. They demand expertise in areas in which the EC/EU has long played an active role and enjoyed particular strength and they require coordinated responses from a group of states in order to achieve the necessary impact. Joint Actions undertaken by the EU have included the monitoring of elections to the Russian Duma in 1993, the control of dual-use exports to unstable areas of the world and support for the Israeli–Palestinian peace process in the Middle East (Regelsberger *et al.* 1997).

Whereas NATO has struggled to prove its relevance in the face of these issues, the legitimacy of EU institutions has never been questioned. With the end of the Cold War these problems are recognised by European publics to be serious in nature. Therefore the fact that the EU can be seen tackling issues such as environmental degradation and organised crime provides a way to gain favour in the eyes of national constituencies, thereby serving to strengthen the case for further integration. The EU also has the benefit of reassuring Russia which does not see the organisation in the same confrontational light as the Atlantic Alliance.

(margin note: Chp 1/3 Securitising issues)

The inclusion of these concerns does not reflect a new agenda of issues. Rather, what has happened is that these issue areas have moved from being either moderately or highly *politicised* to being *securitised*.[4] The process of securitisation did not just occur after the Cold War as the EU had been involved in environmental and societal security for a long time. For example, as Huysmans has suggested, the securitisation of migration resulted from the ratification of the Single European Act which guaranteed the free movement of people (Huysmans 1996). Similarly, environmental issues were being securitised before the end of the Cold War because of events such as the catastrophic fire at the Chernobyl nuclear reactor in 1986. The result has been that the environment has been transformed from a domestic issue to an international one with security implications arising directly from the threat to eco-systems and to humans. This has been reflected in the work of the EU, where the focus of effort has shifted from the state level to international cooperation.[5]

The WEU, albeit to a lesser extent than the EU, has also demonstrated its relevance to the broader agenda of security issues. Because of its ill-defined role in the past, the WEU has proved to be flexible enough to undertake missions that are either quasi-military or civilian in nature. In the Bosnian situation, the WEU carried out, with NATO, the joint monitoring of the UN naval embargo in the Adriatic Sea under 'Operation Sharp Guard' and provided vessels for the monitoring of the River Danube. On the ground in Bosnia, the WEU was requested by the European Council to provide a police force for the EU-administered city of Mostar. This involved personnel from 12 countries, including Austria, Finland and Sweden, and was not brought to an end until October 1996 (*Europe Documents* 1996b). Such unconventional tasks may be a feature of WEU's responsibilities in the future as west European states employ it as an organisation that can be adapted to suit unique circumstances.

Not only have the security remits for the EU and the WEU been expanded in post-Cold War Europe, but the geographical extent of their responsibilities have also increased. Whereas the traditional focus of military security concerns used to be the former Soviet Union, new threats and risks are perceived to emanate from a multiplicity of directions, with implications for western Europe in terms of instability and the movement of economic migrants or refugees. Included on this list are CEE countries but in addition are states in the Balkans, North Africa and the Middle East. During the Cold War, these areas were either part of one of the Superpower's sphere of interest or their importance was judged to be secondary in the face of the East–West confrontation. In North Africa there have been a number of states, such as Algeria, who have experienced violent unrest or economic decline and, since 1991, the Balkans has demonstrated its capacity to degenerate into chaos. The level of European interest in the Balkans was exemplified by the fact that out of the $588 million donated by the international community for reconstruction in the Balkans by September 1996, $239 million had been given through the EU (*Economist* 1996b: 51).

The EU and the WEU have acknowledged the growing importance of the southern region to the interests of their members. The prospect of offering membership to states in the area has not been considered appropriate and consequently the emphasis has been placed on dialogue and financial assistance. The French and Spanish Presidencies in 1995 did much to focus attention on the issue – the European–Mediterranean Conference of November in Barcelona was designed to signal the interest of west European countries in the region's stability (Barbe and Izquierdo 1997). The WEU has also witnessed efforts among states with

Mediterranean coastlines, notably France, Spain and Italy, to assemble cooperative military frameworks that could intervene in an area during a crisis: EUROFOR has been created as the land component while EUROMARFOR represents the maritime element.

The acknowledgement of an EU interest in the security of the southern region as well as the East has balanced up the sense of vulnerability among the member states who were hitherto almost solely preoccupied with eastern Europe. This has been a positive factor for the internal consensus within the EU and has contributed to the willingness of some countries to proceed with deeper integration. For example, controlling the influx of illegal immigrants from North Africa has been an extremely costly affair, particularly for Spain. The EU has helped with the cost of maintaining border controls, obliging Spain to accept a similar deal for some of the other receptor countries. It has also led it to accept that the problem must be addressed through economic aid to the countries in distress, which has consequences for the structural development fund from which Spain currently benefits. Integration is thus carried forward incrementally through the perceived need for action in areas that have previously been national responsibilities, but which increasingly emerge as common problems.

However, the development of the EU and the WEU in the field of security has been important for reasons other than contributing to the external capabilities of Europe. The institutional process of change has a useful internal dimension, in the sense that it furthers integration and strengthens the core. Despite the fact that there has only been modest progress towards building a common defence and security policy within the EU, it remains a process which acts as a constraining factor on national foreign policies, and therefore works against the forces of fragmentation.

The global dimension

There remains an ambivalence about the future role that the EU will play: whether it will become a truly world power or whether it will remain focused on regional issues. At present, in economic terms, it is indisputably a global power. Similarly, as a model of political stability for states on its periphery, the EU possesses global status and thereby exerts a strong sense of attraction. Yet whether all its members want to see the EU develop into a multicompetent actor on the world stage remains open to question. If they decide that they do seek such an objective, then it will require the EU to develop a more cohesive external identity and a genuinely common foreign policy. This will certainly influence its view of its security interests: whether it must assess threats on a global scale or concentrate on regional matters. In turn, a security policy that looks beyond the continent will have implications for its defence requirements and may demand considerable investment from the member states over a sustained period of time.

The role that the EU will play will depend to a large extent on how it defines its relationship with the United States. The US has traditionally provided the security leadership in western Europe and hence for Europe to assert itself will require a redefinition of trans-Atlantic relations. Successive American administrations have actively promoted European integration. Yet they have opposed European efforts that would have risked challenging their leadership position or the central role of NATO on the continent. Nevertheless, the US has made it clear that in the post-Cold War situation it would welcome a greater European contribution to peace and stability, providing EU efforts were compatible with US policies. The US appears to want to encourage the development of a European subordinate, while many EU countries, such as France, desire Europe to become an equal partner.

An insight into US thinking on this subject was provided by the signing of the 'New Trans-Atlantic Agenda' in Madrid in December 1995, between President Clinton, EU President Santer and Spanish Prime Minister Gonzalez. The document was built on the earlier 'Trans-Atlantic Declaration' that had been signed in 1990. The cooperative framework that was established in Madrid demonstrated a strong emphasis on 'soft' security issues in which the US believed that the EU could make an effective contribution. Issues such as terrorism, organised crime, drug-trafficking and the environment were singled out for special attention. Not only were these subjects that were of increasing importance to the US, but they were matters that drew upon the economic strength of the EU and had little relevance to military capabilities. The US has shown its desire to improve cooperation with the EU, but only in particular issue areas. The US still does not see the European Union becoming a meaningful defence actor in the immediate future. Nor, in the meantime, does it regard the defence capabilities of the WEU as significant. Until the EU and the WEU demonstrate the political will to act in a more muscular fashion in the defence field, the US is unlikely to treat them seriously.

Conclusion

Evaluating the WEU and the EU's contribution to a stable post-war security system is a complex task. Critics point to the limitations that have been evident in the development of both organisations in the security and defence fields. The WEU has found itself in an awkward institutional position, poised between the EU and NATO. The support for its development has depended on a membership containing states with very different visions for the organisation, while the resources placed at its disposal have always been small by comparison with NATO. Its status as a core group of west European states in defence has been put into question by the prospect of offering membership to CEE states. As regards the EU, there has been a failure to fulfil the early expectations that were invested in the CFSP. It has proved, in the words of Commission President Jacques Santer, to be little more than an attempt 'to seek the least costly consensus' between the members (*Europe Documents* 1996a). Now, with the vigorous integration of the late 1980s and early 1990s appearing to have come to a halt, the future of the Union and its relationship with central and eastern Europe depends on the outcome of the Intergovernmental Conference.

Yet this is too negative an assessment of both organisations. It fails to acknowledge that the WEU and the CFSP were starting off from modest beginnings and are still in their early stages of development. The environment in which both organisations have sought to expand their competencies has been characterised by uncertainty, both in the interrelationship with other institutions and in the nature of the threats that must be countered. The WEU has concentrated on developing its operational capabilities and, although not a rival to NATO, it has created the foundations for undertaking small-scale tasks. The EU proved its relevance to the problems of the continent by addressing the broader agenda of security issues that lie outside the ambit of other institutions. Matters such as economic stability, environmental degradation and migration pressures are now firmly within the EU's sphere of competence. Henceforth, these are likely to be the security issues which preoccupy the attention of European capitals and publics alike.

As suggested by Waever, perhaps we should evaluate the institutions of the EU and the WEU not so much in terms of what *has* happened in Europe since the end of the Cold War, but rather in terms of what has *not* happened (Waever 1996: 249). Europe has not fallen prey to the classical rivalry predicted by neo-realists (Mearsheimer 1990), nor have the institutions themselves collapsed into disarray. Both widening and deepening is taking place, albeit slowly and incrementally, and it is accepted that there is a role for both the EU and the WEU in these processes. The consensus that the new Europe will be based on a plurality of institutions is now so widely accepted, that any alternative security order emerging seems out of the question (van Ham 1994: 197). The EU must be said to be the most important of all because of its relevance for all the new aspects of security, and because of the magnetism it presents to the CEE countries. It symbolises, on the one hand, a European sense of identity, while on the other, it serves as a powerful economic engine that will contribute to the economic well-being of the whole continent.

Notes

1. The need to speed up integration as a means to increased European security is very much an élite point of view which has not filtered into general public opinion.
2   The term EC is used before the ratification of the Maastricht Treaty in November 1993, whereas the term EU is used subsequently and when the period of time under consideration straddles the two periods.

3   For example, NATO's 1991 *Rome Declaration* (para. 5) makes a specific
     reference to the new broader security concept.
4   The terms 'politicised' and 'securitised' are taken from Waever 1995:
     46–86.
5   Interviews with Ritt Bjerregaard (EU Commissioner for the Environment)
     in *EUROPA*, October 1996, and with Thorvald Stoltenberg, *EUROPA*,
     June 1996.

References

Amsterdam European Council Summit (1997) Title V, Common Foreign and
  Security Policy, June.
Barbe, E. and Izquierdo, F. (1997) 'Present and Future Joint Actions for the
  Mediterranean Region', in Holland, M. (ed.) *Common Foreign and Security
  Policy: The Record and Reforms*, London: Pinter.
Buzan, B., Kelstrup, M., Lemaitre, P., Tromer, E. and Waever, O. (1990) *The
  European Security Order Recast. Scenarios for the Post-Cold War Era*,
  London: Pinter.
Buzan, B. (1991) *People, States and Fear*, London: Harvester Weatsheaf.
Cahen, A. (1989) *The Western European Union and NATO*, London: Brassey's
  Atlantic Commentaries No. 2.
Declaration on the Western European Union (1992) Treaty on European Union.
Economist (1996a) 'Europe's Iron Chancellor', 13 January.
Economist (1996b) 'Bosnia's Lingering Peace', 9 November.
Europe Documents (1994) No. 1887, 12 May.
Europe Documents (1996a) No. 6830, 11 October.
Europe Documents (1996b) No. 6834, 17 October.
Europe Documents (1997) No. 6952, 11 April.
Flockhart, T. (1996) 'The Dynamics of Expansion: NATO, WEU, and EU', *Eu-
  ropean Security*, 5(2): 197–219.
Foreign and Commonwealth Office (1996) 'A Partnership of Nations. The Brit-
  ish Approach to the EU Intergovernmental Conference 1996', *UK White
  Paper*, HMSO, March.
Huysmans, J. (1996) 'European Identity and Migration Policies. Socioeconomic
  and Security Questions in a Process of Europeanisation', *British Interna-
  tional Studies Association Paper*, Durham, December.
Laurent, P.-H. (1990) 'European Integration and the End of the Cold War', in
  Armstrong, D. and Goldstein, E. (eds) *The End of the Cold War*, London:
  Frank Cass.
Mearsheimer, J. (1990) 'Back to the Future: Instability in Europe after the Cold
  War', *International Security*, 15(1): 5–56.
Petersberg Declaration (1992) Western European Union Council of Ministers,
  Bonn, June.
Rees, G. W. (1993) (ed.) *International Politics in Europe: The New Agenda*,
  London: Routledge.
Regelsberger, E., Schoutheete, P. de, Travarent, P. de and Wessels, W. (1997)
  (eds) *Foreign Policy of the European Union: From EPC to CFSP and Be-
  yond*, London: Lynne Rienner.
Rühle, M. and Williams, N. (1995) 'NATO Enlargement and the European
  Union', *The World Today*, May.

78 *Rethinking Security in Post-Cold War Europe*

Rummel, R. (1997) 'The CFSP's Conflict Prevention Policy' in Holland, M. (ed.) *Common Foreign and Security Policy: the Record and Reforms*, London: Pinter.

Serfaty, S. (1996) 'Ameria and Europe Beyond Bosnia', *The Washington Quarterly*, Summer.

Treaty on European Union (1992) *Common Foreign and Security Policy*, Title V, Article J4.2.

Udenrigsministeriet, (1995) *Dagsorden for Europa*, Copenhagen, Udenrigsministeriet.

United States Information Service (1996) 'President Clinton Calls for "Next Historic Step" in Evolution of NATO', *Washington File*, 23 October.

van Ham, P. (1993) *'The European Community, Eastern Europe and European Unity: Discord, Collaboration and Integration since 1947*, London: Pinter.

van Ham, P. (1994) 'Can Institutions Hold Europe Together?', in Miall, H. (ed.) *Redefining Europe*, London: Pinter.

Waever, O. (1994) *Security and Identity Unlimited,* Copenhagen, Working Papers 14, Centre for Peace and Conflict Research.

Waever, O. (1995) 'Securitisation and Desecuritisation', in Lipschutz, R. D. (ed.) *On Security*, New York: Columbia University Press.

Waever, O. (1996) 'The European Security Triangle', in Wilde, J. de and Wiberg, H. (eds) *Organized Anarchy in Europe: The Role of Intergovernmental Organizations*, London: Tauris Academic Studies.

WEU Council of Ministers (1987) 'The Platform on European Security Interests', The Hague, 27 October.

PART TWO

Post-Communist Europe

CHAPTER 5

Central Europe and European security

PAUL LATAWSKI

Introduction

Since the end of the Cold War, the former communist east has contributed two distinct bodies of thinking to the debate over the future of European security. The central European countries have advocated the enlargement of existing institutions such as NATO and the European Union (EU) to form the core of the new architecture. Further east, the Russian Federation has led the camp that advocates European security built on pan-European cooperation by developing institutions such as the OSCE. This chapter explores the central European reconceptualisation and assesses its impact on the post-Cold War debate on the architecture of European security.

The expression 'central Europe' is used here to reflect a common security approach rather than a geographical area. 'Central Europe' refers to those states which have argued for the enlargement of western institutions (NATO, WEU and EU) eastward. The countries that advocate security architecture based on enlarged western institutions are the three Baltic States: Estonia, Latvia and Lithuania; the Visegrad group: Poland, the Czech Republic, Slovakia and Hungary; Romania and Slovenia. A caveat, however, must be added about Slovakia. While its external policy has consistently held the goal of membership in western institutions, the attitudes and style of governance of its current political leaders has cast doubt about the depth of Slovakia's official commitment to joining western institutions (Hamberger 1996: 5–18). There are also two states that hover on the fringes of central Europe. Bulgaria has important strands in its domestic debate that are decidedly lukewarm about membership in western institutions, despite official pronouncements to the contrary. Bulgarian commitment to this position is far from concrete (Todorov 1997: 29–38). Ukraine has not completely dismissed the idea of eventual membership in western institutions but its official policy has been heavily constrained by the views of its large eastern neighbour, the Russian Federation (Goncharenko 1995; Kremen 1997).

The central European concept of post-Cold War security is the product of the changes sweeping the European security environment. The collapse of communism in both eastern Europe and the Soviet Union between 1989 and 1991, with the attendant dissolution of the Warsaw Treaty Organisation (July 1991), ended the bipolar security harness in

Europe. Central European commentators often characterised the situation as a 'security vacuum' or 'security limbo'. Despite the uncertainty, the new security environment produced undoubted opportunities for central European states along with a strong desire to avoid the security predicaments that dogged the region earlier in the century. It was in this context that the distinctive rethink of security on central Europe emerged.

Security legacy: lands between

The current central European view of security in post-Cold War Europe cannot be divorced from the historical experience of this century. In this setting, 'central Europe' means less a group of states sharing common security aspirations than a region with common threats, vulnerabilities and catastrophes in the European political arena. The question to be considered here is what are the historical security legacies stemming from this experience? There is a great emphasis in post-Cold War analysis to produce 'historical lessons' that are meant to promote understanding of central Europe's place in the new security architecture. Such lessons paint the region as a cauldron of fanatical nationalism with every village a potential Bosnia or as geopolitical meat sandwiched between a German and Russian power centre (Brzezinski 1989/1990; Bender 1972). In fact, these historical paradigms are *faux amis*. It is dangerously misleading reductionism to see history as an unending repetition of patterns. History is important, indeed vital, to understand the current security debate. However, it is less important for providing so-called lessons of history than for supplying the necessary historical perspective to bring into clear focus the differences that dominate today's foreground.

For most of this century, central Europe has faced an insoluble security dilemma. This region has been a shatter belt or *zwischeneuropa* between German and Russian power centres. Whether in the guise of ramshackle empires (Habsburg and Ottoman) or independent states, the region was the object of the pressures and ambitions of Berlin or Moscow. During the First World War, Germany and Russia made plain in their war aims the desire to annex or control large portions of the region. German concepts of *Mitteleuropa* and dreams of building zones of influence from 'Berlin to Baghdad' or Russia's aims to augment its share of the Polish lands and to control the Straits had overt imperial agendas (Dallin 1963; Fischer 1967). With the emergence of the successor states in the power vacuum that resulted from the First World War, the Habsburg and Ottoman Empires may have departed from the region for good but the dramatic changes to the European political map did not put to rest German and Soviet (Russian) pressures.

Versailles Europe: collective insecurity

The construction of the Versailles security system after the First World War had a number of components that were meant in theory to cater for the security of the states occupying the middle zone of Europe. The League of Nations, through the principle of collective or cooperative security, was to be the agency responsible for maintaining the general peace of Europe. The League also had the responsibility of supervising the national minority protection regime established in central Europe by the post-war treaties. France, however, emerged as the key guarantor of the security of the middle zone through a series of bilateral collective defence treaties in 1921 with its key partners in the region: Poland, Czechoslovakia and Romania (Wandycz 1962). This was supplemented by regional collective defence arrangements that included bilateral alliances (e.g. Poland and Romania) as well as multilateral defence pacts such as the Little Entente (Czechoslovakia, Romania and Yugoslavia). French collective defence arrangements were buttressed by the tough disarmament regime imposed on Germany. Moreover, as long as the French occupied the Rhineland and held bridgeheads across the Rhine, their security guarantees in central Europe had real military credibility against the emergence of a German threat to France's eastern allies. The one serious flaw in the French collective defence arrangements was the lack of British support. Britain declined to enter into collective defence arrangements with France because its eastern alliances risked an implied British commitment. In a European crisis, French policy-makers would quickly face the dilemma of choosing between Britain and their eastern allies. In fact, France wasted little time in making its choice.

Less than five years after the Versailles system was constructed, the collective defence guarantees that underpinned the security of France's allies in the middle zone of Europe were rendered worthless. With the Locarno agreement in October 1925, France agreed to give up the Rhine bridgeheads and withdraw from the Rhineland in exchange for German guarantees of the permanency of the German western frontier. The Locarno agreement did not extract a similar promise on Germany's eastern borders. At a stroke, the French eastern alliance system lost its military credibility. France's eastern allies saw their major partner accept as open to revision their borders with Germany. Soon afterwards, France began building its Maginot line of frontier fortresses with all that they implied for the possibility of future French offensive operations against Germany. Kazimierz Smogorzewski, a well-known Polish commentator on international affairs, summarised the consequences of the Locarno agreement on the security of central Europe:

> One of the greatest political and psychological
> mistakes made after the last War was the attempt
> to appease the Germans' expansionist ambitions
> by giving them a free hand to the East . . .

> Munich was the culminating point of the policy
> expressed in the Locarno Pacts, which divided
> Europe into two 'security zones', the western
> one, which was guaranteed, and the eastern one,
> which was not guaranteed.
>
> (Smogorzewski 1943)

Locarno also meant that the onus of security resided in the cooperative arrangements of the League of Nations. For the middle zone, the League held little promise. From the start the organisation was flawed in its incomplete membership. The United States never joined and Germany and the Soviet Union only later. By the 1930s, the Abyssinian crisis demonstrated the manifest failures of the principle of collective security to all in Europe. The League also provided a vehicle for Germany to fuel instability in central Europe by exploiting the minority protection regime to forward a German irredentist agenda whatever real shortcomings existed in the treatment of national minorities in the region (Sierpowski 1992). The League had passed into irrelevance during the twilight of Versailles Europe. The appeasement policy begun at Locarno culminated at Munich in September 1938 with the destruction of Czechoslovakia. By March 1939, Britain ironically was handing out 'soft' guarantees to central European states threatened by Germany despite its earlier reluctance to underwrite the French system of eastern alliances. For the states between Germany and the Soviet Union, the legacy of Versailles Europe was collective insecurity.

Yalta Europe: security by limited sovereignty

The history of the region during the Second World War is a grim reminder of the brutal consequences of the failures of Versailles Europe. Nazi Germany and the Soviet Union, first as partners (1939–41) and later as bitter rivals (1941–45), pursued their ambitions with horrific consequences. The Molotov–Ribbentropp agreement (23 August 1939) partitioned the region into spheres of influence. The totalitarian partnership shared in the division of Poland with the Soviet Union annexing the Baltic States and Bukovina and Bessarabia. The remainder of the region fell into the German orbit. The German invasion of the Soviet Union (June 1941) placed the entire region in the Nazi 'new order' to be followed in 1944 by Soviet 'liberation'. The Sovietisation that followed between 1944 and 1948 not only imposed a political, social and economic order modelled after the Soviet Union but, in security terms, it created a unipolar hegemony in the region.

The historic paradigm of Great Power domination of the region now involved under communism only one player – the Soviet Union. Security for the region was now to be defined solely in terms of Soviet interests. The defence policy of each state was made an extension of that of the Soviet Union. A web of bilateral defence treaties bound the countries of the region to their fraternal ally to the east (Wandycz 1956). When the multilateral Warsaw Pact treaty was signed in 1955, it made little real difference in terms of security links. The officially designated 'threat' to the Warsaw Pact states was American-led NATO and West German revanchism. In fact, the most apparent threat to the states of the region came not from the West but another direction.

The *de facto* threat to central Europe was not from 'German revisionism' or 'western imperialism' but from its chief fraternal ally: the Soviet Union. When communist party newspapers filled their pages with articles about 'geopolitical realities' lauding the indispensable role of the Soviet Union to guard against German 'revanchism', it was really coded language warning against any challenge to the Soviet Union's hegemony from within the region. The real 'geopolitical reality' was the presence of Soviet garrisons in many of the central European states and a willingness to employ them in defence of the 'socialist commonwealth' as was so brutally illustrated in Hungary 1956 and Czechoslovakia 1968 (Linden 1982).

Intervention in defence of the Soviet imperium spawned the famous 'Brezhnev Doctrine' which underscored the limited sovereignty of the states making up what was now dubbed 'Eastern Europe'. The semantic change was important. It signified that the political centre of gravity for a group of states had shifted eastward despite their location in the geographical centre of Europe. Communism delivered a kind of security to the region that could only be threatened by internal ideological deviation that triggered 'fraternal' intervention or by Soviet adventurism against western Europe. In the world of bipolar confrontation, this security arrangement for eastern Europe had its attractions for the West. The West oscillated throughout the Cold War between exploiting discontent and tacitly accepting Soviet domination to maintain 'stability' in the region. Despite the public furore over the leak of the so-called 'Sonnenfeldt Doctrine' in the mid-1970s, calling for American policy to support the creation of an 'organic' relationship between eastern Europe and the Soviet Union, it demonstrated the degree to which western policy saw Soviet security arrangements as bringing stability.[1] Security, however, for the eastern half of Yalta Europe was ultimately built on Soviet bayonets. The combination of endemic economic failure and internal political opposition brought about Communism's terminal crisis. Mikhail Gorbachev's unwillingness to maintain the 'socialist commonwealth' by force led to the demise of a security system for 'Eastern Europe' predicated on limited sovereignty.

Security landscape: the 'New West'

The end of communism in the east has led to a fundamental security transformation. With the elimination of the German Democratic Republic (GDR) through unification with the Federal Republic and Austria's entry into the EU, central Europe now directly borders western Europe. In the east, the region has acquired a completely new set of neighbours. The demise of the Soviet Union created a belt of successor states on central Europe's eastern border (Belarus, Lithuania, Moldova and Ukraine). Russia, with the exception of the Kaliningrad enclave, has become a distant neighbour. For the countries of central Europe, the security centre of gravity has shifted westward.

For the region, this geopolitical realignment represents a major break with historical patterns. The collapse of communism between 1989 and 1991 created a radically new security reality. The unification of Germany within the framework of German membership in western institutions and the break-up of the multinational Soviet Union shattered the old constraints on central Europe. No longer partitioned between hegemons or in the grip of one imperial centre, central Europe acquired some room for political manoeuvre. This situation represents a security change far more favourable and fundamental than that experienced by the emerging successor states in 1918. At the conclusion of the First World War, central Europe entered a power vacuum soon to be refilled by Nazi Germany and Soviet Russia. The post-1989 security vacuum, although equally temporary, is one no longer sandwiched by the same historic hegemons. The communist implosion not only swept away totalitarian regimes, more importantly, it destroyed the last vestiges of the security order that had determined the fate of the region for much of this century.

The key to the new security reality is the post-war transformation of Germany into a democratic state that is firmly anchored in western institutions. With German unity taking place in this context, it brought not renewed menace but the dawn of German *rapprochement* with its eastern neighbours. The improving bilateral relations with Germany's eastern neighbours are being built on the solid foundation of the settlement of the outstanding issues left over from the Second World War. German *de jure* recognition of the Oder-Neisse (Odra-Nysa) frontier in 1990 as the Polish–German frontier and subsequent 'friendship and good-neighbourliness' treaties with both Czechoslovakia and Poland, closed bitter historical chapters and set in motion a revolutionary transformation in bilateral relations (Latawski 1994). German goodwill has been matched by that of the central Europeans who have come to see Germany less as a potential opponent than as a partner. The enormous distance travelled in this process of reconciliation has been done in a comparatively short period of time. Although it has had its problems to overcome as the lingering difficulties in Czech–German relations indicate, on the whole, the reconciliation continues to mature with growing economic, political and military ties. The significance of Germany's reconciliation with its eastern neighbours is comparable in European security terms to the post-war Franco–German reconciliation.

The end of the Soviet Union put in train similarly important security changes on central Europe's eastern periphery. The former Soviet

Union's most powerful successor state, the Russian Federation, did not inherit an imperial border in central Europe but a distant ethnographic one shared with other Soviet successor states. The Kaliningrad enclave, a kind of Guantanamo Bay of the Baltic, is the only remaining *de jure* piece of Russian-controlled territory in the heart of Europe. Although Belarus may be considered a *de facto* extension of Russia, it remains for the time being a nominally independent state. The net effect of this change in the east has been to match the economic, military and political separation of Moscow from its former Warsaw Pact allies with a physical one. The physical separation of Russia from central Europe, however, has not been matched by a psychological one among Russian élites. The vociferous Russian opposition to NATO enlargement suggests that acquiring a *droit de regard* or veto of the security arrangements of central Europe remains a Russian policy goal. Such a policy may be grounded in the fact that Russia has yet to adjust to post-Cold War circumstances and failed to define its national interests in the light of the new security conditions (Baranovsky 1997). More worrying has been a tendency, in the absence of such a fundamental revaluation of policy, to fall back on old geopolitical impulses grounded in Imperial Russian and Soviet foreign policy toward the region. This aspect of Russian policy is astounding given the bitter legacy of Tsarist and Soviet imperialism in central Europe. If the past suggests anything it is that a more fruitful approach would stress reconciliation rather than recidivism. Moreover, post-communist Russian policy ignores the reality of the shift westward of central Europe.

The implications stemming from the post-Cold War security realignment of central Europe are profound. The political, economic, social and security consequences of the changed security structure mean that central Europe will gravitate to the neighbouring region to the west. It is a new security reality not artificially created by imperial ambition and maintained at the point of a bayonet but one in which the new circumstances allow and promote a natural process of integration to take place. To label central Europe as the 'New West' simply recognises the security consequences of the end of Communism.

Central European security complex: threats, vulnerabilities and goals

In order to understand how the new security environment led the central Europeans to favour the enlargement of western institutions, we need to consider post-Cold War threats and vulnerabilities as seen from central Europe and how these relate to the goal of membership in western institutions. The 'security complex' pioneered by Barry Buzan provides a useful analytical tool to develop an integrated model of central European security thinking (Buzan 1991). This chapter employs a definition of the security complex developed by Wojciech Kostecki, a central

European member of the Buzan school: 'A security complex is a politi-cal constellation of states which is constituted by their mutual security concerns and aspirations' (Kostecki 1996: 35). It is particularly com-patible with the more holistic definition of 'security' that must be employed to describe the broader spectrum of threat prevalent in post-Cold War conditions. Moreover, the security complex offers an integra-tive perspective that can incorporate the anarchical characteristics of states with their growing interdependence (Kostecki 1996: 53–5). Given the breakdown of bipolarity (with the increased scope for competition or rivalry among states) and the central European vision of the enlarge-ment of western institutions eastward (a process promoting wider inte-gration), this feature of the security complex model is well suited to presenting the security vision of the region.

The relatively straightforward threat of a major East–West military confrontation has been replaced by a diversity of threats. Modelling the multifarious threats and vulnerabilities requires an integrated perspec-tive encompassing various levels and sectors (Kostecki 1996: 62–3). In Table 5.1, the levels adopted include system (Europe), sub-system (sub-region), unit (state) and sub-unit (internal state) to illustrate how threats and vulnerabilities impact on various layers of the international order. The model employs five sectors: military-diplomatic (questions of war and peace), political (factors shaping political systems), economic (fac-tors shaping economic performance), societal (factors leading to disin-tegration and conflict) and environmental (factors causing degradation and public health deterioration).

Within the framework of the integrative model presented in Table 5.1, we can identify threats and vulnerabilities that sweep across sectors and levels. These threats fall into a number of broad categories: internal (political stability, failure of economic reform), trans-border (migration and environmental problems), nationalism (minority separatism, ethnic conflict) and the danger of the re-emergence of a military threat (exter-nal hegemon). Most of these threat categories are 'soft' rather than 'hard' (Landgren 1992; Zielonka 1992). Although it must be recognised that problems of nationalism can manifest themselves across a spectrum that encompasses both soft and hard threats. The overall picture, how-ever, is of a threat environment more complicated than in the Cold War era even if none of the threats are so apocalyptic in consequences. We cannot exclude, however, the possibility of a new external threat emerg-ing to central Europe with Russia providing the most obvious candidate for this role. At present it is recognised by most of the states of central Europe (the Baltic states excluded) that Russia today poses no immedi-ate threat. The nature of the majority of threats and vulnerabilities found in post-Cold War central Europe are such that a purely military re-sponse in most cases is wholly inappropriate.

Given the diversity of threats and vulnerabilities and the lack of a major external military threat, the question arises as to why the central Europeans made integration into western institutions their principal

Table 5.1 Central European security complex: threats/vulnerabilities

Level	Military-diplomatic sector	Political sector	Economic sector	Societal sector	Environmental sector
System (Europe)	Renationalisation policy Limitations on sovereignty (involuntary) Hegemony	External limits domestic politics Ideological menace	Restricted market access Low investment Migration Organised crime	Global culture Migration Organised crime	Ecosystem crisis Energy crisis Transborder disasters Food and health problems Migration
Sub-system (sub-region)	Frontier disputes Minority problems State disintegration	Instability in neighbours Refugee influx	Restricted market access Migration Organised crime Transit restrictions	Cultural/religious conflict	Ecosystem crisis Energy crisis Transborder disasters Food and health problems Migration
Unit (state)	Lack of policy consensus Weak defence forces Technology gap	*Failure reform:* Weak political system Political fragmentation Problems civil-military relations Minority separatism	*Weak reform:* Slow privatisation Weak marketisation Weak banking and financial system Slow reform law and regulation Protectionism Crime/corruption	Weak civil society Corruption Organised crime Weak human rights regime Archaic class structure Minority discrimination	Crumbling infrastructure Ecosystem crisis Energy crisis Transborder disasters Food and health problems Migration
Sub-unit (internal state)	Internal collapse Regional separatism	Political extremism Extreme polarisation Massive protests/strikes	Unemployment Recession/depression Organised crime Corruption	Human rights violations Organised crime Corruption Xenophobic nationalism	Crumbling infrastructure Ecosystem crisis Energy crisis Transborder disasters Food and health problems Migration

aim. The answer lies in the goals of the transformation process in the region and its impact on the different levels of the security complex model. For the central Europeans emerging from the rubble of Soviet communism, western societies provided the model of transformation for reconstructing their social, economic and political systems (Staniszkis 1995: 31–50). Table 5.2 sets out the internal and external goals of the central European security complex across the different levels. At whatever level we consider these goals, it is quite clear that the western model is guiding the process of transformation. The central European states are striving to put into place western models in their internal political and economic reforms, in the context of relations with their neighbours or membership in the major security institutions. The goal of seeking western models at all levels of the central European security complex is seen as the best way of addressing the threats and vulnerabilities described in Table 5.2.

Table 5.2   Central Euopean security complex: goals

Level	Goals	
	External	*Internal*
System (Europe)	Prescriptive membership: NATO WEU EU	Normative membership: Council of Europe
Sub-system (sub-region)	Prescriptive bilateral links: Friendship and Cooperation Treaties Binding Subregional Cooperation: CEFTA	Cooperative sub-regional Multilateralism Infrastructure development Environmental issues
Unit (state)	Cooperative reform: Meet external membership criteria: NATO/WEU/EU Market access/ open borders	Prescriptive reform: Democratic political system Market economy
Sub-unit (internal state)	Cooperative links: Cross-border development: Euroregions	Cooperative reform: Democratic political system Market economy

Moreover, in the central European view, there is a clear interrelationship between the system level and the subsidiary levels. Indeed, membership in NATO is seen as buttressing the process of transformation to western models in the subsidiary levels of the security complex. In a speech given in October 1993, President Václav Havel stressed the linkage between membership in NATO and the broad thrust of 'western-isation' under way in the region:

> We belong and have always belonged to the Western
> European cultural area and we subscribe to all
> fundamental values of the Euro-American civilisation,
> to such values as are civil society, parliamentary
> democracy, pluralistic political system, the rule of
> law based on respect for the individual human beings
> and their rights and freedoms, liberal market economy.
> Quite naturally we thus share exactly the same values
> which NATO is to defend. What is more: we not only
> share these values but we feel to be their co-creators
> who do not subscribe to them from the outside but who
> have contributed to their creation and development
> throughout [the] centuries. Why should we not therefore
> participate also in their collective defence?

(Havel 1993)

The moral tone in Havel's argument is unmistakable, but beneath the language of shared 'fundamental values' is a hard pragmatic point. The stability of the region, state or internal political, economic and social order is very much contingent on security arrangements at a Europe-wide level. Many examples can be found of political figures in central Europe stressing the same point. The then Polish Minister of Foreign Affairs, Wladyslaw Bartoszewski, mirrored Havel's speech when he said in May 1995: 'We are convinced that the enlargement of the Alliance to the east will consolidate political stability and enhance the development of democracy and the market economy in all OSCE member countries' (Bartoszewski, May 1995). More recently, the Hungarian Defence Minister, Gyorgyi Keleti wrote: 'Our admission to NATO would not be aimed against anyone; instead, it would fulfil our goal which is to modernise Hungary. It can only be conducted as part of the Euro-Atlantic integration that we view as a sweeping process' (Keleti, *Zycie Warszawy*, 17 May 1997). His Czech counterpart, Miroslav Vyborny, offered the best summary of central European thinking when he wrote that 'the Czech Republic views the full-fledged membership in NATO and the EU as an actual conclusion of the transformation process at the international level' (Vyborny, *Zycie Warszawy*, 17 May 1997).

The central European argument that integration into a military alliance at the system level enhances security at subsidiary levels and buttresses the process of internal transformation has found support in the western community. Most notably, the 'Study on NATO Enlargement', produced in December 1995, echoes central European arguments. In the broad criteria set out in the enlargement study, the document indicates that such things as a functioning democracy, a market economy and democratic-civilian control of the armed forces are necessary prerequisites to Alliance membership. The implication is clear that NATO is meant to uphold these features and that its role extends beyond the collective defence of the territory of its members. For NATO it is precisely its credible collective defence role that allows it to contribute to the internal political, social and economic stability of its members. The link between providing collective defence and internal stability has been underestimated during the Cold War years, obscured as it was by the massive external threat faced by the Alliance. As a consequence, as NATO emerged into the post-Cold War era, questions were immediately raised about an Alliance that no longer faced a large external threat. On a wider theoretical plane, many commentators continue to believe that alliances need threatening enemies to survive.

Conclusion: commitment versus collective security

The perpetuation of NATO since the end of the Cold War has defied the conventional wisdom about collective defence arrangements in the international order. Such wisdom holds that military alliances can only survive in the face of a strong unifying threat. The demise of the Soviet Union seemingly put an end to NATO's *raison d'être* (Mortimer 1994; Palmer 1994). With no barbarians at the gates, who needs the castle let alone its multinational garrison? Despite everything that commentators have said, NATO has endured for a variety of reasons. The more cynical would cite organisational inertia and the survival instinct of the bureaucracy in Brussels and Mons. More charitable explanations have been the need to keep the United States involved in European security and the benefits of an integrated military structure so recently demonstrated with IFOR (Implementation Force) and SFOR (Stabilisation Force) in Bosnia. The key to understanding NATO's survival, however, has been the central European role in rethinking the Alliance's *raison d'être*.

Despite the theoretical impossibility of NATO's continued existence after the Cold War, the central Europeans have continued to champion a system of European security based on NATO's *collective defence* instead of a system founded on the concept of cooperative *collective security* as in the OSCE. In a 1993 speech, Havel summarised the central European thinking on the core security concepts that ought to govern European security:

> The lesson we were taught in Munich is still within
> living memory. And Munich meant not only a failure
> of the Western democracies face to face with the Nazi
> evil coming to power, a failure for which the West
> had to pay dearly, but a failure which also meant the
> collapse of the then system of European collective
> security. This lesson taught us how important it is
> for a country situated in such an exposed place to

firmly incorporate – both in our own and in general interest – into a system of functioning collective defence. Whoever are the top representatives of this state they, if they are responsible, must realise this need. Flirting with the isolationist idea of a third road in the form of a special nonalignment would be, particularly for our country and particularly in the present uneasy situation when Europe has been dramatically seeking a new image, not only very short-sighted from the security point of view but could also dangerously exclude us from the community of countries participating in this search in the spirit of jointly shared responsibility for jointly shared values.

(Havel 1993)

The central European desire to have collective defence as the bedrock of European security has provided the Alliance with new arguments to support its collective defence role in the absence of a major threat against its members. What the central Europeans have argued for is a system of European security based on mandatory commitment rather than voluntary cooperation. Such a system of *commitment security* with collective defence as the binding obligation at the core of the concept has deterrence value against diffuse or unforeseen external threats; while internally among its membership it precludes or dampens (Greece–Turkey example) the development of competition and rivalry that could be destabilising or lead to conflict. The denationalised and integrated military structure is the key to commitment security. It provides military capability that offers real deterrence against a potential aggressor while limiting the scope for competitive defence policy at the national level.

The central European concept of commitment security is best understood when compared with its rival system of cooperative security promoted by the Russian Federation for post-communist Europe. In Table 5.3, the concepts of 'commitment' and 'cooperative' security are compared. The mechanisms of each model are the familiar collective defence with its obligatory features for states and collective security which assume voluntary collaboration between states. The process that each imparts on international order is, however, very different. Commitment security with its mutual binding obligation promotes integration between states within the context of a broader security system. In contrast, cooperative security with its voluntary cooperation between states actually promotes an international order governed by the balance of power and adaptation. Ironically, the mechanism of collective security was meant to militate against such features in the international system. The legacy of the League of Nations in Europe, or more broadly its successor the United Nations, does not point to a successful record of blunting the worst effects of disparities in states' power or competition in the international order.

Table 5.3 **Security complexes compared**

	Central Europe	Russian Federation
Complex features		Versus
Concept	Commitment security	Cooperative security
Mechanism	Collective defence	Collective security
Process	Integration	Balance of power/ adaptation
Characteristics	Prescriptive	Normative

The central Europeans have preferred commitment security because its chief characteristic is its prescriptive qualities based ultimately on the mechanism of collective defence with its 'automatic' mutual defence guarantees. The alternative of cooperative security based on the OSCE offers at best a normative guide for the interaction of states. NATO's Secretary-General noted in a speech in London that the 'collective defence of Alliance territory remains at the heart of NATO' (Solana, 1997). The fact that collective defence has survived as the core mission of the heart of the Alliance owes a debt to central European thinking on European security. Their argument regarding the benefits of enlargement have made clear that the Alliance's cohesion rests on more than simply having a common enemy for 40 years. The shift from collective defence against a massive military threat to collective defence of a 'zone of stability' sharing common values still ultimately rests on NATO's binding military obligations to its members. For the central Europeans, this fact makes NATO the embodiment of a system of commitment security in post-Cold War Europe.

Note

1. See 'United States National Security Policy *vis-à-vis* Eastern Europe', Hearings Before the Subcommittee on International Security and Scientific Affairs of the Committee on International Affairs of the Committee on International Relations House of Representatives, Ninety-Fourth Congress, Second Session, 12 April 1976: 2.

References

Baranovsky, V. (ed.) (1997) *Russia and Europe: The Emerging Security Agenda*, Oxford: SIPRI Oxford University Press.
Bartoszewski, W. (1995) Address of the Polish Minister of Foreign Affairs to the Diet, 24 May.
Bender, P. (1972) *East Europe in Search of Security*, Baltimore: The Johns Hopkins University Press.

Brzezinski, Z. (1989/90) 'Post-Communist Nationalism', *Foreign Affairs* (LXVIII): 1–25.

Buzan, B. (1991) *People, States and Fear*, London: Harvester Wheatsheaf.

Dallin, A. (ed.) (1963) *Russian Diplomacy and Eastern Europe 1914–1917*, New York: King's Crown Press.

Fischer, F. (1967) *Germany's Aims in the First World War*, New York: W. W. Norton.

Goncharenko, A. (1995) *Ukrainian–Russian Relations: An Unequal Partnership*, London: Royal United Services Institute Whitehall Paper Series.

Hamberger, J. (1996) 'Slovakia's Geopolitical Situation', *International Studies*, 2: 5–18.

Havel, V. (1993) Address to the House of Deputies of the Parliament, 12 October.

Keleti, G. (1997) *Zycie Warszawy*, 17 May.

Kostecki, W. (1996) *Europe After the Cold War: The Security Complex Theory*, Warsaw: PAN-ISP.

Kremen, V. (1997) 'The East Slav Triangle', in Baranovsky, V. (ed.) *Russia and Europe: The Emerging Security Agenda*, Oxford: SIPRI Oxford University Press: 271–88.

Landgren, S. (1992) 'Post-Soviet Threats to Security', in *SIPRI Yearbook 1992: World Armaments and Disarmament*, Oxford: SIPRI Oxford University Press: 531–57.

Latawski, P. (1994) 'Germany's Reconciliation with its Eastern Neighbours', *The RUSI Journal*, 139: 65–9.

Linden, R. H. (1982) 'The Security Bind in East Europe', *International Studies Quarterly*, 26: 155–89.

Mortimer, E. (1994) 'In search of a unifying threat', *Financial Times*, 7 December.

Palmer, J. (1994) 'Can we now put NATO on ice now the Cold War's over?', *Guardian*, 22 November.

Sierpowski, S. (1992) 'Mniejszosc niemiecka na tle aktywnosci mniejszosciowej ligi narodów', in Wrzesinski, Wojciech *Polska – Polacy – mniejszosci narodowe*, Wroclaw: Ossolineum: 77–90.

Smogorzewski, K. (1943) Address on the Future of Europe, Le Play Society, Somerville College, Oxford, 2 January.

Solana, J. (1997) 'Only Winners in New Security Structure', *The World Today*, April.

Staniszkis, J. (1995) 'In Search of a Paradigm of Transformation', in Wnuk-Lipinski, Edmund (ed.) *After Communism: A Multidisciplinary Approach to Radical Social Change*, Warsaw: ISP-PAN: 19–56.

Todorov, I. T. (1997) 'The Bulgarian Political Parties and NATO', in Ivanov, A. (ed.) *Bulgaria and NATO: The Debate at Five to Twelve*, Sofia: Center for Strategic and Applied Studies: 29–38.

Vyborny, M. (1997) *Zycie Warszawy*, 17 May.

Wandycz, P. (1956) 'The Soviet System of Alliances in East Central Europe', *Journal of Central European Affairs*, 16: 177–85.

Wandycz, P. (1962) *France and her Eastern Allies 1919–1925: French–Czechoslovak–Polish Relations from the Paris Peace Conference to Locarno*, Minneapolis: University of Minnesota Press.

Zielonka, J. (1992) 'Security in Central Europe', *Adelphi Paper*, 272, London: International Institute for Strategic Studies.

CHAPTER 6

A New Russia in a New Europe: still back to the future?

WILLIAM PARK

The new context

Historically, Russian–European security has been a two-way street. Whether positively or negatively, by design or by default, it has rarely been possible for non-Russian Europe to pursue security policies for the continent without reference to Russian domestic developments or to Russian foreign and security concerns. Russian history, on the other hand, not least in the last two centuries, can be read as a compelling saga of the vulnerability of both Russian state and society to turbulence and dynamism to its west. At least from a security perspective, then, Russia has been an intrinsic part of Europe (Ruhl 1997). This is and will continue to be so in post-Cold War Europe. However, this observation does not offer any simple guide as to how best to construct the Russian–European security relationship – if it ever did.

The task of analysing Russian–European security relationships is today complicated still further by the historically unprecedented geopolitical and geostrategic configuration of the Russian state which emerged from the December 1991 break-up of the Soviet Union (Dunlop 1993). The emergence of independent and sovereign states in the Baltic region, Belarus, Ukraine and Moldova, to say nothing of Georgia, Armenia, and Azerbaijan too, serves to physically separate Europe's largest and most populous state from the European geographical heartland. Although both the existence of the Kaliningrad enclave and the still unsettled relationship between Russia and other former Soviet (FSU) states weakens the observation a little, the collapse of the Soviet Union represents about as profound a geopolitical shift as any that European history has produced. Four centuries of Russian territorial advance and annexation has been wiped out, leaving as a residue a Russian state with a territorial configuration quite unfamiliar to modern European diplomatic history. The loss to Moscow of her *glacis* in east-central Europe, acquired at the end of the Second World War, emphasises still further the profundity of recent geopolitical and geostrategic changes. For the countries of east-central Europe, Russia can in some respects now be seen as a distant neighbour, impoverished, with little of positive value to offer, and with tendencies towards anti-social behaviour. To extend this analogy, western Europe by contrast has become a more proximate, welcome and (perhaps ambivalently) beckoning neighbour, promising to raise the tone of the whole neighbourhood.

Indeed, we could reasonably ask ourselves in what senses does post-Soviet Russia possess either the resource base or the geographical configuration to make much of a positive contribution to the European security order at all? Certainly its residual military capability, its associated capacity for mischief, the weakness and vulnerability of many of its neighbours, all serve to render Russia a major factor in and potential problem to any new European security arrangement – in other words, Russia today constitutes an integral element of any European security order, as ever (Legvold 1997). On the other hand, that its population and economic strength roughly equate it to Brazil (Mihalka 1994: 35) should alert us to how incomplete Russia is even as a 'Great Power', let alone as a Superpower. Furthermore, the unpredictable and unsettled political, social and economic conditions in Russia also caution against any analysis based on the assumption that Moscow can play the part of a 'Great Power' in European security affairs in the years to come. The sheer incoherence in the making and conduct of external policy in Moscow serves to weaken still further Russia's impact and effectiveness in Europe's diplomacy (Allison, *et al.* 1996; Arbatov 1997a, 1997b). Such is the instability and uncertainty there that any analytical conclusions we might arrive at are in grave danger of being overturned by unforeseen and even dramatic developments. Are we peering into an abyss, consisting of some frightening mix of political chaos, economic collapse, civil conflict, widespread criminality, environmental disasters, coups and inter- and intra-state wars? Or are we looking towards the sunlit uplands of stable democracy, a thriving market economy and the emergence of civil society? Is Russia on the road to joining some pan-European zone of peace and cooperation, or is it in the process of imploding, and forming a major threat to any such zone of peace? Given this unpredictability, what *is* today's Russia to European security?

We must also take account of the fact that western Europe, if not yet central Europe, is also very different from what it has been in the past. This makes a difference, too, for the Europe from which Russia is differentiated, or within which it is to be slotted, or with which it might cooperate on security affairs, or from which it might be excluded, or to which it might pose a threat, is in many ways, more integrated, more whole, than in previous periods of history. This takes two forms. First, there is the overlay of institutions, functioning as for a multilateral and cooperative diplomacy, as instruments for the management and even intensification of economic and security interdependence, and as a means by which norms might emerge and adherence to them be encouraged. The European Union, WEU, NATO, OSCE, and the Council of Europe, all have a part to play here. Second, there is the widespread commitment to the norms, values and practices which underpin this institutional network: political democracy, human and minority rights, market economics, free trade, open societies, cooperative diplomacy and the like (Wallace 1992). That both the institutional memberships and adherence to the prevailing norms embrace other parts of the industrialised world too, and most notably North America, is also a central feature of the 'Europe' which has developed since 1945. Certainly from a security perspective, the United States is part of Europe too, although the tightness of trans-Atlantic relations are increasingly being questioned in the light of the Cold War's demise (Gordon 1996).

Although there is always politics and diplomacy in the relations between states, and differing interests and perspectives, there is nothing quite like a 'balance of power' system in today's Europe, no imperial competition, no 'billiard ball' model of the politics of European security (Jervis 1991–2), in which Russia as one player might expect to play or balance other players in the system off against each other as was possible in previous historical eras. It is not at all clear that Russian policy-makers fully appreciate the centripetal nature and instincts of modern Europe. It can also sometimes appear that Russian thinking on foreign and security policy has been quite by-passed by the kind of 'new thinking' Gorbachev seemed to have had in mind (Bialer 1988), and instead retains its attachment to crude measurements of power, balance-of-power diplomacy, the significance of 'Great Power' status, confrontational rather than cooperative diplomacy, zero-sum games and the like. This is not necessarily to assert that Europe will never return to its competitive and conflictual past, not least as a consequence of the removal of the Soviet threat and of Europe's Cold War divisions (Mearsheimer 1990). But for the foreseeable future this Europe will resemble a pillar, albeit one within which active and sometimes fractious debate takes place, which Russia could join or be excluded from, with which it can cooperate or which it can confront. Will Russia join this pillar, or form a separate one, or even be 'quarantined' in some way, as a source of instability, chaos, threat, and 'un-European' activities? In any case, Russian behaviour, internal and external, will be judged by the norms of this Europe, not least as they are represented by its institutions, and will be a crucial factor in how Russian–European security relationships are to evolve into the future.

Even prior to this post-1945 'Europeanisation' of western Europe, Russia's particular uniqueness had always been recognised – so much so that its 'Europeanness' has itself been questioned throughout history, both within and without Russia (Neumann 1996). It is a uniqueness that is multidimensional, and takes physical, military, political, historical, cultural and economic forms. Russia has perhaps always been too big, too poor, too Asiatic to be properly 'European' – whatever that might mean. One could argue that this peculiarity, this distinctiveness, was perpetuated – albeit in a novel form – in the wake of the Bolshevik Revolution in 1917, when Russia – in the shape of the Soviet Union – embarked on its remarkable and ideologically inspired experiment in social and economic engineering. After 1945, Russia – now accompanied by its newly acquired central and south-eastern European satellites – in some ways diverged still further from what we might regard as Europe's mainstream or prevalent evolutionary pathway, as the (broadly) western half of the continent flourished under the forces of political democracy, economic marketisation and transnational integration. Russia's experiment with communism, and the West's integrationism, has meant that once again Russia has missed out on what has been a profoundly formative experience for much of the rest of Europe. Given that the West's institutional and political cohesion has a strong security dimension to it, this carries quite serious implications for Russia's future place in the European security order.

Indeed, it is not easy to know how to characterise, analyse and grapple with the unique Russian Federation that emerged from the ashes of the Soviet Union at the end of 1991. We could note, for example, that with over 80 per cent of its population of Russian ethnicity it more closely resembles both a nation-state and an ethnically European state than either its Soviet or Tsarist predecessors. On the other hand, we could draw attention to the fact that, compared with the past and notwithstanding the Kaliningrad enclave, the territory under Moscow's direct (and indirect) control is now proportionately more east of the Urals than west of them, comparatively more geographically Asian than European, further from Europe's central European heartland than it has been for centuries. Notwithstanding the loss of Central Asia, when we take into account the enormous eastward extension of the territory of the Russian Federation, for this reason too today's Russia can plausibly be perceived as *less* European than was either the Soviet Union or Tsarist Russia, as a kind of European backyard geographically as well as a backwater economically, politically and socially.

Russia and the West

The Soviet Union's military and nuclear might – its Superpower status – also separated it out from other European states after 1945. With the collapse of the Soviet system came the collapse of the political, military and ideological confrontation of the Cold War. The Cold War had cast Russia as the main protagonist to the other major European powers, and had forced them into alliance both with each other and with the United States. Now, for Russian reformers at least, and notably Andrei Kozyrev, the new Russia's foreign minister, the collapse of the Soviet system offered an historic opportunity for Russia to become a normal European state, even if after a period of necessary 'apprenticeship' (Neumann 1996: 200), and to reconstruct the country's security relationships with her European neighbours on the basis of cooperative rather than confrontational behaviour. They shared with central Europeans, but not necessarily with their conservative compatriots in Russia, a feeling of victory over the Soviet system. They believed that the West would welcome Russia with open arms, that Russia would be regarded less as a defeated Cold War adversary and more as a fellow victor and a partner in the construction of a new European order. They were 'integrationists' with the West rather than '*re*integrationists' with the other FSU states. The cause of the Organisation of Security and Cooperation in Europe (OSCE), as it became known, was championed as the basis for 'a unified, non-bloc Europe' to which other organisations such as NATO and the Commonwealth of Independent States (CIS) would be subordinate (Kozyrev 1994: 65; Mihalka 1994: 37–8; Baranovsky 1995a: 47–8; Arbatov 1997b). In such a 'non-bloc' Europe, the divisions between Russia and western Europe would, along with other divisions, in time dissolve. Such was the drive to 'return to Europe' in Moscow in the year or two following the collapse of the Soviet Union that relations with other parts of the world, including those with whom the Soviet Union had formerly enjoyed close relationships or towards which had conducted an active and engaged diplomacy, and most especially the former Warsaw Pact and Soviet states, were generally almost totally neglected (Bowker 1995; Davydov 1997: 372–5).

Inspired by what former Russian Ambassador to Washington, Vladimir Lukin, dubbed this 'romantic masochism' (Simes 1994: 79), and having turned their backs on Russia's Asian hinterland in this way, Moscow's reformers had not anticipated that Russia might simply become Europe's 'backyard', psychologically and politically as well as geographically (Kortunov and Kortunov 1994: 269). In the initial euphoria, the risks of Russia's exclusion from the western world were not really considered. Moscow failed to appreciate that west Europeans would prefer to stick to the certainties of NATO and the EU rather than risk all on an untried and probably ineffective OSCE which offered to serve no particularly useful purpose other than to give Moscow a veto over the conduct of their security business. Paying very little attention to the similarly newly liberated countries of central Europe, nor did Moscow's reformers foresee that these countries would shift so rapidly from their initial pan-European security preferences once they saw that the West's institutions would be preserved and predominant even in the wake of the Cold War. Nor did they anticipate that the West would more readily move towards accommodating the aspirations of the central Europeans to 'return to Europe' than they would Moscow's (Baranovsky 1995b).

For all that the West undoubtedly welcomed the collapse of the Soviet Union and recognised Yeltsin's contribution to that collapse, both in Moscow and in the West a tendency to regard Russia as the Soviet Union writ small revealed itself. Moscow was not much trusted to respect the independence and sovereignty either of the former Warsaw Pact allies or of FSU states. Although the Soviet Union had been the Cold War adversary, and it had been the Soviet Union that had experienced 'defeat', Russia as the successor state at times appeared to be required to 'go through a long period of reflection and redemption akin to that of post-war Germany and Japan' (Simes 1994: 77). As such, the

West was in no hurry to embrace Russia into the European fold in either the economic or security spheres. Economic aid was not forthcoming in the quantities needed or expected, and private commercial investment in the post-communist economies has been far greater in the central European and Baltic states than in Russia. There was indeed little interest in the construction of a pan-European security structure providing for the elimination, or at least the subordination, of 'blocs'. Instead, NATO appeared to be ready to embark on a process leading to its enlargement by incorporating the central Europeans, potentially including the three FSU Baltic states, but not – or at least not for some time yet – Russia. It was not too surprising that Moscow tended to see in this the message that the – imagined, as Moscow saw it – security fears of the central Europeans were more important to the West than were those of Russia. Across a whole range of issues, from arms sales to CFE revision to Bosnia, there was an increasing sense in Moscow that the West was riding roughshod over Russia's interests and sensitivities.

Still championing partnership with the West, but deeply disillusioned – above all, perhaps, with the prospect of NATO's enlargement (Buszynski 1995; Kozyrev 1995; Lieven 1995) – Moscow's reformers came to fear that insufficiently sympathetic western responses to Russia's plight and to its overtures to the West could combine with the 'Great Power' and 'Russian interests first' mentality of the 'Eurasianists' and nationalists to isolate Russia once again from mainstream economic and political processes in Europe and elsewhere. This fear of Russia's isolation and marginalisation formed the root of the reformers' opposition to NATO enlargement. Beginning with his now famous 1992 Stockholm speech, Kozyrev repeatedly sought to warn the West that a failure to respond positively to Russia's offer of partnership, and take into account Russia's legitimate concerns and interests, might indeed strengthen the position of the conservatives, and he might have had a point (Griffiths 1994). It became harder for the increasingly chastened, even embittered, westernisers in Moscow to resist, or even to disagree with, the fears of western encirclement and containment which were gaining such widespread currency on the Russian right. Again, as Andrei Kozyrev put it, it could appear 'that it does not matter to our partners who is sitting in the Kremlin – advocates of partnership with the West or champions of imperial policy' (Kozyrev 1995: 12). And for some in the West – most famously Zbigniew Brzezinski, who argued that neither autocracy nor imperialism were yet dead in Russia (Brzezinski 1994) – Russia did, and does, remain an adversary, perhaps an enduring one. If Moscow's reformers dreaded Russia's continued isolation from the European mainstream (Pierre and Trenin 1997: 7–9), some western opinion and the corollary of some western policy trends appeared to threaten precisely that.

There are more benign explanations for what might appear to be the West's neglect of Russia and its concerns. First, there appears to be an assumption, probably well-founded, that even if Russia's 'return to

Europe' – or whatever other form Russia's 'normalisation' might be expected to take – is eventually to happen, it is still a long way off. Russia's greater economic backwardness, the duration of its communist past, its more limited experience of democracy and market economics, are all likely to delay Russia's reintegration into the European and global community as a western-style state (Stemplowski 1995). In support of this thesis, it might be noted that the less advanced states of central and south-eastern Europe, such as Bulgaria, Romania and Albania, have also been less well-received by the West than have their more northerly neighbours. The same might be said to be true of western attitudes towards Ukraine (Larrabee 1996).The sheer size of the country, and the daunting peculiarities of its economy, make progress in Russia even more problematic than in many other post-communist states, even though Moscow's reformist credentials may be more impressive than some others. In fact, modern economic, technological and political trends might make it impossible for Russia to achieve isolation from the rest of the world, even if it wanted to and despite the obstacle of Russian history, culture and circumstances (Braithwaite 1994; Malia 1994). In this way, Russia's fusion into the European mainstream could be presented as simply a matter of time.

Still on the positive side of the equation, western policy has, broadly speaking, aimed to integrate Russia into the global system economically and politically – through measures as diverse as inviting Russia to attend G7 meetings, involving Moscow in the 5-power 'contact group' dealing with the Bosnian situation, incorporating Russia into the Council of Europe, extending both the Partnership for Peace programme and the prospect of a special NATO–Russia strategic relationship to Moscow, and supporting the International Monetary Fund (IMF) plan to reform the Russian economy. Western support for President Yeltsin, including its acquiescence in the Chechen affair – in which Russia's behaviour hardly heralded her acceptance of modern Europe's behavioural norms – is alone testimony enough that the West is concerned to preserve a working diplomatic relationship with Moscow. The western, and especially American, preference that Russia assume the mantle of the Soviet Union in the international system – with respect to membership of the UN Security Council, for example, or the Soviet Union's nuclear weapons power and obligations – are testimony to a Russo-centric strand in western responses to the post-Cold War scenario from the very beginning. Indeed, other former Warsaw Pact or FSU states have sometimes been unsettled by what they have perceived as the West's Russo-centric bias. In fact, it is the economic and political stability of the country that has probably become the West's main policy objective – or wish – towards Russia. Some have argued that this is more important than the development of a fully-fledged democracy in Russia (de Nevers 1994: 76).

In any case, the immediate problem is that the rest of Europe will not stand still while Russia 'catches up'. The three FSU states in the Baltic region, and the central European states of Poland, the Czech Republic and Hungary in particular, are economically growing at a rapid rate and are economically, socially and politically increasingly mirroring and integrating with western Europe. Their desire to join NATO and other, western, institutions, and the readiness in some quarters in western Europe and North America to grant their wish, cannot easily be held in check pending some far-distant and probably unspecifiable 'normalisation' or 'westernisation' of Russia's political and economic circumstances. This is not to say that at the moment the West is doing much to enable Russia to close any economic, social and political gaps between itself and other European countries – which is also not necessarily to imply that there is much the West can do, or that Russia could not do far more for herself. At the same time, Russian–European relations cannot simply be frozen until it is possible to build a new, institutionalised relationship at some future date when Russia is deemed to have 'caught up' or served its 'apprenticeship'. Any real or imagined exclusion, isolation or marginalisation of Russia will have an effect now, as well as in the future. In effect, what the West is in the meantime endeavouring to do – and it is the United States and Germany which take the lead here – is engage Moscow in a security dialogue aimed at weaning Russia's foreign and security policy élite from its rather Hobbesian, *realpolitik* view of the world. Moscow is being advised that in an interdependent and norm-governed world, behaviour such as the attack on Grozny, or threats to and unilateral military action in other FSU states, or the pursuit of unconstrained arms-sales policies, are not acceptable. Similarly, NATO enlargement should not be read as military encirclement but rather as the extension of a desirable security and stability westwards towards Russia's borders. A NATO–Russia strategic partnership could be developed to emphasise the constructive and non-threatening nature of this development. It is in Russia's own best interests, domestically and internationally, to cooperate with western governments, institutions and norms. Only in this way can Russia hope to avoid the marginalisation and isolation that might otherwise befall it (Kugler 1996; Pierre and Trenin 1997).

Russia as Eurasia

However, both in Russia itself and in the rest of Europe, Russia's 'Eurasian' character, which has geographical, historical, economic and cultural dimensions, has sometimes been regarded as the ultimate testimony to that country's immutable distinctiveness from the rest of Europe (Hauner 1992). Again both in Russia and in the rest of Europe, this 'Eurasianism' is sometimes seen as the foundation on which not only Russia's uniqueness, but also its strength and its claim to be a 'Great Power' is based. For this strand of thinking, separation from Europe can be seen as inherent, unavoidable and natural, and control of or at least influence over the territory of what is now the 'near abroad' can seem imperative (Brusstar 1994: 617–18; Kortunov and Kortunov 1994:

270). According to this argument, in order to be a 'Great Power', even in Europe, Russia needs to be truly Eurasian. And this line of thinking is indeed usually quite obsessively concerned that Russia retains its status as a 'Great Power'. In the wake of the Soviet collapse, Russia – and the other former Soviet states – have also had to deal with the very real economic interdependencies, ethnic problems and security complexities left behind.

Two observations follow from this Russian attachment to the 'near abroad' as the very foundation of the country's character and power. First, Moscow can be very sensitive to anything smacking of 'outside' interference in what it regards as its own, FSU, sphere of influence, in its European no less than its Asian dimensions. Many of Russia's immediate neighbours are vulnerable, weak and unstable, and Moscow often seems inclined to the premise that, should Russian influence wane, other – perhaps more dynamic – power centres will fill the vacuum. Perhaps we should not be too surprised at this, given that these spheres of Russian influence in what is now the FSU were indeed wrested from or otherwise acquired as a result of struggle with competing powers in what has been characterised as '. . . a long-term and never-ending reconfiguration of empires and states . . .' (Blank 1995: 634). This angle of vision is bound to see NATO or EU interest in the Baltic states or Ukraine in a provocative light. Those familiar with Washington's Cold War 'domino theory' will recognise these thought processes, and it should be borne in mind when we seek to understand Russian policy towards the 'near abroad' (Kortunov and Kortunov 1994: 271). One analyst indeed claims that 'a full-blown domino theory has taken hold' in Moscow (Blank 1995: 632).

In any case, and certainly towards the furthest end of the spectrum, occupied variously by those of a nationalistic/Slavophile/communist disposition, it can be easy to slip into an assumption of the inevitability of conflict with those external, and especially western, forces, which are believed to want to weaken, contain or otherwise marginalise Russia, and thus deny or constrain its 'Great Power' status. What others might perceive as 'globalisation' or 'modernisation' can here be regarded as American hegemonialism or as a means to undermine Russia's sovereignty and autonomy in world affairs. It is far from clear that this strand of thinking in Russia is at all ready to accept that Russia's interests lie in its voluntary subordination to any global, interdependent, institutionally governed and American-sponsored world order. Indeed, this sentiment, or identity, can at times incorporate or imply a pessimism about Russia's prospects of ever successfully catching up with or truly 'belonging' to the West. Disbelief that Russia will ever compete successfully in the economic or technological spheres can convert into a self-justifying anti-materialistic rejection of and opposition to western values and influence. This can in turn provide the foundations on which Russian antagonism towards the West, or at least a stand-off from it, can be built.

For the Russian nationalistic sentiments which often attach themselves to 'Eurasianism', there is, according to a former British Ambassador to Moscow, sometimes a romanticised view of Russia as a victim,
and an emotional stance incorporating both despair and defiance,
'placed with a growing indifference, indeed with paranoia and hostility,
towards the outside world' (Braithwaite 1994: 14). As one Russian
diplomat has expressed it, 'For a variety of reasons rooted deep in its
history, it would be psychologically easier for Russia to slide into
renewed confrontation with the West than to concede that it must accept
limitations on its freedom of action' (Sokov 1994: 915). Talk of
NATO's enlargement, criticism of Russian 'neo-imperialism' in the former Soviet space, and the creation of closer relationships between FSU
states and external powers, can all serve to reinforce this conflictual and
paranoid tendency – or, if one prefers it, this *realpolitik* mind-set. At
minimum, Moscow can appear to want a 'free hand' in dealing with
problems in the FSU space, and even the more moderate Russian 'Eurasianists' might wonder why Moscow should be denied the freedom afforded to other 'Great Powers' such as the United States to police its
own 'backyard' (Simes 1994: 77–8). Within a couple of years of the
emergence of the Russian Federation from the ashes of the Soviet
Union, most elements of Moscow's foreign and security policy élite appeared resigned to a recognition that Russian and western interests and
perspectives in the FSU space might simply not coincide (Arbatov
1997b).

The second observation to be made is that, if Russia's 'Eurasian'
character is perceived as the basis for the country's power and status,
then economic and social objectives might have to be subordinated to
the needs of 'empire'. Many would argue that this has precisely been
the course of, and explanation for, Russian history over a much longer
term, and for its differentiation from mainstream development in much
of the rest of Europe (Afanasyev 1994; Braithwaite, 1994; Garnett
1994). Today, sections of the military, and Russian 'nationalists' and
communists more generally, who appear to find it hard to envisage a
Russia with 'Great Power' status but without extensive 'imperial' sway,
are often committed to a more centralised, state-directed economic system than that envisaged by more reformist elements. They are 'statists',
and have a foreign policy orientation to match (Kugler 1996: 25–159).
Their identity and well-being have been so entangled with the Soviet
system in all its manifestations (Covington 1995: 447–8). However, this
emphasis on the FSU space as the location of Russia's national interests, combined with continuing domestic political and economic weakness, could produce 'a supernova state, expanding slowly outwards on
its periphery while collapsing internally' (de Nevers 1994: 6–7). The
military and economic resources which might have to be devoted to the
pursuit of Russia's interests there, and the need to handle political opposition at home, might reinforce the link between external expansion and
domestic collapse, or at least stagnation (Garnett 1997).

In this context, Russia's behaviour in the former Soviet space can become something of a touchstone for Russian–western security relationships more broadly (Royen 1997). It cannot be said that the West's interpretation of Russian 'near abroad' activities have been any clearer or more consistent than have those activities themselves (Kremeniuk 1997). There has at times been frustration in Moscow with the contrast between seeming western indifference to Russia's problems in the 'near abroad', and opposition to Russian activities there. The Russian inclination to regard the former Soviet space as its more or less exclusive sphere of influence where it has concrete interests and in which it is entitled to a 'free hand', is sometimes recognised as inevitable and even desirable (Braithwaite 1994) as a means to maintain order and prevent competitions for influence which might get out of hand – between Russia and Turkey, for example, or Russia and China. Partly in keeping with this willingness to concede Russia its sphere of influence, the West has in any case been generally unwilling or unable to provide any useful contribution to the problems of instability in the FSU space. The international community's failure to respond to Georgian requests for help in the face of that country's internal fragmentation, or Russia's in the face of the Tajik civil war, might be offered as examples. The domestic political crisis of late 1996 in Belarus was similarly initially left to Moscow to deal with. The Baltic states have been the exception, to some extent from Moscow's point of view as well as that of the West (Asmus and Nurick 1996). It might even be possible to detect the emergence of a tacit understanding between Russia and the West that western interest in the Baltics and in the Ukraine be recognised in Moscow in return for a Russian 'freer hand' elsewhere in the former Soviet space (Marantz 1994: 739). Any such 'understandings', however, are surely ambiguous and unstable, and would in any case intensify Russia's exclusion from Europe's mainstream.

Russian 'misbehaviour' in the 'near abroad' would inhibit Russia's incorporation into Europe's institutions, or the development of closer relations with them. This would be doubly so if assertive behaviour towards her neighbours was associated with a slackened commitment to, or continuing failure in, political and economic reform on the domestic front. Were the West to react sharply to perceived Russian heavy-handedness in the former Soviet space, then the prospects for economic and probably political progress too could recede still further. In this way, Russian domestic developments, relationships with other FSU states, and the evolution of pan-European security arrangements, are all closely intertwined. It can sometimes seem as if there is a structural problem obstructing the development of healthy Russian security relationships with the rest of Europe. Certainly, Russia can hardly be expected to be taken seriously when in effect it seeks a veto over the security policies of its western neighbours, or proposes that NATO subordinate itself to a reformed OSCE, while simultaneously it jealously guards its special rights in the FSU. Moscow has never cleared up this contradiction in its professed preference for a 'bloc-free' Europe, and it constitutes part of the explanation for Moscow's isolation in its championing of the OSCE as the basis for a pan-European order (Borawski 1996).

In fact, Moscow's attitude towards the FSU, or the CIS, seems far from settled. For example, it is possible to gain the impression that although there is widespread agreement in Moscow that closer economic and security integration with the CIS states is desirable and in accordance with Russia's vital interests, and that there is also a concern with the fate of Russian minorities, many fear the burdens involved and the risks entailed – not least of being drawn into quagmires. There is some speculation about alternatives to a CIS-wide zone of integration – the establishment of buffer zones, of inner-and-outer cores and multitiered relationships within the CIS, differentiations between predominantly economic and predominantly security-based relationships, and the like (Olcott 1995; Russell 1995). Perhaps as a result of this debate and indecision, Russia's 'neo-imperialist bark has been worse than its bite; aggressiveness has been more a matter of words than deeds' (Adomeit 1995: 59). A recognition of the realities and the limits to Russia's power may have constantly nagged at the desire to be resolute. Russia has acquiesced in permitting a role for the OSCE, albeit a limited and as yet undeveloped one, in Georgia, Nagorno-Karabhak and even Chechnya. The inviolability of borders has been accepted in Moscow, and although the status of Georgian and Tajik invitations to send Russian troops to help quell domestic turmoil may be questioned, there have been no bald and incontrovertibly illegal or even unambiguously unhelpful invasions of sovereign territory by Russian troops. Russian economic policy and practices, not least her insistence that accounts be settled in hard currency or that her energy and other raw material exports to other FSU states be at world market prices, have hardly enhanced the cause or contributed to the progress of CIS integration.

In any case, all CIS states to some degree, and some to a great degree, have been active in pursuing alternatives to over-reliance on Russia, and they have met with some success. There are divergences of interest, and these have become clear, and for some CIS states the institution represents little more than a civilised means towards the achievement of full independence from Russia. The Baltic states have in effect flown the nest, for all the sensitivity about their possible incorporation into NATO. Ukraine has been free to develop relationships with Washington and with European states and institutions, and may be in the process of becoming freer still, notwithstanding the requirement to balance these with the maintenance of Kiev-Moscow lines of communication (Larrabee 1996). Russia has not – quite – obstructed the development of relationships with NATO via the Partnership for Peace programme, with China, Turkey and Iran, and with western commercial interests, on the part of other FSU states. The sovereignty, actual and aspirational, of CIS states is now a reality with which Russia must deal, and by and large has dealt with, and may not be prepared to pay the price to prevent. This might apply even in the wake of NATO enlargement, for all Moscow's rhetoric to the contrary. Cost-benefit calculations of foreign relations are made in all CIS capitals, including Moscow. Moscow's behaviour in its 'near abroad' has been differentiated and largely bilateral rather than systematic and hegemonial (Olcott 1995).

Russia's national interests

Indeed, it is hard to see how Moscow can pursue a consistent, long-term and active foreign policy towards the FSU without first securing a more sound economic base and a more coherent and reliable political decision-making system than exists at present (Kortunov and Kortunov 1994: 276). The Chechen débâcle might have the paradoxically beneficial effect of persuading at least some of those who are most keen on the pursuit of Russia's 'Great Power' interests that there are indeed limits to what military power can achieve, given the current disastrous condition of Russia's armed forces. They might even come to appreciate that economic and political circumstances preclude any rapid reconstruction of a more effective military arm (Garnett 1997). They might in time understand that, as Russia's trade with other FSU states declines and its trade and economic interaction with the rest of the world expands, CIS economic reintegration might inhibit Russia's integration into the world economy – and this might be something Russia's élites might be increasingly disinclined to sacrifice – and impose on the Russian economy burdens and disadvantages (Becker 1996–7). These élites might come to recognise more clearly that the key to the country's integration into the world economy really does lie with the West in general and the European Union in particular. On the other hand, some observers are quite pessimistic about the learning curve of many of Moscow's foreign policy élite, and fear that the 'imperial' basis of 'Great Power' status will be seen as more central to Russia's interests and identity than economic regeneration and political reintegration into global, including European, structures (Covington 1995: 447–8; Becker 1996–7). A further possibility is that, at least in the near future, an insufficiently reconstructed Russia, feeling let down by the West, might see its economic and political future elsewhere, in the development of relationships with China, Iran, Iraq, Libya and the like. An aggressive arms and nuclear-related sales push could be at the forefront of this. Russia might in a sense become a 'rogue' state, befriending other 'rogue' states and recklessly fueling global and regional instabilities – or, put another way, fueling challenges to Washington's 'new world order'. The sale of anti-aircraft missiles to Cyprus represents just one example. This too could inhibit the development of better Russian–European relationships.

This seemingly middle position between the unrealistic and unrepresentative position associated with the 'westerners' on the one hand, and the more extreme nationalist and expansionist approach on the other, while incorporating some elements of the thinking of both ends of the spectrum, can be read as testimony that 'a mainstream standpoint, centred between the post-imperialist and nationalist perspectives, has emerged' (de Nevers 1994: 38). It can suggest that 'a more pragmatic group of people' (Brusstar 1994: 614) determines Russia's foreign policy. It can be consistent with the view that a whole range of options and opinions exist along a continuum from which individuals and factions pick and mix in a way not necessarily consistent (Adomeit 1995: 51). It can suggest a genuine consensus, some kind of meeting of minds, has been achieved (Aron and Jensen 1994: 23) or, alternatively, that there is little in the way of consensus, but that there has been some success, via improved control over the policy process, in combining 'some of Russia's diverging foreign policy tendencies' (Griffiths 1994: 711). It might imply some kind of pact or coincidence of interest between the government on the one hand and powerful economic lobbies on whom it has to depend on the other (Malcolm and Pravda 1996: 549–51). The very fact that such a divergence can exist about who is in power in Moscow, how choices are made, and to what ends, is a clue to the continuing messiness of policy-making in Moscow, and to the continuing flux and scope for unpredictable developments. Moscow's policy-making too must settle down before the West can truly be judged on the quality and content of its security policies *vis-à-vis* Russia.

Questions for the future of Russian–European security relations

We cannot predict what twists and turns might still be to come in the domestic political development and debate in Russia, yet much in Russian–European security relationships will hinge on this. We can, however, seek to identify the complexity of Europe's security *interdependencies,* to explore what assumptions are made throughout the European zone about what are and are not regarded as legitimate security concerns and actions. Only then might we be able to identify the risks, opportunities and pathways to a more tolerable and even mutually beneficial set of security arrangements. Again, the emphasis here is on the reconceptualisation of the Russian–European security nexus, not on the itemisation of its current difficulties. And we should not necessarily presuppose that some harmonious set of assumptions, interests and institutional arrangements awaits only our uncovering of them.

1. Will Russia seek to dominate the FSU and, if so, in what ways and to what extent? It appears that since early 1996 and Yvgeny Primakov's appointment as foreign minister, Moscow has intensified its attempts to construct an effective and Russian-led CIS. Although this could be presented as a counter to Moscow's

losses in the West, as a means to block 'external' interference and influence in Russia's 'traditional' sphere of influence, and as a means to restore the country's status, many have argued that the West should not be alarmed. Russia, so the argument goes, does have vital economic, human, political and security interests, and these should be recognised and respected. Furthermore, the threats that Russia perceives – of Asian military expansionism, of Islamic fundamentalism, of chaos and conflict around its periphery, of exploitation of these difficulties by others – could be seen as unwelcome to the West too. In other words, a strong Eurasian Russia could actually be in the interests of the West (Kortunov and Kortunov 1994: 270–1).

However, Russia does not self-evidently have a great deal to offer its now-independent FSU neighbours. Investment, technology, know-how, markets and even cultural affinities might best be found elsewhere. This is particularly true for the European FSU states, but it applies to central Asia and even the Caucasus, if not now then certainly into the future. Indeed, Russia's own far east might gain more from establishing closer relationships, at least in the economic dimension, with the USA, Japan and China, thus threatening the fragmentation of the Russian Federation itself (Goure 1994; Clark and Graham 1995). On current trends and as time passes, Russia might find itself with fewer and fewer levers at its disposal except the military one. But the use of force in the 'near abroad' would obviously be unacceptable to other FSU states, and might do little more than worsen the chaos and instability that Moscow's policies would ostensibly be designed to eradicate. Judging by the performance of Russia's armed forces in Chechnya, any resort to their employment in the FSU might be quite ineffective. In other words, Russian endeavours to dominate the former Soviet space, regardless of how indulgent the West was prepared to be, might not be effective, could make matters worse, and could have adverse consequences for Russia's own political and economic progress. The real danger could be neither Russian aspirations nor capabilities, but the discrepancy between the force of the former and the weakness of the latter.

2.   How indulgent in fact will and should Europe, the West and the international community more generally be to any Russian claim to a more-or-less exclusive sphere of influence in the FSU? The answer depends a great deal on the measures Moscow employs. For Europe, Russian pressure on, interference in, or direct threat to or encroachment in, the Baltic states and the Ukraine would be received quite differently from similar behaviour in, say, central Asia. On the other hand, the attainment of independent statehood on the part of the former Soviet republics does introduce the question of whether the international community is in practice to regard the sovereignty of these states as in some way reduced or

limited. As the FSU states expand their networks of international diplomatic, economic, security and cultural relationships – and they are doing just that, again not least in the cases of the Baltic states and Ukraine – then there is likely to be greater international sensitivity to any Russian disregard for their independent and sovereign status. In effect, the end of the Cold War has meant that a world has been ushered in, in which the norms of international behaviour are set by Russia's former adversaries. If it wishes to participate in and cooperate with that prevailing order, Russia must abide by these norms. Otherwise, it must recognise the consequences could be negative, ranging from active hostility from the West to Russia's exclusion and marginalisation from Europe's affairs and institutions (Sokov 1994).

3. How will Russia's desire to exert some influence westwards, into Belarus, the Baltics, Ukraine, and central and south-eastern Europe, and Europe's desire to extend its institutional membership and its less formalised influence eastwards, be resolved? This is currently the primary issue around which Russian–European security relationships are revolving. In the space of just a few years, central Europe shifted from being Moscow's top security priority to a region which, at least until midway through 1993, Moscow appeared almost to have forgotten about (Bowker 1995). Now its concerns in the region are almost exclusively focused on central Europe's membership of NATO, and the forms it might take. The Baltic states especially, and Ukraine too, raise still more difficult issues for Russian–European relations because of their status as former Soviet states, the Russian populations there, the economic interdependencies, and the security considerations involved. The crux of the matter, though, is that the former communist states to Russia's west – FSU and non-FSU – are, arguably, simultaneously less attracted to what Russia has to offer and more attracted to the regional, European, alternatives, than is the case for other parts of the former Soviet bloc. Unless Russia itself develops more successfully along democratic and market economy lines, and is incorporated much more fully into the European institutional club, this desire to 'return to Europe' and escape from Moscow's sphere of influence, is likely to intensify over time. Thus, the more Europe seeks to institutionally and in other ways embrace the central, south-eastern and FSU European states, without simultaneously finding effective and acceptable means of also bringing Russia into the fold, the more Europe's *de facto* policy towards Russia will be one of its exclusion and isolation from Europe. It would certainly be perceived this way across the Russian political spectrum and, whatever consequences ensue, they are unlikely to be comforting. Europe would, in effect, be acting so as to weaken Russia, or to encourage it to base its strength on its Asian rather than its European dimension.

4. The final question relating to Russian–European security relationships perhaps lies beyond anyone's direct control. That is, will Russia survive as a functioning entity, or will it degenerate into chaos, disorder, further fragmentation and perhaps civil war? The possibility of such developments cannot be ruled out, and the possible consequences – of territorial adventurism and other forms of direct and indirect involvement on the part of Russia's neighbours, of large-scale and even nuclear battles spilling across Russia's borders, of large-scale famine, population movements and environmental disasters – could be incalculable, and are almost too horrendous to contemplate. Yet such a chain of events arguably poses as big a threat to Europe's security as ever a massive Warsaw Pact military aggression did. And it may be no less likely to happen.

References

Adomeit, H. (1995) 'Russia as a "great power" in World Affairs; Images and Reality', *International Affairs*, 71 (1): 35–68.

Afanasyev, Y. N. (1994) 'Russian Reform is Dead; Back to Central Planning', *Foreign Affairs*, 73 (2): 23–6.

Allison, R., Light, M., Malcolm, N. and Pravda, A. (1996) *Internal Factors in Russian Foreign Policy*, Oxford: Oxford University Press.

Arbatov, A. (1997a) 'The Vicissitudes of Russian Politics', in Baranovsky, V. (ed.) (1997): 77–89.

Arbatov, A. (1997b) 'Russian Foreign Policy Thinking in Transition', in Baranovsky, V. (ed.) (1997): 135–59.

Aron, L. and Jensen, K. M. (eds), (1994) *The Emergence of Russian Foreign Policy*, Washington: The US Institute of Peace Press.

Asmus, R. D. and Nurick, R. C. (1996) 'NATO enlargement and the Baltic states', *Survival*, 38 (2): 121–42.

Baranovsky, V. (1995a) 'Russian Foreign Policy Priorities and EuroAtlantic Multilateral Institutions', *The International Spectator*, XXX (1): 33–50.

Baranovsky, V. (1995b) 'Russia and European Security', *EuroBalkans*, 19 (Summer): 4–17.

Baranovsky, V. (ed.) (1997) *Russia and Europe: The Emerging Security Agenda*, Oxford: Oxford University Press/SIPRI.

Becker, A. S. (1996–7) 'Russia and Economic Integration in the CIS', *Survival*, 38 (4): 117–36.

Bialer, S. (1988) '"New Thinking" and Soviet foreign policy', *Survival*, 30 (4): 291–309.

Blank, S. (1995) 'Russia and Europe in the Caucasus', *European Security*, 4 (4): 622–45.

Borawski, J. (1996) 'If not NATO Enlargement, what does Russia want?', *European Security*, 5 (3).

Bowker, M. (1995) 'Russian Policy towards Central and Eastern Europe', in Shearman, P. (ed.) (1995): 71–91.

Braithwaite, R. (1994) 'Russian Realities and Western Policy', *Survival*, 36 (3): 11–27.

Brusstar, J. H. (1994) 'Russian Vital Interests and Western Security', *Orbis*, 38 (4): 607–19.

Brzezinski, Z. (1994) 'The Premature Partnership', *Foreign Affairs*, 73 (2): 67–82.

Buszynski, L. (1995) 'Russia and the West; towards Renewed Geopolitical Rivalry?' *Survival*, 37 (3): 104–25.

Clark, S. L. and Graham, D. R. (1995) 'The Russian Federation's Fight for Survival', *Orbis*, 39 (3): 329–51.

Covington, S. (1995) 'Moscow's Insecurity and Eurasian Instability', *European Security* 4 (3): 438–56.

Davydov, Y. (1997) 'Russian Security and East-Central Europe', in Baranovsky, V. (ed.) (1997): 368–84.

de Nevers, R. (1994) 'Russia's Strategic Renovation', *Adelphi Papers* 289, London: International Institute for Strategic Studies.

Dunlop, J. (1993) *The Fall of the Soviet Union and the Rise of Russia*, Princeton, NJ: Princeton University Press.

Garnett, S. W. (1994) 'The Enduring Elements of Russian National Power', *Conflict Studies Research Centre*, E72.

Garnett, S. W. (1997) 'Russia's Illusory Ambitions', *Foreign Affairs*, 76 (2): 61–76.

Gordon, P. H. (1996) 'Recasting the Atlantic Alliance', *Survival*, 38 (1): 32–57.

Goure, L. (1994) 'The Russian Federation; Possible Disintegration Scenarios', *Comparative Strategy*, 13 (October–December): 401–15.

Griffiths, F. (1994) 'From Situations of Weakness; Foreign Policy of the New Russia', *International Journal*, XLIX (4): 699–724.

Hauner, M. (1992) *What Is Asia to Us? Russia's Asian Heartland Yesterday and Today*, London and New York: Routledge.

Jervis, R. (1991–2) 'The Future of World Politics; Will it Resemble the Past?', *International Security*, 17(3).

Kortunov, A. and Kortunov, S. (1994) 'From "Moralism" to "Pragmatism"; New Dimensions in Russian Foreign Policy', *Comparative Strategy*, 13 (July–September): 261–76.

Kozyrev, A. (1994) 'The Lagging Partnership', *Foreign Affairs* 73 (3): 59–71.

Kozyrev, A. (1995) 'Partnership or Cold Peace?', *Foreign Policy*, 99 (Summer): 3–14.

Kremeniuk, V. (1997) 'Post-Soviet Conflicts; New Security Concerns', in Baranovsky, V. (ed.) (1997): 246–66.

Kugler, R. L. (1996) *Enlarging NATO; the Russia Factor*, Santa Monica: RAND.

Larrabee, F. S. (1996) 'Ukraine's Balancing Act', *Survival*, 38 (2): 143–65.

Legvold, R. (1997) 'The "Russian Question"', in Baranovsky, V. (ed.) (1997): 42–69.

Lieven, A. (1995) 'Russian Opposition to NATO Expansion', *The World Today*, 51(10).

Malcolm, N. and Pravda, A. (1996) 'Democratisation and Russian Foreign Policy', *International Affairs* 72 (3): 537–52.

Malia, M. (1994) 'Tradition, Ideology and Pragmatism in the Formation of Russian Foreign Policy', in Aron, L. and Jensen, K. (eds) (1994): 35–49.

Marantz, P. (1994) 'Neither Adversaries nor Partners: Russia and the West Search for a New Relationship', *International Journal*, XLIX (4): 725–50.

Mearsheimer, J. J. (1990) 'Back to the Future: Instability in Europe after the Cold War,' *International Security*, 15 (1): 5–56.

Mihalka, M. (1994) 'European–Russian security and NATO's Partnership for Peace', *RFE/RL Research Report,* 3 (33): 34–45.

Neumann, Iver B. (1996) *Russia and the Idea of Europe*, London and New York: Routledge.

Olcott, M. B. (1995) 'Sovereignty and the "near abroad"', *Orbis*, 39 (3): 5–18.

Pierre, A. J. and Trenin, D. (1997) 'Developing NATO–Russian Relations', *Survival* 39(1).

Royen, C. (1997) 'Conflicts in the CIS and their implications for Europe', in Baranovsky, V. (ed.) (1997): 223–45.

Ruhl, L. (1997) 'The Historical Background of Russian Security Concepts and Requirements', in Baranovsky, V. (ed.) (1997), 21–41.

Russell, W. (1995) 'Russian Relations with the "Near Abroad"', in Shearman, P. (ed.) (1995): 53–70.

Shearman, P. (ed.) (1995) *Russian Foreign Policy since 1990*, Boulder and Oxford: Westview.

Simes, D. (1994) 'The Return of Russian History', *Foreign Affairs,* 73 (1): 67–82 .

Sokov, N. (1994) 'A New Cold War? Reflections of a Russian Diplomat', *International Journal*, XLIX(4): 908–28.

Stemplowski, R. (1995) 'Sailing in the Same Direction: Central Europe, Eastern Europe and the Russian Federation Reintegrate into the World System', *Journal of the Royal United Services Institute*, 14(1): 23–6.

Wallace, W. (ed.) (1992) *The Dynamics of European Integration*, London: Pinter/RIIA.

PART THREE

Regions on the Edge

CHAPTER 7

The Baltic–Nordic region

CLIVE ARCHER

Introduction

The Nordic area is a fairly distinct region in the minds of its occupants and – at first sight – on the maps of Europe. A closer appreciation of those maps will normally reveal that only the southern area of the Scandinavian peninsula is shown and that Iceland and Greenland are similarly absent. There is plenty of opportunity for cartographic trimming as the Nordic region is normally taken to include the five Nordic countries of Denmark, Finland, Iceland, Norway and Sweden which stretch from Greenland in the west to the Finnish–Russian border in the east, and from Svalbard in the north to Slesvig in the south. This chapter examines two regions that have come to be associated with the Nordic area – the Barents region and the Baltic region – in the light of the rethinking about security that has occurred in Europe since 1989. It is claimed that these two areas, with the Nordic area as their linchpin, have seen a major battle between new and old concepts of security. The 'new' ideas have been somewhat familiar to the Nordic decision-makers, though the new political environment in post-Cold War Europe has provided the opportunity for the development of these ideas and their adoption further afield. The older notions – based on zero-sum views of a country's security and on military power – are clearly still present in Russia (see Chapter 6) but were also a dominant strand in the thinking of many of the decision-makers in the new Baltic republics for much of the early 1990s.

There seems to have been a contest for the minds of those decision-makers. Should they stay with the 'old thinking' and try to ensure the military security of their countries or should they attempt to view their 'security dilemma' in a different light and thus choose more varied solutions? Similarly should the area onshore from the Barents Sea be viewed as one of confrontation between the military of the former European power-blocs, or should emphasis be placed on cooperation across frontiers to deal with a seemingly greater threat to the security of the residence of the area, that of the pollution of the environment, not least by the decaying carcasses of the Cold War itself?

The question of region

One definition of region involves a group of territories with geographic propinquity, significant interaction in one or more spheres, and a recognition, both by the actors involved and those outside, that the area stands out from its surroundings (Castberg, Schram Stokke & Østreng 1994: 71). Saarikoski (1995: 228–9) has defined regionalisation as 'a "natural" and passive process without a conscious or programmed human activity' whereby a subjective identity emerges over a period of time, during which the political and cultural frontier areas create an objective essence. Region-building is 'an active process with a conscious human subject', often based on regionalization (*ibid.*: 229) and can either be made from above (by the political powers) or below (by the citizens and subjects) (*ibid.*: 230).

Iver Neumann distinguishes between an 'inside-out' and an 'outside-in' approach to regions. The 'inside-out' view emphasises cultural integration and a centre or core-area where such 'cultural traits are *more* similar' (Neumann 1994: 54). The latter approach is geopolitical and stresses systemic factors (*ibid.*: 56). Barry Buzan utilises both concepts to describe a 'security complex', being 'a group of states whose primary security concerns link together sufficiently closely that their national securities cannot realistically be considered apart from one another' (Buzan 1991: 189–90). This provides an important link between the concept of a region and its security implications.

Neumann also claims that regions are imagined communities whose existence is preceded by that of region-builders, 'political actors who ... imagine a certain spatial and chronological identity for a region, and disseminate this imagined identity to others' (Neumann 1994: 58). If this is the case, then we should be looking for those who have built the Baltic and Barents region and examining the way that they have defined who is within and who outside these regions. It is the contention of this chapter that the Nordic governments have played a key part in the creation of these regions which have included the Nordic states (or parts of them), and the areas between them and the Russian Federation, as well as parts of that federation. The Nordic countries, and non-governmental organisations within them, have sought to establish these two areas not just for trade and commercial reasons but as zones wherein the Nordic governments can impart some of their ideas about security.

Whether the Baltic or Barents area can be defined as regions depends partly on whether the more permissive definition of Castberg, Schram Stokke and Østreng is adopted or the more inclusive ones of Saarikoski and Neumann. The post-Cold War answer seems to be that there is one region in the making – the Baltic – and one struggling to be a region – the Barents – with the Nordic states as the link between the two. Those states have been active in creating these potential regions as they have seen it in their wider interest to have stable and developing areas flanking them to the north-east and south-east.

The Baltic

The Baltic Sea has historically been both a battleground for Great Powers, including Denmark and Sweden in the fifteenth to eighteenth centuries, and a major trade route. From the thirteenth century, the tentacles of the Hanseatic towns and later their Federation (formed in 1343) stretched out from the Baltic's southern shores from Norway and Sweden down into the Rhineland, and from the east coast of England to Russia. Their strength lay in their preferential trade system and the order that they brought for merchants plagued by bandits and pirates. By the late sixteenth century, the Federation had been severely tested by rising sovereign states such as England, the Dutch Provinces and Denmark, and the Thirty Years War saw the effective end of the Federation. From then onwards, the Baltic Sea became a point of contest for the major trading countries, and a zone where the battles of the wars of the seventeenth to nineteenth centuries could be fought (Klinge 1994: 72–114).

The Baltic republics were born both as a result of war – the First World War that saw the collapse of the German and Russian empires – and peace, that of Versailles. Their birth was uneasy, with revolution, civil war, nationalist uprisings and Great Power intervention. By 1920 the three republics had made their peace with the Soviet Union, as had Finland, another part of the Czarist empire. Poland and Lithuania remained in dispute over the areas of Klaipeda (Memel) and Vilnius. The inter-war southern Baltic coast was typified by two originally weak powers, Russia and Germany, that were to rearm throughout the 1930s, and a series of weak governments in the Baltic republics. These countries became border states in an area suffering a power vacuum. The rise of Nazi Germany threatened to fill that vacuum as the 1930s progressed and the Soviet Union started to look nervously to the defences of the approaches to Leningrad.

In March 1939 Lithuania was obliged to cede Memel to Germany and by the winter of that year Russia had struck at Finland in an attempt to give some depth to the defence of Leningrad. After the Ribbentrop–Molotov pact in August 1939, Russia placed pressure on the three Baltic republics and by November Soviet troops had entered those states. The Soviet advance into Finland was stopped by staunch Finnish resistance, though by March 1940 that country sued for peace. By mid-1940 governments friendly to the USSR had been installed in the Baltic republics, and these applied to become part of the Soviet Union. After Germany attacked the USSR, the Baltic became a German-dominated lake with only Leningrad holding out and Sweden remaining neutral. Finland carried out its own war against the USSR. The citizens and the small armed forces of the Baltic republics became pawns in the battle of the two Powers and were badly used by both sides.

After the war the balance of power in the Baltic shifted again. Germany's shoreline shrunk and was divided between East and West. The

Baltic republics had been incorporated into the USSR which also took over the Königsberg enclave, renaming it Kaliningrad. Poland soon came under Soviet hegemony, making the southern shore of the Baltic one dominated by the Soviet Union. To the north Sweden and Finland remained neutral, with Finland's 1948 Treaty of Friendship, Cooperation and Mutual Assistance acting as the framework for Finnish relations with its Soviet neighbour.

The Cold War had come to the Baltic. With the formation of NATO and its later extension to the Federal Republic of Germany and the subsequent creation of the Warsaw Treaty Organization (WTO) to include the Soviet Union, Poland, and the German Democratic Republic, the southern shore was ideologically and politically divided between the Soviet bloc to the east and the Federal Republic and Denmark to the west. However, the presence of the two neutrals, Finland and Sweden, and the configuration of Nordic security policies, helped to create a lower level of tension in the Nordic region than that experienced on the continent of Europe. One writer has described the status of the Baltic Sea during this post-war period as being 'almost totally without an identity of its own. It has been a rather blank spot on the mental or metaphoric map of Europe' (Joenniemi 1991: 149). However, as the quotation implies, there was some identity: unlike the border zone between East and West Germany and between the East and the West in Germany, the Baltic Sea did have a 'grey zone' of two states outside the alliance, one of which was reasonably strong militarily. Furthermore, the Nordic states – as will be seen below – tried to keep the tension level low there. Nevertheless, the overlay of the Cold War stifled any significant separate development of the region.

The major military power in the Baltic was the Soviet Union. By the end of the 1970s, it had built up a formidable presence in the sea which, together with their Polish and German allies, had a nuclear element and an amphibious capability.[1] By the start of the 1980s the Soviet Baltic Fleet had held a number of large exercises which over the years had moved closer to the Baltic approaches (SNU 1986a: 164–5). Against the WTO's presence, the two NATO allies in the region, Denmark and the Federal Republic of Germany, had a more modest inventory.[2] These two NATO states placed the emphasis on maintaining control of the Baltic approaches rather than the sea itself; and even for that, they depended on outside reinforcement, most notably from the United States and the United Kingdom (Lindhardt 1981). The defence forces of Sweden and Finland, especially the former, were seen as important, but – at that stage – were considered by some western analysts to be running down and any how were politically unreliable (Ørvik 1979; Lindstrom 1981; Vego 1982)

By the mid-1980s the Baltic Sea was seen in the established context of the East–West strategic balance. Much of the debate that took place was about the military 'bean count' or about such policies as a nuclear-free zone or ending port visits of nuclear-armed vessels (SNU 1986b), but all this took place within a wider framework determined by the nuclear stand-off between the US and the USSR.

Already in the mid-1980s, it was clear that the Soviet navy was not giving the sort of priority to the Baltic Fleet it had had in earlier decades, though a strong amphibious capability was still being built up (SNU 1986a: 147). However, the major change to take place was the coming to power of Mr Gorbachev in 1985 and the change in strategic thinking and domestic policy that he undertook. His introduction of new concepts of security based on common security, and the West's response, especially after the Reykjavik summit of November 1986, brought about a number of arms-control agreements within a few years, and started a dismantling of the Cold War structures. Perhaps more important, Gorbachev's domestic reforms led to a weakening of the Communist Party's grip in the USSR and the Soviet's hold over eastern Europe. The events of late 1989, which swept away Communist power in eastern Europe, started a similar process within the Soviet Union. The Baltic states were not unaffected by this tide.

The end of the Cold War has seen a re-emergence of the Baltic region concept: the idea of a new Hansa, or a Euro-Baltic region, was mooted. After a period of military confrontation and tension, preceded by a bloody conflict, the opportunity arose for the countries in the region to switch the emphasis away from such negative relations towards cooperation. Old divisions were to be healed; new partners sought. A selective memory of a past history – the Hansa period – that stressed trade and cooperation helped in this process. Second, there was the danger that the states in the region – especially the Nordic states, the new Baltic Republics and Poland – could become marginalised from the dynamics of the European integration process in the early 1990s, centred as it was on Germany, France and the Benelux states. Even within Federal Germany, there was the consideration that the Land of Schleswig-Holstein, whose minister-president Björn Engholm strove towards greater Baltic cooperation, could become more of a rim state, especially once the new länder of East Germany had joined the Federal Republic. The prospect of encouraging some horizontal (i.e. west–east) networks in the area, as opposed to the existing vertical ones (north–south, especially to Bonn), proved to be attractive (Engholm, cited in Joenniemi 1991: 148).

This period of German interest in creating – or recreating – a Baltic region was soon replaced by one in which the Nordic states, especially Denmark, Sweden and Finland, became actively engaged. Pertti Joenniemi, writing in 1991, advised that 'the Nordic countries should try to steer themselves into the position of rather central actors' (in the Baltic), but that 'such a Nordic policy is yet to be formed' (Joenniemi 1991:158). In the five years following this recommendation, the Nordic states have not only followed the writer's advice, but a Baltic region has been emerging.

What evidence is there for the creation of a Baltic region? During the 1990s a number of institutions have been created that have linked the littoral states of the Baltic Sea:

- The Council of Baltic Sea States has been set up and there have been increased meetings of ministers to discuss particular functional problems ranging from the environment to culture (Joenniemi and Stålvant 1995: 39)
- The Baltic Council has been established between the three Baltic republics, based on the model of the Nordic Council
- The Parliamentary Conferences on Cooperation in the Baltic Sea Area have been called on a Finnish initiative
- Meetings of the Nordic and Baltic prime ministers have resulted in common action
- A Baltic 'Regional Table' of the OSCE has dealt with security issues such as minority and border questions in a non-confrontational manner
- Membership of states of either NATO or NACC and participation in Partnership for Peace, with a Baltic Battalion being created for peace-keeping purposes, has drawn the region more into the NATO security framework.

Furthermore the trade patterns in the Baltic have changed. With the inclusion of Sweden and Finland in the European Union, and of Norway in the European Economic Area (EEA), the Nordic section of the region has become more westward-oriented in its trade and commerce. This has also been the case for Poland, the three Baltic republics and the St Petersburg region (Joenniemi and Stålvant 1995: 47–8) The change in the strategic situation has spurred a willingness to rethink the area in terms that suggest a different security agenda than that which dominated in the Cold War period.

The Barents region

Two authors contributing to a study of the Barents region wrote in 1994 that from 'a geographical point of view the territory of the Barents region has a set of common properties, while functionally its main characteristic is weak internal interaction' (Kazantseva and Westin 1994: 105). Perhaps more so than the Baltic region, the Barents had to have its past reinvented. As the political necessity for a cooperative region between the northern cap of the Scandinavian peninsula and north-west Russia arose, so histories were printed of the 'Pomor' trade that had existed along the coasts of this area over an era, especially from the seventeenth to nineteenth centuries (Niemi 1992; Saariniemi 1992; Sæther 1992).

More recent history had shown this area both to be on the fringes of Europe and not one of particularly intense cooperation. This was partly because of the sparse population in the area and its fairly prohibitive climate and terrain, but was also a result of political factors. During the period when Norway was under Danish rule, the northern frontier was relatively undefined and, inland, nomadic peoples moved across fairly grey border areas. When Sweden and Norway were joined in one kingdom, Finland came under Russian control, politically dividing the northern part of Scandinavia. During this period, there seems to have been 'flourishing trade between northern Norway and the Archangel area' (Planleggingsavdelingen 1992: 2). With the independence of Finland in 1917, the potential for cooperation between that country, Norway and Sweden in the north rose, but the closed nature of the Soviet Union created a new barrier, one that moved west with the USSR's annexation of Finland's northern coast. The Cold War froze that East–West division with Norway on one side and the growing power of the Soviet Union on the Kola Peninsula, on the other.

In the post-Cold War era, a deliberate effort has been made – especially by the Norwegians – to build up the area as 'the Barents Euro-Arctic region'. The area's history was resurrected (Det konglige Utenriksdepartement 1993; Nielsen 1994: 87–100; Finnish Barents Group OY 1996: 7–10) and schemes drawn up for intense contact across state frontiers. However, this was accompanied by a warning that this history had a double edge, with one side showing the tendency to extreme centralisation in the Russian state.

The opening-up came after an initiative by the Norwegian foreign minister, Thorvald Stoltenberg, who was concerned that the end of the Cold War division between Norway and Russia should not be replaced by economic and environmental barriers (Stoltenberg 1994: ix). He foresaw a long-term development that would help to link together the northern Nordic area and north-west Russia. There was little doubt that the initiative also aimed at increasing Norway's standing as it negotiated membership of the EU (a deal later rejected by its electorate) and at increasing the interest of the Union in the northern region (*ibid.*: x; Stokke and Tunander 1994: 1). It was also based on the Danish–German initiative for a Council of Baltic Sea States, launched in March 1992 (Scrivener 1996: 5).

The Barents initiative was launched at a meeting of the Nordic and Russian foreign ministers at Kirkenes in January 1993. A Barents Council was established with membership from Russia, the five Nordic governments and the European Commission, and with observer status for Canada, France, Germany, Japan, The Netherlands, Poland, the United Kingdom and the United States. An innovative element in Barents cooperation was the setting up of a Regional Council with representatives on it from the three northernmost counties of Finland, the northernmost county of both Finland and Sweden, the Murmansk and Arkhangelsk oblasti, and the Karelian Republic in Russia. A representative of the Saami people was also present.

The main tasks of the Barents Council have been concerned with economic cooperation and with environmental problems in north-west Russia, not least those associated with nuclear power and with decommissioned nuclear submarines. Norway, and the other Nordic states, have spent large amounts of money in dealing with Russian environmental problems in the region, but the level of success of the enterprise has relied on the ability of the Russian local authorities to act effectively – which has not been much in evidence – and on the interest of the Russian government in the region, which cooled after Mr Kozyrev was replaced as foreign minister. Furthermore, the Barents Council has not been the only game in town. After Norway decided to remain out of the EU, it has been in a weaker position than the Baltic area in applying for the European Communities regional funding. Also the activities of the Arctic Environmental Protection Strategy have overlapped in some of the environmental fields and the establishment of the Arctic Council in 1996 could take some of the political attraction away from the Barents Council as substantially the same countries can discuss the same issues but in a geographically wider context.

The Nordic bridge

The Nordic region has acted as a bridge between these two sets of regional plans. However, it seems that the concept of the Nordic region may itself be suffering because of the end of the Cold War and it is reinventing itself in the Baltic context (and to a much lesser extent in the Barents context). After all, the Nordic region managed to flourish during the Cold War period, and many of the aspects of 'Nordicity' are those that have been exported into Baltic and Barents cooperation. In both cases, Nordic governments are using the schemes to make themselves relevant to – yet still somewhat apart from – the wider European venture, especially that centred on Brussels as the EU/WEU/NATO headquarters.

The challenge to the concept of the Nordic region has come in several guises. First, the area had managed to develop its own security configuration during the Cold War that had meant the area was recognised as being one of low tension. This formula had involved not only the neutrality of Finland and Sweden but also the low level of armaments in the Nordic NATO states, Denmark, Iceland and Norway (see below). With the end of the Cold War and with Swedish and Finnish membership of the EU, their neutral status changed to that of being 'alliance-free'. Second, the membership of the EU of Finland and Sweden – as well as Denmark – and of Iceland and Norway in the European Economic Area has led to less emphasis on Nordic cooperation. The Nordic Council has been streamlined as the Nordic states have conducted economic policy, environment cooperation, regional policies and even educational links within the context of the EU. Third, internal strains have been seen to undermine the special nature of the Nordic countries which were renown for their inclusive welfare policies and social solidarity. Economic recession and unemployment in the early 1990s led to a trimming back of the welfare state, especially in Sweden and Finland,

and to a move away from reliance on the state in economic matters. Together, these factors have been seen as meaning that the Nordic region is less 'special' in the post-Cold War Europe (Waever 1991; Neumann 1994; Heurlin 1995).

Their involvement in the Barents and Baltic regions has allowed the Nordic countries to enjoy a privileged position again. These two areas are clearly ones in which the Nordic states have the comparative advantages of proximity and interest. The governments of Denmark, Finland and Sweden in the case of the Baltic area, and Norway in the case of the Barents region, have been willing to take advantage of the opportunities provided by the end of the Cold War by adopting activist policies in the two regions. To that extent, they have also been able to alleviate some of the loss of a 'special nature' by the Nordic region, perceived to have taken place in the 1990s.

Security agendas

During the Cold War the northern area of Europe – including the Barents region, the Nordic states and the Baltic – seemed to be deeply enveloped by the Superpower agenda and notions of security. However, there was a sub-text in the Nordic region that demonstrated perhaps a widespread willingness to be slightly apart from the core concepts of the Cold War. Nordic ideas of security policy were ones based on a broad understanding of the term and did not adhere just to defence aspects. Furthermore, the position of the five Nordic countries in the East–West divide allowed for some variation. The attempts by the Nordic states to maintain their part of Europe as one of 'low tension', while at the same time not undermining their alliance adhesion (in the case of the NATO members) or their national defence (in the case of Finland and Sweden) led to criticism internationally and internally, but nevertheless produced a distinct Nordic security profile.

The Nordic region had long since ceased to be an area that provided Europe with Great Powers and from the start of the nineteenth century it found itself surrounded by three power influences: those of Russia from the east, the dominant continental power to the south and the maritime strength of Britain to the west. During that century the continental power changed from being Napoleonic France to the German Empire. Prussia had already trimmed Denmark of the duchies of Schleswig-Holstein. In 1809 Russia took Finland from Sweden, and in 1905 British influence was key in securing Norway its separation from Sweden. The three Nordic states – Denmark, Norway and Sweden – kept their neutrality during the First World War, but only just. Both the British and German navies had their eyes on Denmark, most of the Norwegian merchant fleet was subcontracted to the Allies, and the Swedish military showed sympathy for the German cause. The bloody birth of the Soviet republic in 1917 also allowed Finland to grab its independence, though it was soon caught up in both the Russian and its own civil war. In the inter-war period, the Nordic states gave full support to the League of Nations until it became clear that the League system could not protect small states. With the coming of the Second World War, Finland was invaded by the Soviet Union, Denmark and Norway by Germany; and Iceland was taken over by the British and then the Americans. Only Sweden remained substantially untouched.

After the Second World War, the Nordic countries embraced the UN concept of collective security and for a while remained free from Great Power entanglement. Once the Cold War became apparent in continental Europe, the three Scandinavian states tried, during 1948, to form a defence union of their own but this failed once it was clear that the strategic needs of each state was different. Norway, and to a lesser extent Denmark, wanted assistance in holding off any threat from the Soviet Union and in rearming themselves. Sweden realised that such a task through a neutral union would be near impossible and that weapons from the United States for Norway and Denmark would mean those states joining some sort of defence agreement. Finland signed an agreement with the Soviet Union – the 1948 Treaty of Friendship, Cooperation and Mutual Assistance – that could have led to Soviet 'assistance' under certain circumstances, but which allowed Finland to remain a democracy and to develop a policy of neutrality. Sweden built up its own forces and developed its neutrality into a more active policy on the world stage.

The geostrategic position in which each of the five states found themselves in the post-war period meant each had a different set of policy options and their historical experience, together with internal factors, helped to determine their choices. There was an extra dimension to the security policies of these states: none of them acted in a way that endangered the position of any of the other Nordic countries and all attempted to keep their region as one of comparatively low tension. This link was sometimes quite explicit and was often known as 'the Nordic balance' (Brundtland 1966), though that metaphor may give a somewhat mechanistic functioning of the relationship between the states (Noreen 1983). Nevertheless, Denmark and Norway did restrict allied military exercises on their territory, forbad foreign bases on their metropolitan territories and also banned the peacetime siting of nuclear weapons on their soil. Both the Finnish and Swedish armed forces were defensive in their postures and procurement, and all countries (with the exception of Iceland which had no armed forces) took part in UN peace-keeping (Archer 1990).

The Nordic states readily embraced – and developed – concepts of common security even before the end of the Cold War. Indeed, Olaf Palme, the Swedish prime minister, chaired the international independent commission that made the concept of 'common security' more widely accepted. An important contribution was made to the Palme report by Johan Jørgen Holst, a Norwegian academic who subsequently became Norway's defence minister and then its foreign minister. The core of the concept of common security is the notion that security is not a 'zero-sum game', which means that one state's security can be enhanced without other states suffering. This helped in escaping from the 'security dilemma' so common in the Cold War period, that steps taken by countries to improve their own security situation (for example, increasing their armaments) seemed also to make the world a more dangerous place. An acceptance of the tenets of common security meant that states could take actions – such as mutual disarmament – that improved general global security without undermining their national position. This had very much been the idea behind the sort of restraints that the Nordic countries had introduced during the Cold War period. It was not that these countries tried to deny the power politics nature of the Cold War divide: it was just that they tried to ameliorate its impact in northern Europe by giving consideration to each other's feelings (and to those of the Soviet Union) in their security policies.

Both the aims and the means of the defence policies of the Nordic states during the Cold War went beyond the purely military. In each of these small countries the defence of society was emphasised. A Swedish example is the emphasis given in official pronouncements on security policy on the need to preserve and develop 'our society politically, economically, socially, culturally and in all other respects according to our own values' (cited in Andrén 1975: 1). Concerning the means of defence, the Nordic states also took an expansive view. The concept of 'total defence' was adopted whereby both the military and civilian side of life would offer an integrated response to any attack (NOU 1992: 19). In the words of H. C. Hansen, the Danish prime minister, in 1959, 'we must think not only of the military sector, but also of the civil, and the latter consists not just ... of civil defence, but the whole administrative, economic and psychological side of preparedness' (cited in Christensen 1983: 4).

Thus, ideas of comprehensive security emerged easily from this already-existing wider understanding of security. Nordic concepts of security were developed rather than reconceptualised. After the end of the Cold War, the Nordic states started to adopt very much a liberal institutionalist view on international security that contained elements of common security and comprehensive security. The common security element could be seen in the wider Soviet and NATO approach at the end of the 1980s and early 1990s, where the common concern was controlling the arms race and, in particular, reducing the number of nuclear weapons. Indeed, the Danish political establishment showed concern at the end of 1989 that events in eastern Europe might undermine the move to common security and arms control and disarmament agreements (Archer 1994: 601–2). Eventually all of the four main Nordic states came to emphasise the need to develop the aspects of international society which exist when a group of states 'conceive themselves to be bound by a common set of rules in their relations with each other, and share in the working of common institutions' (Bull 1977:13). To this end, the Nordic countries have given support not just to the OSCE and its idea of cooperative security (see Chapter 2), but also a range of other institutions including those in the Baltic and Barents areas. The notion has been to bring in states undergoing political transition and, in particular, Russia to forums where security, in its widest sense, is discussed. The hope is that Europe will not only escape from the power divisions of the past but will be able to prevent a descent into new insecurities such as those experienced in the former Yugoslavia.

The Baltic republics, on the contrary, emerged into a Hobbesian world where it seemed that their existence could well be 'nasty, brutish and short'. Their governments' view of the world was moulded by both their wartime and post-war experience, with intransigence being one of the key political attributes of many of their leaders. They had understood that the compromises made by their countries in the lead-up to their Soviet wartime invasion had not prevented the inclusion of the three republics into the Soviet Union and that it had been the insistence of the Baltic peoples on the return of their sovereignty in the 1989 to 1990 period – even in the face of Soviet military action – that had led to their independence.

However, the object of their zero-sum game – the Soviet Union – disappeared and, during 1991, Boris Yeltsin and the Russian Federation made common cause with the Baltic states against the faltering power of the Soviet Union. Once the Russian Federation took over from the USSR, the Baltic states transferred their suspicions to the new political entity. Many of the Baltic republics' decision-makers remained unconvinced that the Russian bear had had its claws drawn, and their experience of negotiating with the new Russian leadership, especially over troop withdrawals from their territory, did little to change their views. The Russian Federation provided the Baltic states with an enemy image. It had kept troops in their country long after they were welcome; it had threatened or hinted at military action should the Baltic governments not comply with certain wishes; it had made common cause with the Russian-speaking minority within the three states, who were often seen as threatening the new nations from within. The Second World War and events after 1990 seemed to suggest to the Baltic leaders that the power relationship in their region would be the most important element in their survival, and in the early 1990s it was clear that they had little power compared to that of the Russian Federation. The most immediate way around this problem was to bring in outside power to assist the new fledgling states. Thus the Baltic governments decided that membership of NATO was desirable (*Joint Statement* 1996: 2; Helveg Petersen 1996: 7), with the expectation that this would give them the protection afforded by the North Atlantic Treaty's Article V.

From 1990, there has been a sort of security dialogue between the Baltic republics and the western states, with the Nordic countries in the lead. The Nordic states, together with Germany, have brought the three republics – and Poland – towards an acceptance of the new security agenda. However, there is an acceptance – not least in the Nordic states – that, because of their position and their mind-set, the Baltic states will need to deal with 'traditional security threats' for some time.

The new security agenda has placed an emphasis on institutions. In the Baltic region, the Nordic Council acted as model and stimulus for the creation of a Baltic Council between the three Baltic republics, and a Danish–German initiative led to the creation of a Council of Baltic Sea States, on which is represented the governments of all the Baltic coastal states, as well as Norway and Iceland. This has provided a wider forum for the Baltic republics and the Russian federation to discuss their mutual problems. Another useful instrument has been the OSCE and its Baltic Regional Table, established consequent to the European Stability Pact of March 1995 (see Chapter 4) and which has dealt with minority and border questions in the area. The OSCE itself has helped in monitoring the withdrawal of Russian troops from the Baltic republics (Viksne 1995: 80). The Baltic republics – and Poland – have also come closer to both the EU and NATO. All four countries are members of the North Atlantic Cooperation Council (NACC) and have been active participants in NATO's Partnership for Peace (PfP) (see Chapter 3). They have also signed Europe Agreements with the EU and should at least be at the starting post for the next round of membership negotiations.

The content of much of the discussion within the institutions covering the Baltic has been decidedly 'new agenda' security. The Council of the Baltic Sea States has produced an Action Programme for Baltic Sea States Cooperation that has the aim of increasing people-to-people contacts and 'civic security' (against crime), economic cooperation and integration and strengthened environmental protection (Council of the Baltic Sea States 1996). These elements were identified as the non-military elements of 'soft security', which in itself was defined as 'all aspects of security short of military combat operations including the defence of the national territory' (Helveg Petersen 1996: 1).

The other – military – aspects of 'soft security' were addressed in the programme of cooperation undertaken within NACC and PfP, but also by the Nordic states in the way that they encouraged Baltic defence cooperation as a contribution to UN peace-keeping. A Baltic battalion was established and trained by the Nordic states and the United Kingdom (Haab 1995: 10). Later the Nordic–Polish brigade deployed in IFOR in 1996 contained contributions from the Baltic states folded into the Danish battalion (Hækkerup 1996: 11-13).

In the Barents region, the Norwegians, in particular, have attempted to insinuate a new security agenda, but their success in relation to Russia has been mixed. An ambitious programme of environmental cleansing and of economic development has been undertaken particularly by Norway (Utenriksdepartementet 1993). Within 20 months of the founding meeting of the Barents Council at Kirkenes in January 1993, a range of regional and functional cross-border activities had been promoted in the areas of the environment, economic cooperation, educational and scientific cooperation, transport and communications, tourism and health (Barents Euro-Arctic Council 1994). In 1996 the Norwegian foreign minister's evaluation of Barents cooperation was that it had done much in a short time with respect to contact between peoples, political links and confidence-building work. Though a lot had been achieved in business and the environment, he saw the project essentially as a long-term one (Godal 1996). However, much of the immediate success of Barents projects, particularly those connected with industry or the military, is dependent on the reform process in Moscow as recognised by one of the Russian industrial administrators in the area, Yevgeny Komorov (*Barents Nyyt* 1996: 12). Indeed the leading newspaper covering the area had, by August 1996, decided that the Barents region was in crisis (*Barents Nytt* 1996: 1) and diplomats were admitting that the process had run up against the difficulty of dealing with a centralised and inefficient Russian administration. While it has certainly not been the case that the old insecurities have returned between Norway and Russia, the method of coaxing the north-west part of Russia towards an easier security relationship with the West through functional cooperation has yet to be proved.

As mentioned, the Barents Council already had to compete with other functional arrangements in the Nordic north when it was established and its work could be superseded by that of the Arctic Council, formed in 1996. Furthermore, the initiative that drove the creation of the Barents Council came at a time when Norway was considering membership of the EU. With the rejection of membership by the Norwegian electorate, this aspect of Barents cooperation has been weakened. With the growing interest of Sweden, Finland and Denmark in Baltic cooperation, Norway may also find that Nordic enthusiasm for the Barents Council has weakened. To cite one study, 'three years into the Barents scheme, the assessment of the merits of co-operation has been somewhat overcast by an air of despondency and scepticism' (Mitcham 1996: 67). Despite this, Barents cooperation remains as a witness to the Nordic, in this case specifically Norwegian, effort to deal positively with the end of the Cold War. Norwegian decision-makers were not content to allow old security concepts to remain in residue, but were prepared to undertake a bold approach involving a new security relationship with their former adversary.

Prospects for the Baltic–Nordic area

In both the Baltic and Barents areas, a high level of institutional development has been achieved over the past six years, both at the inter-governmental and non-governmental level. Some of this is regional, but increasingly much is linked to Brussels, especially in the Baltic. It could be said that the Nordic liberal institutionalist approach to international security is being extended to the Baltic and the Barents.

The question that the Baltic republics are asking is 'will this be enough?' and they have tended to respond negatively, wanting some 'old-fashioned' security guarantees. Part of the battle over the extension of NATO to include the Baltic states is over the very nature of NATO in the future. The Baltic states want an Article V NATO and want it extended to them, while the Danes want a more 'new security task' NATO and on that basis would be happy to see it extended to cover the three Baltic republics. This also brings in the relationship between NATO and the EU, with some seeing the inclusion of the Baltic republics into the EU as a way of providing them with 'soft' security guarantees while keeping them outside NATO. In the Barents region, the Norwegians, in particular, have tried to deal with the Russian areas at a regional level and have also advanced functional cooperation as a means of turning old security divisions into a new mutually beneficial relationship. As yet, these schemes have had some modest successes but have not fulfilled earlier hopes.

The key element in all these calculations is Russia. Should the Russian decision-makers decide that the cooperative route is worth travelling, as did Mr Kozyrev over the Barents Council in 1993, then progress can be made. However, should those in power, either in the Kremlin or in the armed forces, decide that confrontation is more worthwhile – as seems to have been the case over the Baltic states for much of the time since 1991 – then the response of the newly independent countries in the region is going to be determined by fear and caution. The Nordic states have tried to encourage those elements within Russia that prefer the cooperative approach, but their ability to affect the internal situation in the Russian Federation is limited. They can help the Baltic republics in such a way that threat and conflict become more expensive options for Russia, and they can provide and support the forums within which Russia and the Baltic republics can discuss their disagreements in a peaceful atmosphere.

In many ways, what happens in the Baltic and Barents areas will be a key test for new security concepts. If the 'Nordic approach' is successful, then not only will old security dilemmas be soluble, but some of the newer security problems will be tackled with a variety of institutions. If it fails, there may be a return to rigid divisions within the Baltic and Barents areas, though perhaps not to Cold War frostiness.

Notes

1. At that time the Warsaw Treaty forces included six Gulf II class diesel-powered ballistic missile submarines, 50 diesel-powered attack and patrol submarines, 27 cruisers and destroyers, 25 frigates and escorts, 260 torpedo and missile-armed attack craft, 250 minesweepers, 120 landing

ships, at least 12 Backfire bombers, a Soviet naval infantry regiment, a Polish Sea Landing Division, an amphibious-trained East German Motor Rifle Division, 410 fighter-bombers, 300 air-superiority fighters, a large array of helicopters, strategic forces and ground forces (Furlong 1979a: 525; see also SNU 1986a: 147).

2. Denmark and the Federal Republic could then muster 110 bombers, 58 fighter/attack aircraft, 33 destroyers/frigates and corvettes, 30 submarines, 56 fast-attack craft, 73 mine-ships and sizeable numbers of ground troops on mobilisation (Furlong 1979b: 903–5).

References

Andrén, N. (1975) *Problems of Swedish Security*, Stockholm: National Defence Research Institute.

Archer, C. (1990) 'The North as a Multidimensional Strategic Arena', *The Annals of the American Academy of Political and Social Science*, November: 22–32.

Archer, C. (1994) 'New Threat Perceptions: Danish and Norwegian Official Views', *European Security*, 3 (4): 593–616.

Barents Euro-Arctic Council (1994) *Second Session 14th–15th September 1994 Tromsø. Joint Statement,* mimeo.

Barents Nytt (1996) 8, August.

Brundtland, A. O. (1966) 'The Nordic Balance', *Cooperation and Conflict*, 2: 30–63.

Bull, H. (1977) *The Anarchical Society*, London: Macmillan.

Buzan, B. (1991) *People, States and Fear*, London: Harvester Wheatsheaf.

Castberg, R., Schram Stokke, O. and Østreng, W. (1994) 'The Dynamics of the Barents Region', in Stokke, Olav Schram and Tunander, Ola (eds), *The Barents Region. Cooperation in Arctic Europe*, London: SAGE Publications: 71–83.

Christensen, I. (1983) *Totalforsvaret (Total defence)*, Copenhagen: Forsvarets Oplysnings- og Velfærdstjeneste.

Council of the Baltic Sea States (1996) *Fifth Ministerial Session, Kalmar 2–3 July 1996. Action Programmes for the Baltic Sea States Cooperation*, mimeo.

Det konglige Utenriksdepartement (1993) *Barentsregionen – Et regionaliseringsprosjekt I det nordligste Europa (The Barents region – a regionalisation project in Northernmost Europe)* Oslo: Royal Norwegian Ministry of Foreign Affairs, Aktuelle utenriksspørsmål, 1, April.

Finnish Barents group OY (1996) *Barents: The Barents Euro-Arctic Region*, Helsinki: Ministry for Foreign Affairs.

Furlong, R. D. (1979a) 'The Threat to Northern Europe', *International Defense Review*, 4: 517–25.

Furlong, R. D. (1979b) 'The Strategic Situation in Northern Europe', *International Defense Review*, 6: 899–910.

Godal, B. T. (1996) *Utenriksminister Bjørn Tore Godals innlegg på Finnmark fylkestings temadag om Barentssamarbeidet, Vadsø 6.6.96 (Foreign Minister Godal's address to the Finnmark county council theme day on Barents cooperation)*, Oslo: Royal Ministry of Foreign Affairs.

Haab, M. (1995) 'Estonia and Europe', in van Ham, P. (ed.) 'The Baltic States: Security and Defence after Independence', Paris: Institute for Security Studies, *Chaillot Papers 19*: 37–60.

Hækkerup, H. (1996) 'A Multinational Force Culture', *Enjeux atlantiques*, 13, June: 10–13.

Helveg Petersen, N. (1996) *Security Cooperation and Integration in the Baltic Region. The Role of the European Union: Soft Security* (Speech to conference in Riga, 25 August 1996), mimeo.

Heurlin, B. (1995) 'Security Problems in the Baltic Region in the 1990s', in Joenniemi, Pertti and Stålvant, Carl-Einar *Baltic Sea Politics: Achievements and Challenges*, Stockholm: The Nordic Council, Nord 1995: 35: 55–75.

Joenniemi, P. (1991) (ed.) 'Co-operation in the Baltic Sea Region: Needs and Prospects', Tampere: *TAPRI Research Report 42*.

Joenniemi, P. and Stålvant, C-E (1995) *Baltic Sea Politics: Achievements and Challenges*, Stockholm: The Nordic Council, Nord 1995: 35.

Joint Statement of the Ministers of Defence of the Republic of Estonia, the Republic of Latvia and the Republic of Lithuania (1996), Tallinn, 23 January.

Kazantseva, N. and Westin, L. (1994) 'Missing Networks in the Missing Region – The Challenge of Infrastructure Development', in Jan Ake Dellenbrant and Mats-Olov Olsson (eds) *The Barents Region. Security and Economic Development in the European North*, Umea: Cerum: 105–24.

Klinge, M. (1994) *The Baltic World*, Helsinki: Otava.

Lindhardt, B. (1981) *Allierede forstærkninger til Danmark (Allied reinforcement to Denmark)*, Copenhagen: Dansk Udenrigspolitisk Institut Forskningsrapport, 5.

Lindstrom, T. (1981) 'Nordic Defense', *The Journal of Social, Political and Economic Studies*, December: 307–23.

Mitcham, P. (1996) Continuity and Change in North European *Nordpolitikk* in the Wake of the Cold War, *M Phil thesis*, Cambridge: Scott Polar Research Institute, University of Cambridge.

Neumann, I. B. (1994) 'A Region-building Approach to Northern Europe', *Review of International Studies*, 20 (1): 53–74.

Nielsen, J. P. (1994) 'The Barents Region in Historical Perspective' in Stokhe, Olav Schram and Tunander, Ola (eds) *The Barents Region. Cooperation in Arctic Europe*, London: SAGE Publications: 87–100.

Niemi, E. (ed.) (1992) *Pomor. Nord norge og Nord Russland gjennom 1.000 år (Pomor. North Norway and North Russia through 1000 years)*, Oslo: Gyldendal Norsk forklag.

Noreen, E. (1983) 'The Nordic Balance: A Security Policy Concept in Theory and Practice', *Cooperation and Conflict*, 1: 43–56.

NOU (Norges Offentlige Utredninger) (1992) *Forsvarskommisjonen av 1990 (Defence Commission of 1990)*, Oslo: Statens Forvaltningstjeneste.

Ørvik, K. (1979) 'The Limits of Security: Defense and Foreign Trade in Finland', *Survey*, 24.

Planleggingsavdelingen (1992) *Planene om Barentsregionen (Det euro-arktiske region) (The plan for a Barents region, the Euro-Arctic region)*, Oslo: Det kongelige Utenriksdepartemente.

Saarikoski, V. (1995), 'Regional Alternatives: The Breaking of the Europe Between?', in Clive Archer and Olli-Pekka Jalonen (eds) *Changing European Security Landscape*, Tampere: TAPRI: 228–56.

Saariniemi, P. (1992) 'Pomorhandelen sett med russiske øyne' ('Pomor trade seen with Russian eyes'), *Ottar*, 4.

Scrivener, D. (1996) *Environmental Cooperation in the Arctic: From Strategy to Council*, Oslo: The Norwegian Atlantic Committee, Security Policy Library No. 1.

SNU (Sikkerheds- og nedrustningspolitiske udvalg) (1986a) *Flådestrategier og nordisk sikkerhedspolitik Bind 1* (*Naval Strategies and Nordic Security Policy. Volume 1*), Copenhagen: SNU.

SNU (Sikkerheds- og nedrustningspolitiske udvalg) (1986b) *Flådestrategier og nordisk sikkerhedspolitik Bind 2* (*Naval Strategies and Nordic Security Policies. Volume 2*), Copenhagen: SNU.

Stokke, O. S. and Tunander, O. (1994) 'Introduction', in Stokhe, Olav Schram and Tunander, Ola (eds) *The Barents Region. Cooperation in Arctic Europe*, London: SAGE.

Stoltenberg, T. (1994) 'Foreword', in Stokke, Olav Schram and Tunander, Ola (eds) *The Barents Region. Cooperation in Arctic Europe,* London: SAGE: ix–xi.

Sæther, O. (1992) 'Nordmenn på Murmankysten' (*Norwegians on the Murman coast*), in Niemi, Einar (ed.) *Pomor. Nord norge og Nord Russland gjennom 1.000 år*, Oslo: Gyldendal Norsk forlag: 69–84.

Utenriksdepartementet (1993) *Samarbeidstiltak i Barentsregionen under Handlingsprogrammet for Sentral- og Øst-Europa samt SUS-landene i 1993* (*Cooperation Measures in the Barents Region under the Action Programme for Central and Eastern Europe and the CIS Countries in 1993*), Oslo: Royal Ministry of Foreign Affairs.

Vego, M. (1982) 'The Royal Swedish Navy', *US Naval Institute Proceedings*, March.

Viksne, I. (1995) 'Latvia and Europe's Security Structures', in van Ham, P. (ed.) 'The Baltic States: security and defence after independence', Paris: Institute for Security Studies, *Chaillot Papers 19*: 61–81.

Waever, O. (1991) 'Culture and Identity in the Baltic Sea Region' in Joenniemi, P. (ed.) 'Co-operation in the Baltic Sea Region: Needs and Prospects', Tampere: *TAPRI Research Report* 42: 79–111.

Rethinking or reorienting Europe's Mediterranean security focus?

CLAIRE SPENCER

Introduction

For a number of reasons, the Mediterranean has been the poor relation of the western security debate in the dramatic changes of the 1990s. The Mediterranean as a focus of the attentions of policy-makers and policy-analysts has undoutedly increased in importance since the 1980s, partly as a result of the expansion of both the European Community (EC) and NATO southwards to include Spain (admitted to NATO in 1982 and the EC in 1986) and Greece and Portugal (admitted to the EC in 1981 and 1986 respectively). However, as a component part of European security considerations, the Mediterranean remains a subsidiary region and set of issues, which have yet to be well-integrated within the mainstream of western security thinking.

The underlying causes of this have historical as well as contemporary roots, not least in the ways that security issues are formulated in the minds of their key proponents. Most strategic analysis was shaped and formed in the Cold War era, and much subsequent analysis of European security has not unnaturally focused on the consequences of the demise of the Soviet Union, and the negative as well as positive expectations this has generated. Even where attempts have been made (frequently, but not exclusively, by southern European states) to realign Europe's security focus from an 'East–West' to a 'North–South' axis, the issues raised have been neither sufficiently tangible, nor sufficiently urgent to mesh well with the primary concerns of the European security agenda.

This chapter examines the reasons why Mediterranean security issues continue to pose a challenge for a more integrated and global vision of European security, and considers what this illustrates about western and European security thinking in general. One of the difficulties has arisen at the structural and institutional level, where, for example, debates about the expansion of NATO find little place for the concerns of the non-European states of the Mediterranean. Another has arisen at the level of assessing 'threats' or 'risks' in the Mediterranean in ways that parallel the threat assessments made for the eastern boundaries of Europe. The biggest challenge, however, has become that of incorporating states to the south and south-east of Europe within collective and co-operative security initiatives in ways that are not undermined by

Europe's continuing preoccupation with its own defence against dangers which may arise in the Mediterranean region.

Most analysts agree that the Mediterranean does not present Europe with major military threats (Moya 1995: 12). The collapse of the Soviet Union, and the replacement of its global military scope by the more regionalised reach of Russia in its 'near abroad' has in fact de-emphasised the strategic importance of the Mediterranean, with the exception of residual concerns about the regional proliferation of weapons of mass destruction. Military activity nevertheless remains a concern in the eastern Mediterranean, particularly in the recurrent tensions between Greece and Turkey, in the recent outbreaks of violence in Cyprus and in the regional ramifications of the checkered Middle East peace process. The proliferation of weapons of mass destruction in the region, particularly if these were to fall into the hands of violent opposition groups, is also a preoccupation, but their use against Europe is a matter of debate among analysts (de Rato 1995: 7; Lesser 1996; Lipkowski 1996: 172).[1] In general, however, the most frequently cited risks and challenges in the Mediterranean are non-military in nature, arising from increasing development gaps between southern Europe and northern Africa, and the volatility of states and societies which have yet to achieve the social and political balance of Europe's modern democracies.

In principle, Europe has recognised this fact, and evolved new joint and cooperative security initiatives for the Mediterranean accordingly, most notably in the EU's Euro–Mediterranean Partnership initiative launched in Barcelona in November 1995. This innovative and global approach reflects a consensus among European governments that conflicts and violence in the Mediterranean arise as much from economic deprivation and sociopolitical inequalities as from arms build-ups or conventional intra-state tensions. It also reflects a growing recognition in the West in general that the long-term stability of the Mediterranean will depend on the growth of autonomous public institutions, of accountable governments, respect for human rights and the rule of law, as well as thriving private sectors based on a liberalisation of trade relations within and beyond the region. For the 12 invited partners of the EU (namely, Morocco, Algeria, Tunisia, Cyprus, Malta, Egypt, Israel, Jordan, Syria, Lebanon, Turkey and the Palestinian Authority), all these issues are addressed by the Barcelona process. In terms of Mediterranean security, however, the European agenda remains split between the priorities of assisting partner governments in the Mediterranean to reform and stimulate economic growth, and residual planning to contain the risks of any overspill effects into Europe during the transition period, as well as threats from states, such as Libya, not included in the initiative. While in many ways these approaches are depicted as complementary, in other ways, the 'soft' (that is, non-military) agenda has been relegated to a secondary role by the preoccupations of the 'hard' security agenda (namely, military and defence questions).

Even though Europe's security institutions have evolved more proactive policies towards the Mediterranean region, they still have not provided a comprehensive answer to what is, effectively, a dual dilemma: one consisting of the goals of collective defence as opposed to cooperative security, the other of the distinctions between military and non-military approaches to security. Traditional approaches to security tend to place military concerns (whether of a defensive, preventive, or co-operative nature, and the institutional means to ensure these objectives) at the centre of the debate, while placing issues such as development cooperation, restructured trade relations, cultural and environmental concerns at the periphery. The underlying thinking is that if the latter contribute to a stable and predictable environment on Europe's boundaries, then the security benefits to all concerned are to be welcomed. The essence of security, nevertheless, continues to lie in the kind of contingency planning provided by political and military alliances (and above all NATO), a large part of the debate being focused on the evolution of their internal structures and the interrelationship of their competences with other alliances and organisations functioning in the same or similar spheres (Cornish 1996; Zelikow 1996).

In Europe's relations with east and central Europe, the blurring of the lines within and between these two axes (external defence/cooperative security and military/non-military approaches to security) have mattered less, or at least, have been less apparent than in Europe's relations with the Mediterranean region. Where the convergence of security umbrellas and economic integration has been coextensive with current or future visions of the European continent, then the problem of the current exclusion of individual states from plans to expand the most important security organisations – NATO and the second pillar of the EU – may not be seen as definitive or irreversible. At the time of their exclusion, it may not be to the liking of the individual states concerned, but there have been other ways, such as the EU's development assistance and NATO's Partnerships for Peace (PfP) initiative, to foster cooperation and even to prepare for their integration at a later date. The main question still to be resolved is the thorny issue of the extent to which Russia can be considered European for the purposes of defence cooperation as well as economic integration, not least because some of the main threats to European security are perceived to arise in Russia, whether this is made explicit or not (Mandelbaum 1996: 15).

In the Mediterranean, only Cyprus and Malta have so far been offered the possibility of both EU and NATO membership. For the non-European states of the Mediterranean, namely the Arab bloc, Turkey and Israel, EU membership is not an option, nor is membership of NATO, even if most of the region's Arab governments have so far expressed little interest in this eventuality (de Rato 1996: 2). The regional anomaly is Turkey, whose membership of NATO since 1952 has not (yet) been equated with the kind of 'Europeanness' which would allow for Turkish membership of the EU or the Western European Union (WEU). European reservations are based on doubts about Turkey's maturity as a democratic state (the prominent public role of the military being welcomed as an asset to NATO, but not to the EU), on concerns about human rights violations, and above all qualms about the cultural identity of Turkey, pending a resolution of the current struggle between the secular and religious components of Turkish state and society.

The Mediterranean thus figures in both of Europe's dilemmas (collective defence/cooperative security and 'hard' security/'soft' security) and loses in each case. In the first, it loses because NATO is more comfortable with collective defence – against external threats – rather than cooperative security which would see the Mediterranean as part of the whole regime; and in the second, it loses because while the Mediterranean offers a prime example of the importance of 'soft' security issues, Europeans, and the West in general, are more preoccupied with 'hard' issues. Even where they recognise the salience of a 'soft' security approach, they are doing so within a defensive, more than a collective mentality, and are, in any case, reluctant to commit the necessary resources to address 'soft' security issues.

As a result, the Mediterranean dimension of European security has come to require more than a regional adaptation of experiences based on Europe's relations to the East. More work may in fact be necessary on the rethinking of security to meet the diverse circumstances and needs of the non-European Mediterranean region. However, in the meantime, and given the instruments Europe and the West already have at their disposal, it is perhaps more immediately a question of reorienting Europe's security focus away from its defensive and military roots towards a more genuinely inclusive security agenda, derived as much from the articulated needs of Europe's southern neighbours as from a more detailed analysis of the sources of instability in the region.

The underlying premise of this analysis is that security concerns are likely to become more rather than less important for Europe in the Mediterranean sphere. This is not because threats or risks have become more acute since the end of the Cold War. It is rather because the linkages between cause and effect in the field of security require more complex and multifaceted analysis than they have hitherto received. To cite but one example: the Mediterranean is first and foremost a region of extreme imbalances, which range, for example, between average *per capita* incomes of $20 000 per annum (and rising) in the European states, and around $1 600 (and falling) in the states of North Africa (Marks 1996: 10; Moya 1995: 23 (note 14)). Even though demographic growth rates of 2.5–3 per cent per annum in the southern Mediterranean have been slowing in the early 1990s, according to several estimations, by the early years of next century the bulk of the region's population will be found on the non-European, southern shores of the Mediterranean (Lesser 1996: 4).[2] In the eyes of many analysts, this shift in the region's demographic balance can only mean greater levels of south–north migration, as the young and unemployed of the Maghreb seek work in Europe.

How this eventuality is included within future Mediterranean security planning, however, will depend on how destabilising demographic shifts actually prove to be. It will also depend on whether traditional security approaches will continue to accord more importance to the defence of Europe against a perceived onslaught of unwanted migrants than on the often complex reasons underlying population shifts. In this respect, only when the studies of development and migration specialists (viz Collinson 1996) are fully integrated into security analyses will it be possible to make a full assessment of the challenges to be faced by Europe over the next decades. Without this, western and European responses to Mediterranean security questions run the danger of being piecemeal and unintegrated, reactive rather than proactive, and as imprecisely defined as the problems they seek to redress.

Mediterranean security and the 'Islamic threat'

A major problem facing attempts to refocus western policy towards the Mediterranean stems from the circumstances in which the debate has evolved in the post-Cold War era. Renewed western interest in Mediterranean security issues arose as much from events in the Middle East in the aftermath of the Cold War, as from a realisation that 40 years of East–West confrontation had obscured the complex realities of the region for perhaps too long. In the view that prevailed during the Cold War, the Mediterranean was the 'Southern Flank': in other words, a region of importance because of its proximity, potential instability and hence exploitation by the erstwhile Soviet Union, but of less importance as an 'out-of-area' region in NATO terms. Apart from the provisions under NATO Charter articles V and VI to defend regional NATO member states against external attack from within the region (including against their navies, airforces and shipping), this remains the case (Winrow 1996: 46).

For many years following the Second World War, the southern flank was seen as an adjunct to the central front of the core Cold War confrontation. This, as John Chipman describes, was understandable in that the core division between East and West was more easily discernible and demarcated in central Europe, as well as subject to more rigorous crisis management than the amorphous Mediterranean, 'where political change rather than maintenance of the *status quo* [was] the rule' (Chipman 1988: 2). Even with adjustments from the mid-1980s in the perceived importance of the Mediterranean Basin as a potential theatre of strategic military action (Chipman 1988: 8–9), planning for war or military operations in the region rarely reached a level of operational consensus among NATO members.

This was not just a question of benign neglect. During the Cold War, the juxtaposition of neighbouring Mediterranean states within the sphere of influence of one or other Superpower – or neither – also made the region difficult to define in terms of the 'East–West' bloc structure. Generally speaking, the defence of Europe meant the defence of NATO member states, including Turkey. Even beyond considerations of where Europe stops and starts, coherent definitions of the region in strategic or even political terms continue to pose problems. The question of whether to include only the littoral states of the Mediterranean Basin in regional analyses, to broaden the scope to encompass the broader Middle East, or to focus on sub-regions, such as the eastern and western Mediterranean, has been a function as much of the challenges faced as of the rationale behind attempts to create security structures for the region. As a result, many discussions of Mediterranean security issues still begin with the question: 'What is the Mediterranean?' without reaching a satisfactory conclusion.

In the post-Cold War period, the aftermath of the Gulf crisis of 1990–1 has done most to shape western security perceptions of the Mediterranean region. Less than a year after the collapse of the Berlin Wall, Iraq's invasion of Kuwait focused western attention on the possibility of war in a world no longer defined by Superpower confrontation. The new concern of the West was not so much that of limiting military activity, as of how to shape a new global alliance to counter the Iraqi aggression under circumstances already significantly different from those prevailing under a Soviet threat. The Gulf crisis laid to rest any suggestion that the course of history by 1989 had ended any future prospect of large-scale military confrontation, especially along ideological lines. Even though the UN Allies' brief war with Iraq went beyond the confines of European security (access to Gulf oil supplies being a major objective of most of the developed world), it did however draw attention to the unwillingness of a number of Europe's neighbours to conform to a 'New World Order' imposed from outside.

For the purposes of Mediterranean security, the identification of links across the Arab world which appeared to defy the new prognostications of the post-Cold War era has remained alive in the minds of many analysts. From popular demonstrations in favour of Iraq in Morocco, Algeria and Tunisia, to the reluctance of most Arab states outside the Gulf (except Syria, Morocco and Egypt) to support the UN Allies, to the political support of both Jordan and the PLO for Saddam Hussein, the Middle East demonstrated how rapidly the perceived allegiances of the Cold War world had broken down. As a result, the objectives and intentions of emerging Islamist movements in the early 1990s were frequently analysed in terms of their antipathy to western values of liberal democracy and free markets. In reality, many of these movements had limited objectives such as the replacement of their national governments with (ostensibly) more popular alternatives. The sudden emergence of the Algerian Islamic Salvation Front (FIS) in 1989 was a salient example of a nationally based movement of popular revolt, which in its early years pursued its political aims through the ballot box with at least as much vigour as it strove to impose its moral doctrines and dress-codes on unwilling Algerian women. Attempts by the FIS leadership to raise the movement's international profile in both the Muslim world and the West were, at very least, subsidiary to their national agenda.

It was the emergence of this perceived 'Islamic threat', however, which did more than any other phenomenon to alert the West to the need to reassess approaches to Mediterranean security. To combat the spread of the phenomenon across the Muslim states closest to Europe demanded more serious thinking than merely pointing to Islamist activism as a global threat. In the interim, however, the evocation of an 'arc of crisis' running from the western Mediterranean to central Asia concerned almost exclusively Muslim states and societies (Anderson and Fenech 1994: 14). The outbreak of conflict in former Yugoslavia was also perceived as partly a 'Muslim' crisis. As the UN, rather than NATO, became the forum and vehicle for international responses to that conflict, the Mediterranean became a secondary backdrop to a war which, despite its geographical location in the eastern Mediterranean, was not perceived in security terms to be part of the Mediterranean at all.

Instead, the combination of a growing international focus on Islamic fundamentalism and developments in the Arab–Israeli peace process after the Gulf crisis led to a division in western priorities towards the Mediterranean region from the early 1990s. On the one hand, from the first Arab–Israeli meetings in Madrid in October 1991, and the Oslo process which succeeded it following the Israeli–Palestinian signature of the Declaration of Principles in September 1993, the main priority of the US has been to broker the various stages of a peace settlement in the Middle East. For the Europeans, on the other hand, the focus of attention, although not exclusively, has been with developments in the western Mediterranean, and with evolving a new global EU policy towards the non-European partners in the Mediterranean region. In reflection of this, the outbreak of violence in Algeria has led to different analyses of the security implications for Europe by European and American observers. The European approach has been partly conditioned by the greater consequences for France of the civil war in Algeria, which continued into 1997 with estimates of over 60 000 dead, spilling over into terrorist attacks in France in 1995 and 1996. It has also reflected the growing EU consensus, culminating in the Barcelona Declaration of November 1995, over the need to address the sources of regional popular discontent at root, rather than plan for combatting its excesses alone. The US approach, in turn, has continued to situate Islamic fundamentalism, 'rogue' regimes (most notably Sudan and Iran) and ballistic missile proliferation at the centre of threats, reaching not only across the Mediterranean, but into the Middle East, to the Gulf states and Central Asia, in a broader regional and strategic sweep.[3]

Although not entirely inimical to one another, these approaches have rendered the creation of a new regional order for the Mediterranean more complex. As Fred Tanner writes, '(t)he geo-political perceptions of NATO officials or of American policy-makers' which 'increasingly link the Mediterranean to a greater Euro-Atlantic theatre' appears to be incompatible with EU efforts to create a separate Euro-Med security partnership (Tanner 1996: 290). The overriding objectives of the US government, particularly as regards safeguarding the security of Israel, are not entirely in line with European priorities, driven by Spain, Italy and Portugal, as well as France, to strengthen the Mediterranean's vocation as an integrated European hinterland. Whilst a basic consensus exists on keeping Libya at arms length, the methods to be employed in respect of other regional 'rogues', such as Iran, have given rise to dissension both within the EU itself, as well as between EU members and the US. In debates and discussions over Mediterranean security questions, little of this dissension is made explicit, not least because of the continuing centrality of NATO to any military eventuality which might still arise in the region.[4] It is rather in the details of defining what collective and cooperative security should mean, and how it should be articulated at the institutional and organisational level in the Mediterranean that progress has been slow, or at best, hesitant.

New security architectures and the Mediterranean region

The reorientation of the European security debate in the 1990s has been only partial, despite genuine attempts to extend security agendas beyond military definitions and parameters. Baldwin observes that scholars of security studies 'give low priority to conceptual issues', not least because 'military force, not security, has been the central concern of security studies' (Baldwin 1997: 9). For theoretical and practical purposes, extending the usage of the term to non-military spheres has not increased the conceptual understanding of security, as Baldwin writes again:

> The dimensions of security have not changed with the end of the Cold War, but the substantive specifications of these dimensions that were appropriate during the Cold War are likely to differ from those appropriate to the 1990s. Economic security, environmental security, identity security, social security are different forms of security, not fundamentally different concepts.
>
> (Baldwin 1997: 23)

The present analysis makes no attempt to redress this conceptual deficiency, but merely notes that the term 'security' continues to be extensively used with implicit reference to military agendas and conventional defence. In the years immediately following the Cold War, the imprecise usage of the vocabulary of security may in fact have been beneficial to slowly evolving strategic agendas. Its more recent application to social and human spheres may, however, be counterproductive where not considered as central to the notion of security – as opposed to defence – when used in cooperative ventures (see Chapter 1).

The consequences of this imprecision for European security are problematic when set in the context of the lack of joint security thinking and practice in the non-NATO, non-European states of the Mediterranean with which to complement the West's long experience of common security approaches. This does not mean that states such as Morocco and Algeria, Israel and Egypt, for example, have not sought external support for their defence and security aims, nor that conventional military security – and particularly arms proliferation – are not a widespread regional preoccupation. Limited regional attempts have been made to address common security concerns, such as the article on common defence included in the founding charter of the Arab Maghreb Union (AMU) established by Morocco, Algeria, Tunisia, Libya and Mauritania in 1989 (Joffé 1994: 26). However, for the purposes of constructing a new European security order within the Mediterranean – especially if generated from outside the region – it means that finding common ground in the sphere of security has been harder to achieve with Mediterranean partners than with the former Warsaw Pact states of central and eastern Europe. As a result, and quite apart from the strategic aims envisaged, the incorporation within an expanded NATO of the Visegrad states, for example, has been easier to conceptualise than a similar expansion to the non-European southern Mediterranean, if these states were to seek this in the future.

These difficulties have not gone unrecognised, but neither have they given rise to substantive attempts to redress the institutional vacuum in the region in ways that address the core concerns of Mediterranean states. If Europe and the West largely equate security with defence, then the states of the southern Mediterranean equate their own security more readily with the achievement of social stability through development (de Rato 1995: 1–2). In terms of threat perceptions, southern Mediterranean states may well identify the economic and military might of neighbouring Europe as the greatest threat to their stability, especially where they feel they have less choice and freedom of action than those setting the parameters for the Mediterranean security debate in the West. For this reason, the EU has taken the lead in defining a policy which, at least in intention, encompasses areas of economic, social and political cooperation which the main security institutions can only discuss, but where they have little or no competence to act. The institutional expression of this evolving relationship, however, has yet to develop beyond government-to-government discussions over sectoral issues and related projects which may contribute to security, while more sensitive political and military security concerns are subject to an exchange of views within *ad hoc* fora of a more exploratory nature, the main ambition of which often appears to be one of keeping channels of communication open between participating members.

This is not to say that increasing mutual understanding across and within the Mediterranean is not a creditable and worthy goal in itself. The EU is in fact following in the footsteps of other institutions, including NATO, the WEU, the Organization of Cooperation and Security in Europe (OSCE), the North Atlantic Assembly (NAA) and the Inter-Parliamentary Union, which have all extended their 'outreach' to the Mediterranean since the early 1990s. Both the WEU and NATO have established bilateral dialogues between their respective international secretariats in Brussels and ambassadors of invited Mediterranean partners, the general aim of which being, as expressed at the launch of NATO's Mediterranean Initiative in February 1995, 'to contribute to security and stability in the Mediterranean as a whole, to achieve a better mutual understanding and to correct any misunderstandings of the Alliance's purpose that could lead to a perception of a threat' (NATO, February 1995).

NATO's Mediterranean Initiative has marked a culmination of policies to upgrade the southern flank in the European security agenda since the goal of maintaining 'peaceful and non-adversarial relations with countries in the southern Mediterranean and Middle East' was outlined in Article 11 of the Alliance's New Strategic Concept of July 1990 (NATO 1991: 3). In keeping with the 1994 NATO summit's decision to explore further measures to promote security in the Mediterranean, a number of states in the region (namely, Morocco, Tunisia, Israel, Mauritania and Egypt, joined by Jordan) were invited to participate in a series of dialogues, essentially devised as a confidence-building exercise (Winrow 1996: 52–4). From even earlier, in 1992, the WEU began conducting a similar set of bilateral dialogues with officials from Morocco, Algeria and Tunisia, expanded to include Israel and Egypt, following the formation of the WEU Mediterranean Group in 1993 (Jacomet 1995: 10).

The challenge to these initiatives has been to place proposals of real substance on the table in order to extend their usefulness beyond their initial explanatory purposes. Even if the agreed scope of the NATO dialogue was to cover the political, economic and military aspects of regional security as well as peace-keeping (Moya 1996: 3), neither of these initiatives have gone far towards defining common areas of defence cooperation, largely because of the reservations of individual WEU and NATO members. The second phase of the NATO dialogue from 1996 has opened up the possibility of civilian and military representatives of Mediterranean countries participating in NATO-sponsored seminars and peace-keeping courses. However, since NATO governments have so far dedicated few resources to fund this participation, Moya foresees 'a risk that the failure to lay out the fairly modest sums of money needed ... could significantly damage the credibility of the whole NATO initiative' (Moya 1996: 6). Of more significance in practical terms has been the contribution of forces by Morocco, Egypt and Jordan to the NATO-led IFOR operation in Bosnia, as well as the follow-up SFOR operation. This, however, has neither been dependent on, nor directly related to, the dialogue, but has arisen in an area of NATO activity – namely 'out-of-area' operations – not yet universally accepted as a future norm. While for the foreseeable future there is little prospect of consensus among NATO members over extending their 'out-of-area' activities to the Middle East and North Africa, the greater involvement of North African and Middle Eastern states in joint and cooperative defence activity is likely to remain restricted (Moya 1996: 7).

In turn, the WEU dialogue has, in the words of Moya, 'failed to bear fruit partly because of the widely diverging security priorities of the two sides, and partly because the WEU was not in a postion politically to put something concrete on the agenda' (Moya 1996: 2).[5] The political weakness of the WEU as an institution in fact stems from its still unresolved relationship to the EU and its CFSP. As Moya notes: 'a WEU Mediterranean dialogue is only meaningful in the context of a CFSP' (Moya 1995: 4). Until the CFSP takes shape, moreover, the WEU initiative has been virtually supplanted by the inclusion of a political and security dimension in the EU's Barcelona process. Despite the fact that the Barcelona Declaration covered many of the areas already raised within the WEU's Mediterranean dialogue, the EU neither ascribed a role for the WEU in its follow-up work programme, nor invited any WEU participation in the Barcelona conference itself (Lipkowski 1996: 177).

As regards other initiatives, in 1994 the OSCE reactivated its Mediterranean dimension (which had been largely redundant since the Helsinki process began in 1975) to invite Algeria, Egypt, Israel, Morocco and Tunisia to attend as regular observers to OSCE Council of Ministers' meetings and Review Conferences (de Rato 1995: 14). Through an OSCE contact group, a number of seminars have also been arranged, including the first held in the southern Mediterranean, in Cairo in September 1995, to share the OSCE's experience in confidence-building measures with the five observer states. However, as Lipkowski comments, 'this organization ... was designed to manage East–West conflict, totally different in nature to the problems arising in the Mediterranean basin' (Lipkowski 1996: 179). Just as most of the other regional initiatives, the OSCE's activities contribute to the goals of mutual familiarisation in and across the Mediterranean. Nevertheless, few participants on either side are under any illusion that the key to both resources and the political will to move beyond the *status quo* lie with NATO and EU. To some extent, the very proliferation of regional dialogues and initiatives serves to dilute prospects for tackling the core conflicts within the Mediterranean. At least one of these lies within NATO itself (namely, differences between Greece and Turkey, where progress at last seemed underway in 1997) and another, the Arab–Israeli peace process, of major importance to the Arab states of the region as well as Israel, has been addressed in the bilateral and multilateral processes of the Oslo process, beyond the scope of more broadly conceived Mediterranean fora.

Officials are also aware that the fate of the WEU dialogue echoes that of similar attempts to structure a durable set of security relationships in the Mediterranean, capable of combining flexibility and adaptability with political purpose (as well as, ultimately, producing tangible results). The main endeavours in this respect since the late 1980s have been the so-called CSCM proposal, the '5 + 5' dialogue and the Egyptian-sponsored Mediterranean Forum. The CSCM was an Italo–Spanish initiative launched at the CSCE follow-up meeting in Palma in September 1990 which sought to emulate the CSCE process in the Mediterranean. It failed to gain ground, not only because of the difficulty of reaching agreement over which Mediterranean states and partners to include or exclude, but also because of the lack of northern European and US engagement in the initiative. At a time in the early 1990s when debates about the future role of Europe's existing security institutions were rife, if not competitive, most governments resisted the idea of creating yet more bureaucratic structures for which the purposes were ill-defined.[6]

In the same way, the round-table discussions of the '5 + 5' dialogue were driven by a French initiative in 1990 to bring together five European states (France, Spain, Portugal, Italy and Malta) with the UMA member-states. Its purpose was partly to draw attention to Europe's neglect of the Mediterranean, and partly, according to its critics, to put a pre-emptive French stamp on any Anglo–American-led efforts to rectify this neglect. However, it failed to survive the differences engendered by the 1990–1 Gulf War, the diplomatic exclusion of Libya and tensions between Morocco and Algeria over the Western Sahara (Moya 1995: 6). Its exclusion of Egypt, however, gave rise in 1991 to the Egyptian-sponsored Mediterranean Forum, comprised of ten Mediterranean states (expanded to 11 when Malta was admitted) to engage in informal discussions over a wide range of Mediterranean affairs. As the only initiative to have emerged from within the region, this forum at least provided a channel for the expression of the security and development concerns of the non-European southern Mediterranean states. Until these issues – and even demands – were taken seriously by the entire EU, however, appeals to the southern Europeans involved in the Forum served the useful, but limited purpose, of strengthening Spanish, Italian and French diplomatic efforts to move the Mediterranean further up the EU's agenda of priorities.

One of the main weaknesses of the dialogue approach to confidence-building measures is that it is often assumed that the mere fact of opening up or expanding contacts where they have either not existed, or have been limited in the past, is in itself a confidence-building measure. Yet as Moya writes: '(i)nitiating a dialogue assumes creating a minimum of confidence between the participants, which is inconceivable if one party brands the other as a threat' (Moya 1995: 17). At the same time that NATO and the WEU have been expanding their 'outreach' to the Mediterranean, they have also been planning for Europe's defence.

This has resulted in some uncomfortable juxtapositions between their professed aims to Mediterranean partners and reassurances to their own members. For example, in writing about 'NATO and the Mediterranean' in early 1997, NATO Secretary-General, Javier Solana, stressed the importance of the Mediterranean's 'common space, common concerns and a common heritage' to produce 'enough commonality, in any case, to make dialogue and cooperation with those in the region an effort worth undertaking', closely followed by a reaffirmation of the importance of the 'stabilising presence' of 'NATO's collective defence function' along with the Alliance's duty to provide for the collective defence of its southern members (Solana 1997: 2). Discussions of the future internal restructuring of NATO also include the possibility of promoting the southern command AFSOUTH to a Major NATO Command (de Rato 1995: 10) and of applying the Alliance's Combined Joint Task Force (CJTF) principle for operations – as yet unspecified – in North Africa or elsewhere in the Mediterranean (Winrow 1996: 49).

If not accompanied by clearer explanations of the precise parameters and objectives of the kind of operations envisaged, any future expansion of the 'out-of-area' role of NATO or the WEU runs the risk of being potentially dangerous for the smooth progress of trans-Mediterranean relations. The WEU's creation in 1995 of a call-up of rapid deployment forces for the Mediterranean, for example, raised consternation in a number of North African capitals, such as Algiers and Tunis, not least because the surprise announcement of the initiative appeared to counter the WEU's expressed aim of exploring confidence-building measures in the Mediterranean. As Alvaro Vasconcelos writes: '(i)mprecision concerning the role of EUROFOR and EUROMARFOR, which include naval units and troops from Portugal, Spain, France and Italy are seen by specialists from northern Africa as an indication of their true mission: nothing other than intervention on the southern shore of the Mediterranean' (Faria and Vasconcelos 1996: 11).

Ultimately, the best prospect for combating the deficiencies of earlier cooperative security attempts continues to lie in the EU's Euro–Mediterranean Partnership initiative. For the first time, at least on paper, this fully recognises the multiplicity of factors which go to make up a security relationship in a region where cross-cutting threat perceptions and challenges are not best addressed through traditional defensive alliances. However, while this approach continues to evolve, it does mean that the mainstream of European security concerns have left the Mediterranean on the sidelines, to be considered almost apart from more immediate developments in the traditional spheres of defence and military activity.

The Barcelona process: security through development?

The EU's Euro–Mediterranean Partnership was launched partly 'out of dissatisfaction with the results achieved so far by its overall Mediterranean policy' (EC, 1995a), and partly to fill the void in the debate over security instruments, as the most comprehensive and next-best thing. The fact that security issues have been included at all is not just a means of sealing the fate of the CSCM and related initiatives by agreeing to do something similar but different (that is, without creating any new institutions beyond *ad hoc* coordinating and follow-up committees at ministerial and 'high official level'). It is also because security, defined as a series of 'soft' as well as 'hard' security challenges, formed the basis of the compromise reached across the 15 member states of the EU.

The Barcelona Declaration outlines three broad areas for the founding of a future Euro–Mediterranean Partnership. These are, a Political and Security Partnership to establish 'a common area of peace and stability', an Economic and Financial Partnership to create 'an area of shared prosperity' and a Partnership in Social, Cultural and Human Affairs, to develop human resources and promote 'understanding between cultures and exchanges between civil societies' (EC, 1995b, Barcelona Declaration, pp. 2, 4 and 6). The central ambition is the creation of a Mediterranean Free Trade Area by the year 2010. The underlying philosophy, as Marks describes it, is that:

> (t)he creation of a free trade zone encompassing both flanks of the Mediterranean – and linked to an area stretching north to the Arctic circle and east to the confines of the former Soviet Union – fits into the 1990s dynamic of building large transnational trading and investment blocs, from which closer political and sociocultural relations are assumed to flow.
>
> (Marks 1996: 2)

The European consensus reached at Barcelona was that the root cause of instability in the Mediterranean derives from insufficient levels of economic growth and development. This view also coincides with the expressed security concerns of non-European Mediterranean states, especially in North Africa, where demographic growth has put most pressure on governments to create employment and improve the welfare of the population. Thus, in preparation for launching the Free Trade Area, the EU has placed most emphasis on galvanising private sector investment in the region, in liberalising the access to Europe of the Maghreb's exports (with the exception of agricultural produce), and in encouraging horizontal, that is South–South intra-regional exchanges and integration.

Europe's own security agenda has in turn been addressed through articles committing the signatories of the Barcelona agreement to cooperate in fighting organised crime, in preventing the proliferation of nuclear, chemical and biological weapons and in limiting the development of military capacities to levels compatible with their 'legitimate defence requirements' (EC, 1995b, Barcelona Declaration, p. 3). In other areas, the EU has gained commitments from their Mediterranean partners to facilitate the return of illegal migrants from Europe, in exchange for greater vigilance in the EU's protection of the rights of legal migrants. While the fear of Islamic fundamentalism is not spelt out or mentioned by name, there are provisions for the promotion of religious toleration and human rights, of diversity, democracy and social and political pluralism (in addition to combatting racism and xenophobia, as the implicit '*contrepartie*' of the Europeans).

While the list of provisions has inspired admiration as well as scepticism on both sides of the Mediterranean, as an expression of a new and integrated approach to European security, the Barcelona process still has some way to go. In the first place, although promoted as an inclusive and global approach to tackling both 'soft' and 'hard' security concerns in the Mediterranean, its three chapters are neither integrated nor evenly balanced in terms of priorities. Rather, as Marks has commented, the social and political benefits of the partnership are expected to arise from the economic progress made – more by the southern Mediterranean states than by the EU itself – to liberalise and open hitherto protected markets to outside trade. One of the major criticisms of the EU's partners has been that the official resources dedicated to smoothing the transition – namely the EU's funding to the region of ECU 4 685 million for the period 1995–99 and additonal loans through the European Investment Bank – have been insufficient (Lipkowski 1996: 159–60).

Second, the EU's approach continues to be bilateral rather than multilateral, except at the level of sectoral follow-up meetings. The main path, or stepping stone, to the Free Trade Area, has been through the bilateral negotiation of association agreements with individual Mediterranean partners. In respect of these agreements, there has been no explicit linkage between the economic and political criteria of Barcelona, to the extent that the EU's negotations with Algeria, although delayed and occasionally disrupted, make no apparent connection between the current levels of domestic social and political unrest and the Algerian government's ability to conform to the macro-economic requirements of freer trade with the EU. In other words, there have been few connections made between an individual partner's progress in the sphere of political as well as economic development and liberalisation.

Third, the focus of the follow-up to the Political and Security Partnership remains primarily in the areas of conventional defence and security. Thus, not only have substantive concerns over sensitive political issues, such as human rights and domestic politics in general been avoided, but the discussion and elaboration of confidence-building measures, such as transparency, have characterised the round-table meetings of high officials. This is partly because the dialogue is conducted at the multilateral level, where consensus over the issues to be discussed must be reached by all 27 members. It is also the case that the Barcelona process has given rise to the only multilateral forum to combine representation from Syria and Lebanon as well as Israel (which has not been the case in the Oslo process multilateral working groups, boycotted by Syria and Lebanon, even before they stalled in 1996–7). However, it does mean that by mutual agreement, questions concerning the Middle East peace process have been kept off the agenda. Partly in consequence of this, the EU's proposed establishment of a 'Stability Pact' or 'Charter for Peace and Stability' for the Mediterranean has taken no concrete form, even at the follow-up conference to Barcelona of foreign ministers, held in Malta in April 1997. The southern Mediterranean partners have begun to express their disappointment at the lack of progress (Lipkowski 1996: 160).

Finally, through no fault of its own, the Barcelona process is an imperfect, and even pre-emptive, expression of the EU's CFSP. Until such a time as the EU resolves its own internal debates about the formation, expression, representation and exercise of the EU's external policy under the provisions of Maastricht, the security dimension of the Barcelona process will necessarily be limited by the extent to which multilateral commitments and undertakings can be made to meet the expectations of the EU's southern partners.

Conclusions

The context of the European security debate has changed considerably to take into consideration cooperative security and joint methods of addressing the concerns of non-European states in the Mediterranean region. From the point of view of the southern Mediterranean states themselves, there continues to be a certain dissonance between the West's preoccupation with security and their own primary concern with development. Despite moves in the direction of addressing the development needs of the Mediterranean, European policy responses have still not been sufficiently coherent to tackle the root causes of the very things European states most fear. These might be loosely summarised as the human consequences of partial or even inappropriate social, economic and political development in the Maghreb itself.

The relativisation of Mediterranean security can be found in the ambivalences expressed by Western analysts and policy-makers about cultural relations across the Mediterranean. On the one hand, there has been an increase in efforts to extend and expand Europe's relations southwards to address shared security concerns through collaborative and coordinated approaches. On the other hand, this impulse has often been countered by the desire to limit the overspill effects within Europe of what are perceived as negative cultural influences from the Islamic south. The debate is rarely couched in these terms, especially since most European leaders are at pains to stress the positive values of Islam as opposed to the negative effects of the more violent expressions of Islamist activism. There is nevertheless at the heart of much debate about future Mediterranean security arrangements a set of rarely acknowledged tensions which pull in opposite directions.

Moving in one direction are the EU's cooperative policy initiatives which encompass 'soft' security issues such as migration control, economic development and the EU's projected creation of a Free Trade Area throughout the Mediterranean Basin by the year 2010. The aim has been to move away from confrontational or defensive models of security to search for common motivations and objectives in redressing the kind of economic and political imbalances outlined above. Moving in the other direction, however, are analyses which divide the north from the southern Mediterranean along a notional cultural and political fautline, as suggested most provocatively by Samuel Huntington's much-cited article 'The Clash of Civilizations?'(1993). Here, the aim has been to examine the extent to which divisions in the region are endemic, or unlikely to respond to external policy initiatives, however well intentioned (Holmes 1995: 2; Conry 1997: 115).

The problem for the evolution of coherent policy towards the region is that these two contradictory impulses are not always entirely discreet from one another. The suspicion of a number of Europe's southern partners, for example, has been that the EU's commitment to economic development is only as strong as its commitment to its own security, conceived in traditionally defensive terms (Tozy, 1995). Europe's reassurances about its respect for Islam may also run the danger of strengthening images of an almost exclusively Christian (and occasionally 'Judeo–Christian') Europe which excludes the contribution of both contemporary and earlier generations of European Muslims in the formation of Europe's diversified identities. For the purposes of rethinking security relations in the Mediterranean, moreover, the predominance of Western norms, both cultural and political, can too often be taken for granted, where existing security arrangements (and particularly those represented by NATO and the WEU) so clearly favour the West and Europe.

The more recent vocabulary of 'partnership' employed by the EU in fact shields a much starker reality of European superiority in all the key areas where this partnership is sought. There may be good diplomatic reasons why the economic and military strength of the states on the northern shores of the Mediterranean are not always spelt out to the discomfiture of those on the southern shores. However, when many of the traditional security concerns of the West are expressed in the vocabulary of fear and 'otherness', there is reason to question the viability of future partnerships based on perceived negative factors, such as Islamic fundamentalism, if ambitions for greater political and economic development are not addressed as equally central to the security of populations on both shores of the Mediterranean.

Note

The author would like to thank Ulla Holm of the Copenhagen Peace Research Institute, colleagues at the Danish Institute of International Affairs, Copenhagen and Michael Clarke of the Centre for Defence Studies, Kings College, University of London, for their assistance and comments on earlier drafts of this chapter.

Notes

1. While Lesser, for example, predicts that '(w)ithin ten years, it is possible that every southern European capital will be within range of ballistic missiles based in North Africa or the Levant' (1996: x), Lipkowski, reporting for the Assembly of the WEU's Political Committee, comments that '(a)lthough it does not do to minimise the dangers of developments in ballistic missile technology, it appears that the countries primarily threatened by such developments are the Middle Eastern and North African countries on account of the various regional conflicts between them' (1996: 172).

2. According to Lesser, 'the total population of states around the poorer shores of the Mediterranean will reach some 350 million not long after the end of the century. By contrast, the total population of the current members of the European Union will not exceed 300 million in the same period' (Lesser 1996: 4).

3. The analyses which reflect this division include on the European side works on the Barcelona process as an economic and sociopolitical approach to security or on the prospects for economic and political cooperation in the Mediterranean Basin (see contributions in Aliboni, Joffé and Niblock 1996). On the US side, works concentrate on whether Islamic fundamentalism (or Islamism) poses a major cultural or political threat to European security and/or American global interests (e.g. Fuller and Lesser 1995), or evaluations of the consequences of the establishment of another (i.e. post-Iranian, post-Syrian) fundamentalist regime in the region (e.g. Fuller 1996).

4. This partly explains the French government's position on gaining the command of NATO's AFSOUTH, with responsibilities for the Mediterranean region.

5. This is an assessment shared by Lipkowski: 'It has to be said that given that the WEU has not become involved in the political aspects, the limited dialogue on which it has embarked with these countries has not produced any tangible results' (Lipkowski 1996: 158).

6. The idea of an extended regional CSCME to cover the Middle East including the Gulf states was revived by the former British Foreign Secretary, Malcolm Rifkind, during a visit to the United Arab Emirates in November 1996. The strong support for this initiative in official Israeli circles has meant that it has remained still-born, pending a more comprehensive conclusion of the Middle East peace process (see UK Foreign Office, Speech by the Foreign Secretary, Mr Malcolm Rifkind,

Emirates' Centre for Strategic Studies and Research, Abu Dhabi, 4 November 1996; Gold 1996).

References

Aliboni, R., Joffé, G. and Niblock, T. (eds) (1996) *Security Challenges in the Mediterranean Region*, London: Frank Cass.

Anderson, E. and Fenech, D. (1994) 'New Dimensions in Mediterranean Security' in Gillespie, R. (ed) *Mediterranean Politics 1*, London: Pinter, 9–21.

Baldwin, D. A. (1997) 'The Concept of Security', in *Review of International Studies*, 23 (1) January: 5–26.

Chipman, J. (ed.) (1988) *NATO's Southern Allies: Internal and External Challenges*, London and New York: Atlantic Institute for International Affairs/Routledge.

Collinson, S. (1996) *Shore to Shore: The Politics of Migration in Euro–Maghreb Relations*, London: Royal Institute of International Affairs.

Conry, B. (1997) 'North Africa on the Brink', *Mediterranean Quarterly*, 8 (1) Winter: 115–30.

Cornish, P. (1996) 'European Security: the End of Architecture and the New NATO', *International Affairs*, 72 (4) October, 751–69.

EC (1995a) The Euro-Meditteranean Conference, Barcelona, 27–28 November.

EC (1995b) The Barcelona Declaration, European Council, Barcelona, 28 November.

Faria, F. and Vasconcelos, A. (1996) 'Security in Northern Africa: Ambiguity and Reality', *Chaillot Papers No. 25*, September, Paris: WEU Institute for Security Studies.

Fuller, G. (1996) *Algeria: The Next Fundamentalist State?*, Arroyo Center: RAND.

Fuller, G. and Lesser, I. (1995) *A Sense of Siege: The Geopolitics of Islam and the West*, RAND, Boulder CO: Westview Press.

Gold, D. (1996) 'Israel and the Gulf: New Security Frameworks for the Middle East', *Policy Focus Research Memorandum No. 31*, November, Washington DC: Washington Institute.

Holmes, J. W. (ed.) (1995) *Maelstrom: The United States, Southern Europe and the Challenges of the Mediterranean*, Cambridge, Massachusetts: World Peace Foundation.

Huntington, S. P. (1993) 'The Clash of Civilizations?', *Foreign Affairs*, 72, (3) Summer.

Jacomet, A. (1995) 'Regional and State Security Challenges in the Mediterranean; the WEU's Response' *University of Reading Discussion Papers in European and International Social Science Research, No. 57*, December.

Joffé, G. (1994) 'The European Union and the Maghreb', in Gillespie, R. (ed.) *Mediterranean Politics*, Volume I, London: Pinter.

Lesser, I. (1996) *Southern Europe and the Maghreb: US interests and Policy Perspectives*, Santa Monica: RAND.

Lipkowski, S. (1996) Security in the Mediterranean region: Report submitted on behalf of the Political Committee Proceedings of the Assembly of the WEU, 42nd Session, *Document 1543*, 4 November, Paris: WEU.

Mandelbaum, M. (1996) *The Dawn of Peace in Europe*, New York: Twentieth Century Fund.

Marks, J. (1996) 'High Hopes and Low Motives: the New Euro–Mediterranean Partnership Initiative', in *Mediterranean Politics* I,(1) Summer: 1–23.

Moya, P. (1995) *Frameworks for Cooperation in the Mediterranean*, North Atlantic Assembly, Civilian Affairs Committee, Sub-Committee on the Mediterranean Basin, AM 259 CC/MB (95) 7, October.

Moya, P. (1996) *Co-operation for Security in the Mediterranean: NATO and EU Contributions*, North Atlantic Assembly, Civilian Affairs Committee, Sub-Committee on the Mediterranean Basin, AN 83 CC/MB (96) 1, November.

NATO (1991) The Alliance's New Strategic Concept North Atlantic Council, Rome, 7–8 November (http://www.nato.int/docu/comm/c911107a.htm).

NATO (1995) Statement by the NATO Spokesman on NATO's Mediterranean Initiative, Press Release (95) 12, 8 February.

Rato, de R. (1995) Co-operation and Security in the Mediterranean North Atlantic Assembly, Political Committee, Sub-Committee on the Southern Region, AM 295 PC/SR (95) 2, October.

Rato, de R. (1996) *In Pursuit of Mediterranean Security*, North Atlantic Assembly, Political Committee, Working Group on the Southern Region, AN 102 PC/SR (96) 1, November.

Solana, J. (1997) 'NATO and the Mediterranean', *Mediterranean Quarterly* March, (http://www.nato.int./docu/articles/1997/a)70301).

Tanner, F. (1996) 'An Emerging Security Agenda for the Mediterranean', in *Mediterranean Politics*, I (3), Winter: 279–94.

Tozy, M. (1995) 'Escepticismo en el Sur', in *El País*, 23 November.

Winrow, G. (1996) 'A Threat from the South? NATO and the Mediterranean', in *Mediterranean Politics*, I (1), Summer: 43–59.

Zelikow, P. (1996) 'The Masque of Institutions', in *Survival*, 38 (1), Spring: 1–22.

CHAPTER 9

A region of eternal conflict?
The Balkans – semantics and security

JAMES GOW

South-eastern Europe suffered immediately after the Cold War came to an end. On an obvious level, the pain of the Yugoslav war of dissolution marked this suffering. But there were deeper levels at which a broader region than that covered by the former Yugoslav lands suffered. In part, this was a function of the Yugoslav war – so often dubbed the 'Balkan war', thereby tarring a number of non-Yugoslav countries with the same dismal brush used to colour those involved in war. In part, this is because many were keen to identify different regions and sub-regions in the broader post-Cold War Europe – some of which would be 'in' and others which would be 'out'. In general, although there was a sense that there was something called Europe, there was a line to be drawn to the east.

The problem with any discussion of the Balkans is labelling. The components of the Balkan region are not always taken to include the same countries. Whichever countries are included, it is hard to find a clear rationale which makes sense of grouping them together as a region in contemporary security affairs. Most disturbingly, whichever countries are included, there is a generally pejorative connotation to the term. Thus, there can be a sense in which to discuss the Balkans as a region is to discuss something to be dismissed as dissipatory and difficult. The Balkan region, in common perception, is one of eternal trial and conflict.

The aim of this analysis is to examine security issues in south-eastern Europe and the north-north-eastern Mediterranean. These are many and sometimes linked – and in all cases are critically shaped by the attitude and engagement of the EU, NATO and their members. But the term Balkan, even if it can occasionally be useful, is more generally harmful and there is little, apart from relative proximity, which can be said to define a region. If there is one thing which truly binds the countries of south-eastern Europe, it is the degree to which traditionally, and in the 1990s, they suffered from a bad reputation which, for most countries, most of the time, is not deserved.

The meaning of the Balkans: chaos and conflict?

The Balkans, as a label, has a number of uses and users. The users include those who have no specialist knowledge, but use the term broadly to connote a set of countries about which they understand little. This understanding usually embraces a sense that the region they have in mind is traditionally a troubled one, populated by irrational peoples historically in conflict with each other. This group might often have no clear idea of which countries comprise the Balkans. A second set of users comprises those in the region and outside who appear to believe that, whatever constitutes the Balkans, there is something mystical and different about the region which entails a strong degree of irrationality, which may indeed explain the existence of conflict there.[1] But for this group of Balkan users, there are also, perhaps, periods of peace. Either way, there is clearly something attractive about these peoples which induces a degree of sentimental identification both by indigenous and exogenous users.[2] 'Balkans' is taken as an explication for everything good and bad.

In reality it is an excuse not to provide better and more specific explanations of characteristics and events. This is most clearly to be understood in the confusion of views expressed about the Yugoslav war of the 1990s. Often, those using the term Balkans in this way sought to, or appeared to, equate those involved on all sides as being equal and bearing equal responsibility for the iniquities of that war. Few were aware (or revealed awareness) of the core of the war: the Serbian project to create a new set of ethnically cleansed borders, carved out of Croatia and Bosnia. (Identifying this core element is not to ignore Croatia's later culpability in prosecuting a similar smaller scale project, following arrangements being made with Serbia (Silber and Little 1995: 324–42)). It was a project conceived, planned and executed by the Serbian political, military and security service élite (Gow 1997: Ch.2).[3] In this context, the term Balkan is used, on occasion perhaps knowingly, at the expense of clear understanding.

The third group of users are specialists. On the whole, these might be judged to be specialists whose use of the label Balkan serves to mark out their territory. By analysing this area, individuals in this group are able to mark out territory in which they can be recognised. Because of the relative complexity of the area and its general reputation as being incomprehensible, this makes them needed.[4] It should be noted that, in this context, there is also a more positive use of the term which is possible. This is the use by experts, particularly those from the countries of the former Yugoslavia, who wish to avoid the use of the equally awkward, ugly and painful use of the term 'former Yugoslavia' and find a wider context in which to set reconciliation and reconstruction work.

At a political level, some Greeks have sought to use the term Balkan in a potentially positive way with a view, apparently, to being seen as having a lead role to play within the region on behalf of the European

Union (although, as will be discussed below, Greece has not always played this role most advantageously) (Economides 1992: 27; Couloumbis and Yannas 1995: 393–6). Athens, 'with the best connections to the West', was, according to Thanos Veremis, 'ideally placed to play the stabilising role of the honest broker in the Balkans' (Veremis 1994: 64). Beyond this, the term Balkan has been a useful marketing device and shorthand for some experts and actors regarding the Yugoslav war. Certain volumes which have nothing substantive to do with the majority of Balkan countries (which only appear incidentally in them) nonetheless use the word in their title (Woodward 1995; Owen 1995).

The meaning of the term Balkans is generally not fixed, although there is clearly a conventional understanding among experts. While some use the term Balkan somewhat lazily to mean the former Yugoslavia, others, in non-expert usage, incorporate Hungary as one of the Balkan states. As far as this is explicable, it rests implicitly on the historical imprint of the Turkish Ottoman Empire. However, although the Turks progressed as far as both Budapest and Vienna, Austria is never thought of as 'Balkan'. Similarly, parts of the Middle East which were under Ottoman rule are not included by Balkan users. Conversely, Montenegro, which is part of any definition of the Balkans, always maintained some degree of independence from the Turks.

This somewhat fuzzy use of the term Balkan is in part a function of history and war, particularly associations with the Ottoman presence on the peninsula between the European continent and the Middle East. From the Crusades onwards, the peninsula was the main strategic channel from Europe to the Middle East (Brown 1992: 3–4). As the Ottomans moved towards Europe, then as they were gradually pushed back, there were wars on the peninsula over a period of more than 500 years. These wars were generally matters of empire, although in the course of the nineteenth century and, especially, in the twentieth century, these were also wars of independence and state formation as Turkish rule weakened and national movements emerged, fighting the Ottomans and then each other.

This overall history meant that many different peoples were pushed around the peninsula, settled in different places and among each other, and in many cases became intermingled. It is this intermingling of many different peoples and lands on a relatively small peninsula which most gives sense to characterisation using the term 'Balkans' (although there are other places in the world, such as the Transcaucasus, central Africa, or Indonesia, where there is comparable intermingling and complexity).

Among experts, in the twentieth century the Balkans conventionally comprised Turkey, Greece, Albania, Bulgaria, Romania and Yugoslavia – but not Hungary (Brown 1992). Although the region can be defined geographically as pertaining to the countries and peoples of the Balkan peninsula, other features which are usually taken to characterise a region in terms of international relations are absent, such as shared political or cultural structures and values (Bennett 1995: 215–18). The six countries regarded as Balkan in this context, apart from co-location on the peninsula and a past which had generally included Ottoman occupation, had little in common. Greece and Turkey were both NATO members, but bitter antagonists (see below). Albania and Yugoslavia were both under communist rule, but outside Soviet influence – and generally hostile towards one another. Bulgaria and Romania were both allies within Moscow's Warsaw Treaty Organisation, but the former was Moscow's most docile ally, while the latter was the least integrated member of the pact and conducted an independently oriented foreign policy; in addition, the two countries had submerged disputes, including ones regarding mutual borders. Thus, as far anything defined the region in political or security terms, it was diversity and enmity.

With the dissolution of the Socialist Federative Republic of Yugoslavia in the 1990s, Slovenia and Croatia sought to put as much distance as possible between themselves and 'the Balkans'. Both portrayed themselves as central European countries which have more in common with Austria, Hungary and the Czech Republic than with the other former Yugoslav states. Of the two, Slovenia was considerably more successful, quickly reorienting itself towards central and western Europe, while Croatia's continuing implication in the Yugoslav war (and the near constant references to the war in Croatia and Bosnia as 'the Balkan war') meant that Zagreb's case was less persuasive than Ljubljana's.[5]

The break-up of Yugoslavia became a particular problem regarding use of the term Balkan in at least two ways. First because it raised further issues about which countries the term encompassed – whether or not all the states emerging from the Yugoslav incubator should be seen as Balkan states. Second, the war which accompanied Yugoslavia's fracturing fitted the common corruption of the term Balkan and emphasised it. Here was something typically Balkan, according to this type of understanding: confusion, conflict and irrationality. Trouble in the Balkans, famously not worth the bones of one of Bismarck's Pomeranian Grenadiers, were not worth the effort of proper attention. Aside from the impact of this approach on the Yugoslav war, this attitude had disadvantageous consequences for Bulgaria, in particular (as will be discussed below).

As we have seen, then, the term Balkans can be obfuscatory, indeterminate, contested, counterproductive and even harmful. There can be little sensible discussion of security matters in south-eastern Europe if the starting point is uncertain and likely neither to permit sensible discussion about security questions, nor positive practical action. Most of all the term is problematic regarding definition because there is little, aside from physical location, which defines a clear region in security terms.

The remainder of this analysis looks at security issues affecting the countries of south-eastern Europe co-located on and around the Balkan peninsula. Croatia, Bosnia and Hercegovina, the Federal Republic of

Yugoslavia (Serbia and Montenegro), Macedonia, Albania, Greece, Romania, Bulgaria and Turkey, along with the ambiguous cases of Slovenia and the extra-peninsula case of Cyprus as the focus of Greek–Turkish competition, comprise the countries of south-eastern Europe. Together they represent a diversity of political and security issues which in some cases are linked, but in others are wholly discrete.

The following review of those security issues and relationships starts from the understanding that it is of little practical, or positive, use to incorporate them under a regional umbrella (or label) and will demonstrate the diversity among these countries and the concerns which affect them. Rather, it is only by treating the security questions which emerge on their own merits, as opposed to a subset of questions which hang on a regional context and definition, that it will be possible to address them adequately. One thing which brings unity to these questions is their being significantly affected by international, most notably western, approaches to them. The degree of western engagement will determine the extent to which the different sets of issues affecting discrete sets of countries in south-eastern Europe can be dealt with.

Security issues in south-eastern Europe: Aegean and Mediterranean issues

At the beginning of the Yugoslav war in 1991, there were many voices in parts of western Europe urging their political leaderships to leave the emerging problems alone: what interest, they asked, did France, or the UK, or Spain have in this conflict? Ranged against them in public discourse were those who exhorted their political leaderships to become engaged. However, rarely were the arguments of the interventionists clearly formed as an answer to their opponents' question on interest. Political leaderships were not easily persuaded to drop their reluctance to approach the Yugoslav war as a priority of security policy.

However, the eventual realisation that real interests were at stake, it seems, reflected some sense that the problems of a radically diverse and divided south-eastern Europe are ones which impinge strongly on all European Union member-states, for example, because they touch immediately on the concerns or situation of some members. For any country which has elected to carry out some part of its security policy through membership of a collective body, such as the EU, or NATO, or even, in some cases, the UN, because doing so is thought to have value, this necessarily implicates those countries with the problems of others. Otherwise, the value of the body as an instrument of security policy would itself be undermined: why should any state be a partner, or ally, if the collective body proves unable to address the concerns of some of its members? Maintaining high value (and ultimately security) means commitment for all member-states.[6]

Because of its membership in both the major pillars of security in

western Europe, any concern of Greece becomes an issue for its partners and allies. There were three apparent foci for Greece's immediate
security interests in the 1990s: Macedonia, Cyprus and Turkey. Although through most of the 1990s it was the Macedonian issue which
proved to be the most obvious focus of Greek concern, beneath the sur-
face Greek policy over Macedonia was implicitly driven by its relationship with Turkey and its experience of Cyprus.

The prospective independence of Macedonia as the Yugoslav federation broke up in 1991 presented Greece with a particular concern. Macedonian independence had a variety of implications for Greece. On
one level, an independent Macedonia would be a fragile state which
could become unstable and vulnerable to conflict. This would have
been undesirable. Therefore, as a second strand to Athens' approach to
this issue it formed an informal alliance with the Serbian political
leadership in Belgrade to maintain pressure on Macedonia in the hope
that it would not become independent, or that it would return to the
Yugoslav fold. However, these were diplomatic initiatives subordinated
to a principal policy initiative which was channelled through the EC
and which, in Greek explanations, was seen as keeping open channels
of communication with Belgrade.

There were two stages in this Greek policy. The first was to insert a
seemingly innocuous provision in the text of the guidelines on recognition of the independence of new states emerging from the collapsed
Yugoslav and Soviet communist federations (later, this was also to embrace the division of Czechoslovakia).[7] That provision was that recognition of an independent international personality should only be
granted where the state in question had no outstanding territorial claim
on an EC member-state, or on any other country.

The second stage in Greek policy was to exercise its veto in the European Council after Macedonia's application for recognition by the EC
member-states had been judged to be consistent with the guidelines by
the EC Conference Advisory Commission. Thus, despite a recommendation that Macedonia was suitable for recognition, the European Council did not agree to extend full diplomatic links to Macedonia. Greece
blocked recognition on the grounds that, according to Greece, Macedonia had a territorial claim on Greek territory – which meant that, in
Greek eyes, it was not consistent with the guidelines. This position
caused frustration and bewilderment among other EC member-states, as
well as outside the EC. To most external observers, the Greek position
appeared to be absurd. Greece as a member of both the EU and NATO,
as well as having a modern armed force over 170 000 strong, seemed to
have things out of proportion in claiming that Macedonia threatened
Greek territorial integrity: Macedonia had only two million inhabitants
and a fledgling armed force of only 7000, lacking in significant arms.

The direct basis for Athens' position stemmed from small elements
of the would-be independent country's attributes of statehood. Prime
among these were Macedonia's flag and its constitution, both underpin-

ning a Greek objection to the very name of the country. The former was an issue of symbolic importance as the flag depicted the Star of Vergina (Pettifer 1994: 88). Use of the Star was seen as a claim on Hellenic heritage and a claim to the land where the Star lay. Perverse or unrealistic as it was to construe the use of the Star in this way, it was also not without any foundation. If seen in a broader context, the question of the flag was compounded by that of the constitution. Although the 1991 Macedonian constitution made no claim to Greek territory, one article expressed interest in the cultural rights of Macedonians in other countries. Macedonia made specific written political and legal declarations to the EC that it had no claims whatsoever, as well as making amendments to the constitution,[8] but this was not enough for Greece.

The crux of the Macedonian question was its uncertain position after the collapse of the Ottoman Empire, with Serbia, Greece, Bulgaria and Albania each coveting all or part of it (Poulton 1995: 47). That situation continued to have relevance in the 1940s as communist-ruled Yugoslavia established the Republic of Macedonia against a background of aspiring to create a communist Balkan federation which would incorporate both Bulgaria and Greece, thus uniting all three regions of geographic Macedonia. Thus, aspirations to unite all three Macedonian regions were specific to the foreign policy agenda of communist Yugoslavia in the 1940s. In Greece's official position, therefore, in the 1990s the use of the name Macedonia by the new state was seen as an extension of that agenda which, in itself, constituted a threat to Greek territorial integrity. As a consequence the Hellenic republic vowed to block recognition of the newly independent state while ever it used a name which, according to Athens, was exclusively Greek property. In the context of the EU's emergent Common Foreign and Security Policy, this meant, effectively, a block overall on recognition by any of the EU member-states.

It was only with difficulty and against the grain of national feeling that Greece, having grievously damaged its relations with its western partners and allies by adopting this position on Macedonia, was able, with considerable international encouragement and assistance, to pull back from a policy which neither served its own immediate interests well, nor the regional stability and the interests of the international community. In May 1993, Macedonia was admitted to the General Assembly of the United Nations under the temporary name of 'Former Yugoslav Republic of Macedonia' (FYROM). That temporary name permitted the Skopje government to begin to establish various international links while being involved in international mediation on the name issue and other disputes with Greece. The major breakthrough in international mediation efforts came in 1995 when Macedonia and Greece agreed on a relatively minor (but symbolically major) change to the Macedonia flag. Greece then lifted its trade blockade against Macedonia and began to normalise relations while continuing indefinite negotiations about a formula to end the name dispute. It was not an issue which had gone away, nor one which would be resolved for some time to come. But it was one which had assumed more appropriate proportions.

The real issue for Greece on Macedonia was only partly to do with the newly independent state itself and the ghost of the challenges of the late 1940s. It was also a function of Greece's relationships with Cyprus and Turkey. The issue of Macedonia's name was of primary importance because recognition of the state using that name would imply recognition of the Macedonians as an ethno-national group (Poulton 1993: 178–80). That, in turn, would lead to a situation in which Greece, a country formally without minority groups, would have to accept the existence of the Slav Macedonians in northern Greece. In itself, this might not constitute a problem. However, recognition of one minority would logically lead to recognition of others – Albanians and, especially, Turks.[9]

For Greece, in reality, this was the heart of the issue and it was linked to Cyprus, where experience showed (in a simplistic characterisation) that if you acknowledge the existence of a Turkish minority, that minority then becomes the basis for Turkish invasion and control of territory, followed by the proclamation of a putative independent Turkish republic.[10] This is what had happened in 1974 and continued to be a neuralgic point for Athens. At that time, Greek generals had been contemplating an invasion of their own to unite Cyprus with Greece. However, it was Turkey which invaded the island to facilitate the creation of the so-called Turkish Republic of Northern Cyprus which it sought to unite with Turkey.

The division of Cyprus is the most contentious of the issues which create an antagonistic relationship between Greece and Turkey. In the course of 1996, this issue threatened to erupt in new violence, 22 years after the Turkish invasion. Tension between Athens and Ankara also came close to open armed hostilities over disputed Aegean Islands which were formally sovereign Greek territory, but lie immediately off the Turkish coast. This dispute is significant both as an issue about coastal territorial waters, and as an issue relating to exploitation of seabed resources. The Imia incident saw a stand-off between Greek and Turkish naval forces (Institute of Neo-Hellenic Research 1996). As the countries came close to an exchange of blows, hostility was only tempered by US diplomatic pressure.

The US, in particular, and NATO as a whole had a responsibility in this region. One aspect of this role concerned NATO itself and armaments. During the 1990s, Greco–Turkish tension was compounded by a qualitative increase in armaments in the two countries under the NATO Cascade programme, derived from implementation of the CFE Treaty, which saw surplus modern Treaty-covered equipment in central Europe being transferred to the flank countries. This did not increase the number of weapons on either side, but enhanced the quality of them and was generally perceived as an arms race. That perception was part of the pattern of increasing tension. In the end, a war between Greece and Turkey was avoided, but the issue remained unresolved and looked set to require further US and NATO management in the future.

Following the Imia incident, Greece and Cyprus began to activate a joint defence doctrine which had been declared in 1993,[11] without much attention and which had lain dormant. This was again relatively unnoticed, but a significant step up the ladder of tension. Another step was taken in this context when Cyprus was at the heart of new levels of tension at the beginning of 1997. The Greek–Cypriot government of Cyprus struck a deal (with Greece giving assistance) to purchase a new air-defence system. This was seen by Turkey as a provocative measure and it openly threatened air strikes against Greek–Cypriot installations if the purchase went ahead and was implemented. Again, NATO allies, particularly the US, were engaged in calming tense relations – in this case being unusually unequivocal in criticism of and warnings to Turkey about its threats.

By the mid-1990s, Cyprus was at the heart of international efforts to move towards a resolution of the dispute which had affected the island since independence and, especially, since the *de facto* division following the Turkish invasion of 1974. In that time, there had been a UN peace-keeping force deployed on the island, but little movement towards the creation of conditions for a political resolution which would permit that peace-keeping force to complete its mission and leave. In the 1990s, however, a number of interlinked issues led to initiatives over Cyprus.

One of these was pressure on the UN system and frustration at maintaining long-term commitments in places such as Cyprus. Another was the realisation, following Athens' reaction to the independence of Macedonia, that Greek sensitivity was in part linked to the Cyprus issue and also that Greek compromise over Macedonia might be more forthcoming if there were movement over Cyprus. This was given an added edge, in the context of the EU, of Cyprus' prospective membership of the Union – something which could only become a serious possibility once the security situation on the island had been improved. All this was also linked to a desire on the part of some EU members to influence the internal political situation in Turkey.

During France's tenure of the Presidency of the European Council in the second half of 1994, the priority for Paris was to bring Turkey closer to the EU. The 1990s had seen a number of former communist countries in central and eastern Europe leave Turkey standing in the stakes for prospective EU membership. Turkey, in the meantime, had witnessed a growth in extremist, or ideological, Islamicism. France, deeply concerned about Islamic extremism, saw signals of more positive links with the EU as a means of encouraging European and democratic trends in the country. Turkey's relationship with the EU, as with Macedonia's, had been subject to a Greek veto. France used its position to move all these issues forward. Following this, the former UK Permanent Representative to the UN, Sir David Hannay, was appointed as a

special envoy. Overall, Greece was encouraged to find ways forward on
Macedonia and to relax its position on Turkey, while Turkey was given
some sense of that relaxation as a precursor to encouraging the Turkish
Cypriots to discuss possibilities of a federation – leading to a political
solution which would facilitate the island's potential membership of the
EU. The downside to all this was that once there was movement on an
issue that had been static for over two decades, tension between the two
communities rose again on the island. This showed that although EU
and other international initiatives were necessary for promoting security
in the region, there were no straightforward paths to resolution.

Security issues in south-eastern Europe: eastern Adriatic and Black Sea issues

The international role on Macedonia was equally crucial, albeit of a
wholly different character. Since the end of 1992, the first ever UN
preventive peace-keeping deployment had been based in Macedonia
with a mission, technically, to patrol, monitor and report on the borders
between Macedonia and neighbouring Serbia and Albania. In reality, its
mission was to deter potential cross-border military activity and to seal
the border in the event of armed conflict breaking out. Originally comprising 700 Nordic troops, these were supplemented by 300 US military
personnel in the summer of 1993 and the balance within the force was
later altered to incorporate 500 US personnel and fewer Nordics (Gow
1997: Ch.5).

The force was deployed, following a failure to respond to calls for a
preventive deployment in Bosnia and Hercegovina, in response to a difficult situation in which it was possible that a major armed conflict
could emerge. There were a number of ways in which this might
emerge, mostly focused on the presence of large ethnic Albanian populations in Serbia and Macedonia. Trouble might have stemmed from the
actions of the Serbian government against Macedonia, or in the southern Serbian province of Kosovo where the population was 90 per cent
ethnic Albanian. Alternatively, there was the chance that ethnic Albanians in either Kosovo or Macedonia might initiate hostilities. Finally,
there was the possibility that an incident might accidentally spark conflict.

Whichever route led to the outbreak of conflict, it was clear that a
number of countries would be likely to feel impelled to step into the
fray – Albania, Greece and Serbia among them, with Turkey and even
Bulgaria also in the frame. Although technically unprovable, it seemed
reasonable to suppose that the UN force, accompanied by OSCE and
EU activity, did much to reduce the possibility of conflict implicating a
number of countries. Nonetheless, there could be no absolute com-
placency as, whatever else happened, the core issue of Kosovo remained unresolved and increasingly subject to violent agitation.

This was particularly clear with the emergence of the Kosovo Liberation Army (as reported in the *Nedjenji Telegraf* on 22 January 1997) responsible for carrying out terrorist attacks during 1996 and playing into the hands of Serbian political leaders seeking to maintain repressive control of the province which was the historic heart of the medieval Serbian kingdom. While the situation in Kosovo itself, as an internal matter for Serbia itself, could only be treated with circumspection, there was no doubting that various international efforts in other countries had made for a less volatile situation overall. This was especially so following US initiatives on Albania. Greece's changing and more positive position on its northern neighbour also contributed to regional stability.

Contributions to stability in the region were not always recognised, however. Bulgaria, for example, played a strongly positive role *vis-à-vis* its neighbours in the early years of the Yugoslav war. Historically, Bulgaria has been one of four wolves with its hungry eyes on Macedonian territory. Serbian, Greek and Albanian responses to the dissolution of the Yugoslav federation did nothing to persuade the external observer that historic perspectives had been eliminated. Bulgaria, in contrast, broke the historic mould by being the first country to recognise the independence of Macedonia in January 1992.

Bulgaria's recognition of Macedonia was a positive move, contributing to certainty and stability over statehood and borders in the region (although there would be no formal indication before the signing of bilateral agreements in both Bulgarian and Macedonian languages four years later that Sofia accepted the existence of Macedonians as a distinct ethno-national group). An even more remarkable counterpart to this diplomacy, however, was Sofia's work to secure recognition for Macedonia by both Russia and Turkey in January 1992. The former, although it was not to implement recognition by establishing full diplomatic ties for several months, was a major coup for Bulgaria – taking the initiative with its Slav big brother.

The latter was even more remarkable, on two counts. The first was because of the historical enmity between the former imperial power in the region and one of its former territories. The second was that in the 1980s, the fading communist regime in Bulgaria had sought to bolster its position through a vicious campaign against ethnic-Turks in Bulgaria, forcing them to change their names, or to emigrate to Turkey, in many cases. This put pressure on Turkey and created tension. Following the collapse of the communist regime, the democratic government had expressly set out to redress the transgressions of its communist predecessor, by building confidence with the Turkish minority, even encouraging those who had left the country to return (Carnegie Endowment and The Aspen Institute 1996: 131–2; Poulton 1993:129–71)). A corollary of this was a radically transformed relationship between Sofia and Ankara. It was this positive relationship which fostered the mutual recognition of Macedonia.

In terms of its highly commendable record over the Turkish minority and Turkey, and its recognition of Macedonian independence, Bulgaria had a rough deal. Its contribution to regional stability went unheeded, let alone rewarded. And the government's approach to Turkey and the Turkish minority was a model for others in a period where ethnic tensions and minority rights were being taken as the main themes in European and international security.[12] Yet, this model of good practice was largely ignored.

In time Bulgaria was to receive some international attention, but for negative reasons. With the democratic government being replaced by one of the former communists' Bulgarian Socialist Party, Bulgaria's initially good implementation of the UN sanctions regime against the Federal Republic of Yugoslavia, with Serbia one of its neighbours, began to wither as there was no compensation for the losses implementation brought to the country (Woodward 1995: 371). As a result, the authorities came to be criticised, to some extent unfairly, for turning a blind eye to breaches of the international sanctions regime.

Bulgaria's generally positive role in the region was not noticeably diminished by the arrival of the Socialists. Indeed, under the Socialists, a further positive aspect to Bulgarian policy was apparent. In the summer of 1994, Bulgaria organised one of the first joint exercises to be placed under the umbrella of NATO's Partnership for Peace Programme (PfP), launched earlier that year. Although this was an exercise for which planning had begun before the announcement of PfP, it was quickly identified with the programme as the cooperation it represented reflected not only the nature and intention of the programme, but also a significant measure of confidence-building.

The Partnership for Peace naval exercise held off the Bulgarian coastal town of Burgas, in the Black Sea and called 'Breeze 94',[13] brought together vessels from traditional enemies and antagonists. Those involved were Bulgaria, the US, Russia, Turkey, Greece, Romania and Ukraine. Again, however, despite the US wanting to repeat the exercise as soon as possible, Bulgaria itself got no real credit either for its engagement under the PfP initiative, or for having brought together countries with deep antagonisms such as Greece and Turkey and Russia and Ukraine (which at the time were deeply divided over the fate of the former Soviet Black Sea Fleet). Whatever Bulgaria did that was positive went unnoticed, probably because it was unproblematic.

It seemed that only the prospect of Bulgaria's bankrupt economy generating internal strife and tension with one or more of its neighbours would draw Bulgaria to the attention of the international community. Bulgaria suffered in the 1990s from an internally stalled reform, but crucially from a lack of international encouragement, despite being a meritorious case. Instead, it was seen as a Balkan country and as such was masked by the misleadingly named 'Balkan war' even though it had little to do with most of the countries which could be regarded as Balkan.

As with Bulgaria, Romania too had little connection to the 'Balkan war'. Although its record on reform showed next to no effort, it was also clear that Romania's internal sluggardliness was not translated into international trouble-making. Indeed, the country's three main security concerns lay not with the Yugoslav war, or Bulgaria, to the south in 'the Balkans'. Rather, Bucharest's security interests lay in its relationship with the EU and with NATO, both of which it wished to join and with both of which it engaged in cooperation. Otherwise, its major concerns were Transilvania and Moldova. Its relationship with Hungary over the Hungarian minority in the Transilvanian region within Romania was traditionally an issue of friction between the countries. There were encouraging signs, however, at the end of 1996, with the two countries signing a preliminary agreement on the issue with the encouragement of EU and NATO member-states.

Moldova presented a different kind of problem, being, to a large extent, a second Romanian state – one about which there had been talk of unification in the early 1990s, following the collapse of the Soviet Union. However, Russian military activity in the eastern Moldovan Transdniestr region and the taste developed by political leaders in Chishinau, the Moldovan capital, for running their own independent state meant that unification was removed as a topic of discussion, while Russian activity inside Moldova only confirmed traditional Romanian antipathy to Russia. Moldova, as with Bucharest's other security concerns, had little to do with anything which would traditionally be regarded as the Balkans.

Romania's real concerns, then, are other than 'Balkan'. Apart from a sometimes questionable record on implementation of sanctions in the Yugoslav war (although this improved once the WEU had begun to give assistance on implementation along the River Danube), Romania had little connection with the Yugoslav war. Although not to be cast in as positive light as that which Bulgaria merited, Romania too, to some extent was disregarded by the West – officially seen as part of central and eastern Europe, like Bulgaria, but also like its Black Sea neighbour, not the same as Poland, Hungary and the Czech Republic. As with the other countries and situations in south-eastern Europe already discussed, the crucial factor in Romania's further development could only be its relationship with bodies such as the EU and NATO.

It was the Yugoslav war which overshadowed everything else in south-eastern Europe in the 1990s. The Socialist Federative Republic of Yugoslavia dissolved into five states – four of which were gaining independence and one which represented a new joint state formed by the remaining two states which had previously formerly exercised their sovereign rights through the old federation (Gow 1997: Ch.4). The Yugoslav war, although tinged with historical tones and ethnic dimensions, was essentially a war about statehood. Slovenia secured its statehood and independence at relatively low cost and was quickly able to put distance between itself and the other Yugoslav states, although usually not as much as it would have wanted. Slovenia's focus and identity quickly became aligned with the central European countries.

The core to the war, however, was the clash of state projects between Serbia, Croatia and Bosnia. The essence of the war was the attempt by Serbia to carve a new set of borders incorporating parts of Croatia and parts of Bosnia and Hercegovina to form a 'mini-Yugoslavia' (or a 'Great Serbia', in nationalist eyes). This was countered by Croatia and Bosnia and Hercegovina both of which sought to maintain the integrity of their borders. Croatia, often ambiguous about Bosnia and Hercegovina, made its own efforts to annex territory in western Hercegovina and central Bosnia during 1993. This effort was driven back by Bosnian government forces. But Croatia was still left with control of territory and, as Croatian forces which had received American assistance helped the Bosnian army to push back the Bosnian Serbs in 1995, it gained an increasingly influential position in Bosnia.

With the Bosnian Serbs being granted a 'republic' within Bosnia and Hercegovina and Croatia maintaining an influential position, especially over the Bosnian Croat para-state of Herceg Bosna, there remained some uncertainty and ambiguity over Bosnia's future. While the international community and the Bosnian government sought to ensure the integrity of the Bosnian state, the ambiguity in the agreement required to obtain signatures meant that there appeared to be scope for Serbs and Croats seeking to separate territory from Bosnia to believe that this might still be possible. Thus although the major Serbian initiative and the lesser Croatian attempt to dismember Bosnia and Hercegovina by force had been defeated, in the eyes of those who had been denied, this was possibly only temporary.

The shifting balance of power in 1995 created the conditions for peace talks which were held under American auspices at Dayton, Ohio, in November that year. Thus, it became possible to draw armed hostilities to a close. However, there were two crucial aspects to the success at Dayton. The first was the role international, particularly US, pressure (including military action) had played in bringing the conflict to a close. The second was recognition that only continued international engagement would secure the terms agreed and turn the peace agreement into a genuine peace.

However, the international record during the first year of peace was inconsistent. There was a major international military engagement to implement the military aspects of the General Framework for Peace agreed at Dayton, the NATO organised IFOR (which comprised 53 000 troops from 34 countries, including around 25 000 US military personnel); IFOR, the implementation force (see Chapter 3), was succeeded after one year by SFOR, the 33 000-strong Stabilisation force, for a further 18 months. In all respects, military implementation was judged to have been good.

On the civilian side, implementation was less strikingly successful. Although there could be mitigating arguments pointing out that NATO had, in effect, been planning for deployment at least since 1993, the ci-vilian side of implementation had not properly begun to be conceived until after Dayton. The reality was that the civilian components com-prised five-sixths of the Dayton accords, but that during the first year of implementation, five-sixths of that five-sixths remained to be started. This was a context in which those who still believed in and sought the dismemberment of Bosnia could think that they might still achieve their goal. Although there was a need in the international community for the agreement to work, there was also a dilatory approach to civilian im-plementation with the inevitable corollary that successful integration of the two entities envisaged in the agreement (the Federation of Bosnia-Hercegovina and the Republika Srpska) would be that much harder to achieve.

Clearly, with the US initiating a 'train and equip' programme for the Bosnian government alongside the military peace-implementation forces, there was an implicit fallback position: if peace did not work out and Bosnia's reintegration begin, there would be a return to major armed hostilities, with the Bosnian army seeking to finish off a job it (mistakenly) thought it was prevented from accomplishing in 1995. However, a return to major armed hostilities would be seen as an inter-national failure following such a major commitment to obtaining and implementing peace. Therefore the imperative rested with outside ele-ments, primarily with the US, the EU and its member-states and NATO and the remaining members of the Alliance, to ensure that civilian im-plementation was successful and that Serbs and Croatia and Croats knew that there was no question of an international partition of Bosnia.

As with the other parts of south-eastern Europe, the Eastern Adriatic countries of Croatia, Bosnia-Hercegovina and Serbia have a peculiar set of linked problems and (again as in other cases) these intertwined prob-lems are not connected with other situations in south-eastern Europe (although Serbia is implicated in questions affecting Macedonia and Al-bania, as was seen above). Most of all – again in line with other security issues in south-eastern Europe – it is the influence and engagement of international, especially western, institutions and western countries which will be the single most important factor defining matters of re-gional security and the presence or absence of armed hostilities.

Security in south-eastern Europe and the meaning of the Balkans: EU and NATO commitment

There is no security question in south-eastern Europe which is not cru-cially affected by the international, particularly western, position on it. The salience of this in the most febrile cases (Greece and Turkey, Ma-cedonia and Bosnia-Hercegovina) is self-evident. This is true for all situations and countries in the region. South-eastern Europe is not unique in being significantly affected by western approaches and attitudes.

It is significantly different, however, in the sense that it suffers from the persistent use of the term 'Balkan' which carries with it connotations of blood and confusion. The application of this term is generally prejudicial and detrimental both to understanding of the issues and actors involved and to appropriate engagement in managing or resolving a set of unconnected and disparate issues. In a sense, the term 'Balkans' refers to a non-region in which there is a good number of separate security issues, none of which benefits from being corralled with the others. In most cases, this is not only not beneficial, but it is decisively harmful.

The label 'Balkans' is almost an excuse to dismiss the critical sets of problems which affect the countries of south-eastern Europe. Yet, ultimately, as the Yugoslav war demonstrated, those problems cannot be dismissed. The term 'Balkans' connotes a south-eastern Europe in which there is no political or cultural cohesion. The only way a single south-eastern European region might be expected to form is as a result of western engagement with disparate security questions. Indeed, the only way those questions might be resolved is through western agency. That agency will only make sense if it recognises that there is little or nothing that defines the Balkan countries as forming a region, aside from their geographic co-location and diversity. Any solution to the security problems of south-eastern Europe must begin with the recognition that the problems of the countries in the region are not all one 'Balkan virus', but different infections and afflictions which must be separated out and treated on their own.

Notes

1.   George F. Kennan, for example, wrote in 1993 that historical factors 'had the effect of thrusting into the southeastern reaches of the European continent a salient of non-European characteristics. ... It is the undue predominance among the Balkan peoples of these particular qualities, and others that might be mentioned, that seems to be decisive as a determinant of the troublesome, baffling and dangerous situation that marks that part of the world today' (Kennan 1993).

2.   Sells (1997) exemplifies this, both in itself and in the quotes it uses. For example, Sells himself appears to have a sentimental soft spot for the Serbs whom he describes as 'a paradoxical people' and implies that the other Balkan peoples (by which he seems only to mean south Slavs speaking Serbo-Croat) are the same (p. 34). Sells also quotes a Croat's explanation for the destruction of places of worship in the conflict: '"You don't understand," he said, "this is the Balkans"' (p. 36).

3.   A more extensive interpretation of this project, supported by documents submitted in evidence, was given in testimony at the trial of Du_an Tadi_, the first trial to be held by the International Criminal Tribunal for the former Yugoslavia in The Hague, 7–13 May, 1996.

4. Jonathan Eyal of the Royal United Services Institute in London and Misha Glenny (1992), formerly of the BBC, seem to me to fall into this category. Both write with verve and have carved out a niche as experts on the Balkans, rather than south-eastern Europe, whose explanations, while showing awareness of the Serbian leadership's role in the Yugoslav war of the 1990s, tend to focus their analysis and explanation on the character of the peoples in the region.

5. For example, the Foreign and Commonwealth Office in London gave responsibility for dealing with Slovenia to its central and eastern European Department, whereas Croatia continued to be covered by the eastern Adriatic Department which covered Albania and the other former Yugoslav countries.

6. This also means that there is a requirement for the member-states to behave responsibly.

7. 'Guidelines on the Recognition of New States in Eastern Europe and in the Soviet Union' adopted by the EC Council on 16 December 1991. London: Foreign and Commonwealth Office, 1991; 'EC Declaration Concerning the Conditions for Recognition of New States' adopted at the Extraordinary EPC Ministerial Meeting, Brussels, 16 December 1991, reprinted in Trifunovska, S. (ed.) (1994).

8. Amendment no 1, 6 January 1992, stated explicitly: 'The Republic of Macedonia has no territorial claim on neighbouring states'. Amendment no 2 further clarified the situation: 'The Republic shall not infringe the sovereign rights of other States or interfere in their internal affairs.' This amendment was added to the first paragraph of Article 49 which had expressed Macedonia's 'care for the status and rights of those persons belonging to the Maceodnian people in neighbouring countries'. These amendments were acknowledged by the Badinter Advisory Commission in its opinion that Macedonia met the terms of the EC guidelines to the European Council on 11 January 1992. For references see: Opinion No.6 On International Recognition of the Socialist Republic of Macedonia by the European Community and Its Member States, Paris, 11 January 1992, reprinted in Trifunovska, S. (ed.) (1994): 495–6; 'Constitution of the Republic of Macedonia', reprinted in Trifunovska, S. (ed.) (1994): 391.

9. Greece recognises a Muslim religious minority in Thrace, but this comprises both Turks and Pomaks, while there is very little information on the Albanians (also classed as Muslims) because of the Greek authorities's official position. See Poulton (1993): 182–9.

10. It should be noted that my characterisation is a little simplified for effect. In reality, although there is no acknowledgement of national minority groups in Greece, there is a Turkish consulate in Thrace which liaises with over 100 000 Turkish-speaking 'Muslim Greeks'.

11. In 1986, then Prime Minster Andreas Paparadreou made an explicit commitment that if Turkey were to take armed action over Cyprus again, this would be a *causus belli*. I am indebted to Despina Taxiarchi for clarification on these points.

12. The importance accorded to minority rights could be seen in the work of the EC Conference on Yugoslavia in the second half of 1991, where emphasis was on minority issues. The focus on minority questions could only be seen in various OSCE documents, including the Paris Charter of 1990, the Moscow Document of 1991, the Helsinki Document of 1992

(which established the office of a High Commissioner for National Minorities) and the comprehensive security model agreed at the 1995 Budapest summit of the OSCE.

13. There had been one previous maritime exercise involving a number of countries in the Baltic Sea and two bilateral land exercises, one in Poland with the UK during May and one in the Czech Republic with France at the beginning of June.

References

Bennett, A. L. (1995) *International Organisations: Principles and Issues*, Englewood Cliffs NJ: Prentice Hall.

Brown, J. F. (1992) *Nationalism and Democracy: Security in the Balkans*, Aldershot: Dartmouth/RAND.

Carnegie Endowment and The Aspen Institute (1996) *Unfinished Peace: Report of the International Commission on the Balkans*, Washington DC.

Couloumbis, T. A. and Yannas, P. (1995) 'Greek Security Challenges in the 1990s', in Couloumbis, T. A., Veremis, T. M. and Dokos, T. P. *The Southeast European Yearbook 1994–95*, Athens: Hellenic Foundation for European and Foreign Policy.

Economides, S. (1992) 'The Balkan Security Agenda: Security and Regionalism in the New Europe', *London Defence Studies*, 10, Centre for Defence Studies/Brassey's.

Glenny, M. (1992) *The Fall of Yugoslavia*, Harmondsworth: Penguin.

Gow, J. (1997) *Triumph of the Lack of Will: International Diplomacy and the Yugoslav War*, London and New York: Hurst and Columbia University Press.

Institute of Neo-Hellenic Research (1996) '*Report on the "Limnia-Imia" Islets*', Athens: National Hellenic Research Foundation.

Kennan, G. F. (1993) 'Introduction. The Balkan Crises:1913 and 1993', in *The Other Balkan Wars. A 1913 Carnegie Endowment Enquiry in Retrospect with a New Introduction and Reflections on the Present Conflict*, Washington DC: Carnegie Endowment.

Owen, D. (1995) *Balkan Odyssey*, London: Gollancz.

Pettifer, J. (1994) *The Greeks: The Land and People Since the War*, Harmondsworth: Penguin.

Poulton, H. (1993) *The Balkans:Minorities and States in Conflict: 2nd edn*, London: Minority Rights Group.

Poulton, H. (1995) *Who Are the Macedonians?*, London: Hurst and Co.

Sells, D. (1997) 'Serb "demons" strike back', *The World Today*, 53 (2).

Silber, L. and Little, A. (1995) *The Death of Yugoslavia*, Harmondsworth, London and New York: Penguin and BBC Worldwide.

Trifunovska, S. (ed.) (1994) *Yugoslavia Through Documents: From its Creation to its Dissolution*, Dordrech, Boston and London: Martinus Njihoff.

Veremis, T. (1994) 'Priorities for Athens – a Greek view', *The World Today*, 50 (4).

Woodward, S. (1995) *Balkan Tragedy*, Washington DC: Brookings Institution.

CHAPTER 10

Conclusion

G. WYN REES

After surveying the various chapters in this book, it becomes clear that to try and generalise about security in Europe is fraught with difficulties. This reflects, to a large extent, the enormous diversity of the continent and the problem of defining the boundaries of particular regions. In some cases, such as the territories of the former Soviet Union, the regions have changed beyond all recognition since the end of the Cold War, while in others, as Gow has shown in the Balkans (Chapter 9), diversity has outweighed the similarities between neighbouring states. Just as there were differences between the various regions of Europe during the Cold War, so these variations were magnified when the tension subsided. The straightjacket of the Cold War, that had overlaid regional issues with a system-level confrontation, was swept away. Its place has been usurped by a mélange of different perspectives, some of which preceded the Cold War. There is now disagreement on what the main security issues are, as well as a variety of prescriptions about how best security can be assured.

The continent of Europe may not justify the description of a 'security complex' because the security priorities of many of the actors in the various parts of Europe are different. It can sometimes appear as if the only factor that binds the regions of 'Europe' together is a negative form of interdependence: a recognition of the potential for shared pain that conflict, environmental damage or the movement of refugees in one area could have for all of the others. For example, the prospect of civil war or state disintegration in the Mahgreb could send thousands of refugees flooding into the southern part of Europe, leading to demands that unaffected regions of Europe share the burden. One implication that can be drawn from this study has been that Europe contains a series of regional security complexes that are more compelling than the identification of a continent-wide system. As the evidence of the Cold War system recedes, these regional sub-systems have become more visible.

A useful observation concerns the contrast between the security of western Europe and all the other areas. Western Europe during the postwar period learned to overcome its internal tensions and remove the threat of aggressive nationalism in inter-state relations. The degree of cooperation and the level of integration in the western half was unparalleled in the rest of the continent. As a result, western Europe has evolved into a security community where the threat of force is no longer a consideration between its members. This has made it possible for west European states to evolve towards common views on security problems and aspire to cooperate over crises that take place in areas contiguous to their territories.

The central and east European states have shown themselves eager to integrate into the western security community in order to benefit from its guarantees. They regard this as returning to their historical pattern of development from which they were forcibly diverted by the Cold War and they have expressed their desire to turn their backs on nearly 50 years of enforced bilateral relations with the former Soviet Union. As Latawski has shown in Chapter 5, they are now intent on capitalising on a transformed security environment in which Germany has become a prospective partner and western Europe provides a model for their pattern of development. Meanwhile, sceptics doubt the ability of these states to remain faithful to the western values that they now espouse.

In other regions such as the Balkans, the former Soviet Republics and the Mediterranean, the issues are very different. Here the concept of a security community is alien amid the rivalries and inter-state conflicts that still plague these areas. In the Balkans, for instance, on the one side stand states such as Slovenia that appear to be ripe for inclusion into the western security and economic communities. Yet on the other, are states such as Bosnia-Hercegovina and Albania that are riven by ethnic and civil conflict and dependent on the presence of foreign troops for order and the distribution of humanitarian assistance. Cases such as these served to undermine the optimism of the immediate post-Cold War period that envisaged a collective security regime becoming the security framework for the entire continent. Although the Organisation for Security and Cooperation in Europe embodied that hope, it has never been fulfilled.

It becomes apparent from even a cursory examination of the preceeding chapters that security concerns are not uniform on the continent. First, there are wide variations in the perception of threat. In western Europe, the historical fear of a large-scale military invasion has been replaced by a much more diffuse array of potential risks. Some present a potential military threat to the territorial integrity of western states, such as ballistic missile proliferation and the dissemination of knowledge pertaining to weapons of mass destruction. Yet more of them concern 'soft' security threats such as transnational crime and the danger of instability and societal collapse in areas adjacent to western Europe. As Spencer has indicated, western Europe oscillates in its approach to such soft security problems. Although it acknowledges that most are economic in nature, its approach varies between reaching out with economic assistance to retreating into a siege mentality.

The paucity of direct threats has both permitted and obliged the west Europeans to rethink their security agenda. This rethinking has led to a broadening of the very definition of security which now incorporates environmental matters such as pollution as well as humanitarian issues such as migration and refugee movements. These were issues that were neglected in the past but have been accorded a higher priority in the post-Cold War era. Security now stretches to encapsulate low-intensity threats and issues that could damage the internal fabric of a western society. Concerns such as these are by no means unique to western Europe, but its ability to allocate resources to address them stands in contrast to other regions.

Apart from western Europe, only some of the states within the Nordic region have been able to broaden their definition of security. As demonstrated by Archer (Chapter 7), the Nordic region benefited from less intense confrontation during the Cold War and countries such as Sweden were able to remain neutral, while Denmark and Norway limited their participation in NATO. Ideas of common security were much in evidence in the region before 1989 and therefore the post-Cold War situation has facilitated an exploration of these ideas rather than a fundamental break with the past. Whether or not such ideas can be extended, in due course, to the Baltic states or Russia, remains open to speculation.

In areas such as Russia's 'near abroad' and the Balkans, there has been little evidence of a rethinking of the security agenda. Issues such as environmental degradation continue to be subordinate to more traditional security concerns of a Hobbesian nature. Here, as Gow has related, the issues of greater salience are more likely to be unrest among ethnic minorities, military aggression by neighbouring states or the acquisition of arms by regional powers. While the threats are more complex and varied, the actual agenda of issues has not been transformed in the same way that it has in the West. What has changed, as observed by Hyde-Price in Chapter 2, is the wider context in which these security issues are assessed: namely, the demise of the balance-of-power system on the continent.

A consequence of these variations in regional security issues is that it has become possible to detect the emergence of multiple security discourses across the continent that bear little relation to one another. Whereas during the Cold War there was a common debate about the ramifications of a major East–West conflict, now there can be quite separate debates. For example, the leaking of radioactive materials from Russian nuclear submarines may be a preoccupation of northern European states, while in the south the focus may be on the threat of domestic turmoil and religous discordance in the Mahgreb. Even within regions this process of differentiation has become apparent. Some states within the Nordic region, such as Sweden, may be moving towards a concept of collective security while their neighbours, the Baltic states, fear aggression from Russia and therefore aspire to the collective defence guarantees of NATO membership. Similarly, as Flockhart and Rees have shown in Chapter 4, states within the European Union no longer necessarily share the same security priorities: countries such as Spain and Italy may be concerned with their Mediterranean neighbours, while Germany and Austria may pay most attention to central and eastern Europe.

What has enabled western Europe to move beyond a narrowly power-politics agenda has, to a large extent, been its creation of institutions such as NATO, the European Community/Union and the Western European Union. These institutions have fulfilled a number of important functions. First, they have resolved the tensions between their members, enabling countries such as France and Germany to put an end to the destructive wars that marred their development up until 1945. Economic and political integration through the EC/EU and a collective defence arrangement through NATO has assured the stability of one half of the continent.

Admittedly, this intra-western reconciliation was made possible by the help and direction of the United States. After the end of the Cold War, the role of the US was thrown into question and the drawdown of American personnel from the continent raised the spectre that the US might be preparing to leave. This fear did not materialise and the leadership shown by the Clinton Administration in orchestrating the peace agreement in Bosnia-Hercegovina appeared to strengthen the trans-Atlantic relationship. Yet it would be complacent to assume that the US role in Europe will remain constant forever. The contribution to stability provided by the US should not be taken for granted and could be placed at risk if the west Europeans rely on the Americans to provide leadership in the event of any crisis affecting their interests.

Second, these institutions have prevented western Europe from slipping back into old habits once the Cold War was over. West European integration and collective defence did not unravel after 1990. This confounded the prognostications of realist analysts, such as John Mearsheimer,[1] who believed that only the presence of a powerful external threat, the Soviet empire, had kept the Europeans tied together. Instead, the institutions served as a repository for the progress that had been achieved, while simultaneously facilitating steps forward such as the Treaty on European Union. The future path of integration appears difficult to determine in the light of the modest progress that was achieved at the Amsterdam European Council meeting in June 1997.

This is not to say that the institutions have been exempt from the need to adapt after the Cold War. In the face of the new environment and its challenges, they have been required to demonstrate their continued relevance. NATO, for example, was forced to confront the fact that its territorial guarantee under Article V was largely outdated in the absence of a major threat. It became evident, as Cottey has shown (Chapter 3), that the Alliance needed to take on new roles such as peace-keeping and peace-enforcement. This it subsequently did in the Implementation Force for the Dayton Accords in Bosnia in 1996 and then for its successor, the Stabilisation Force. It also needed to become more flexible to enable its members to participate in only those operations where they perceive their interests to be at stake – hence the Combined

Joint Task Force agreement, which makes possible a WEU-led operation drawing on Alliance assets. In a similar way, the OSCE has developed its work in the spheres of preventive diplomacy and in refugee and national minority problems, not least in some of the continent's newly sovereign states. Adaptation for these organisations has been a painful but necessary task in order to address the needs of their members.

Last, the survival of the major west European institutions has provided a base from which to reach out to the countries of central and eastern Europe in an attempt to export stability. Western Europe represents the core of a model for many of the states to both its east and south, although it is not a universally applicable model because of their variable levels of development. Entry into the main institutions offers a variety of benefits to other states: namely, trade and economic assistance, security guarantees and the prospect of enhanced political legitimacy. The institutions have all made efforts to enlarge: the OSCE did so speedily, while organisations such as NATO, the EU and the WEU have been more cautious, proceeding through the forums of Partnership for Peace and the European Association Agreements. In Madrid, in July 1997, NATO invited three new members to accede to the Alliance; Poland, Hungary and the Czech Republic.

Simultaneously, this has neccessitated clarity from the institutions about what roles they can perform. As Spencer has noted, the western states have not resolved the extent to which their assistance to their neighbours will take the form of trade and investment or whether they wish to focus upon a narrower military agenda. Whereas NATO has a specifically military orientation, the EU enjoys a wider range of competencies which makes it a potentially more appropriate mechanism for dealing with the growing economic demands of aspirant states in the east, south-east and south of Europe. The WEU, on the other hand, has been forced to accept the fact that, because of insufficient strength and lack of political will among its members, it cannot proffer territorial guarantees to central and east European states and must rely on NATO to take the lead.

Within NATO and the EU, the pressure for enlargement has come into conflict with the desire among the current members for closer integration and cooperation. There has been a fear that the cohesion and capacity of the organisations to act effectively will be impeded by the accession of new states with their own security and other priorities. Balancing such considerations has been difficult and has exposed differences of view, such as the French and Italian disagreements with the US over the entry of Romania and Slovenia into NATO. However, emerging from the debate has been the underlying principle that the enlargement of western institutions must take place in order to ensure the stability of the continent. Successive waves of new adherents are now envisaged as the means of incorporating states according to their eligibility and to ease the impact on the institutions.

The proposed enlargement of western institutions – notably NATO first and then the EU and the WEU – has highlighted two facts about the rest of the continent. First, it demonstrates that no organisations have developed within other regions that have been able to satisfy the security needs of these states. There has been no shortage of new forums established since the end of the Cold War, for example, the Visegrad group for the central European states and various organisational structures in the Mediterranean. But all, with the possible exception of the Baltic Council, have focused on narrow sectoral issues rather than addressing the broad sweep of security relationships. As a result, organisations such as NATO have retained their attraction for states that have cause to fear for their long-term safety.

Second, the prospect of enlargement has exposed the cleavages that continue to divide the continent. For enlargement has raised the question of where new lines will be drawn and which states will be excluded from membership of the various organisations. Moscow has stated repeatedly its belief that new lines of tension have been drawn in Europe since the end of the Cold War. Its leaders have proved to be vocal in their opposition to the expansion of NATO, interpreting it as being aimed at Russia and accusing the West of exploiting their country's weakness. The signing in May 1997 of the 'Founding Act on Mutual Relations, Cooperation and Security Between NATO and the Russian Federation' has helped to facilitate NATO's first wave of expansion and will establish a special Joint Council between Russia and the Alliance. Yet few analysts doubt that a multitude of frictions lie ahead between the two sides.

Russia remains, as Park has described, an uneasy partner in European security. Absent now from the heart of the continent, it appears to sit brooding on the edges, uncertain about which way to face and how best to pursue its interests. As Hyde-Price has pointed out, many of the conflicts in post-Cold War Europe have taken place on the territory of the former Soviet Union, such as in Nagorno-Karabakh, Chechnya and Georgia. Efforts to constructively engage Russia in the developments of the continent have met with only limited success: for example, in the Baltic area where Russia has been drawn into forums to discuss shared problems. Despite its own tendency to persist in zero-sum views about security, Russia has called for greater emphasis to be placed on the OSCE. Western nations have proved to be unreceptive to this pressure because of their suspicion of an organisation in which Russia exercises an effective veto power.

The current security environment in Europe is too volatile to forecast future arrangements with any sense of confidence. An optimistic outlook might envisage the steady advance of a western security model, founded on the existing institutions, to central Europe and then to other parts of the continent. This might evolve over time into a pan-European security community, which would assume adherence to western norms of peaceful inter-state relations, conflict resolution, non-intervention and the civilian control over military forces. The export of such a western-inspired order would have to be accompanied by political and economic reforms in the target countries: namely, democratisation, the cultivation of market economies and the nurturing of civil societies.

Yet even this idealistic vision would depend on the willingness of organisations, such as NATO, the EU and the WEU, to foster a process in which successive waves of new members would be admitted. This would depend on two factors. First, the willingness of members to put at risk the cohesion of their organisations by granting access to states with a diversity of needs and interests. This would be pertinent to the EU from the outset of its enlargement programme, because of the complexity of its legal and trading structures. In comparison, NATO's first wave of enlargement is likely to be relatively straightforward whereas subsequent waves, perhaps including the Baltic states, are likely to generate greater controversy. Second, the organisations require internal adaptation to cope with the accession of new states. This may prove to be problematic in the case of the EU, for example, as the recent Treaty of Amsterdam deferred the issue of reweighting voting majorities because of an inability to reach agreement. If the organisations prove incapable of adapting, enlargement may be postponed indefinitely.

An even more pessimistic assessment might reject the possibility of a western security model being adopted across Europe. Post-Cold War events in former Yugoslavia, Albania and parts of Russia have demonstrated the potential for conflict and state disintegration which could derail progress towards building a more tranquil continent. As some of the preceding chapters have outlined, areas of Europe are balanced on a knife-edge of instability. Russia appears to be uncertain whether to constructively engage or implacably oppose the enlargement of western security structures, while North Africa remains a region of considerable turmoil with the threat of civil conflicts, terrorism and refugee movements. In the face of such instability, western Europe may seek not to throw open its doors to admit new states to its community but rather to pull up its drawbridge and defend the walls of its fortress.

Note

1. See the arch-exponent of this view in Mearsheimer, J. (1990) 'Back to the Future: Instability in Europe after the Cold War', *International Security*, 12(1) Summer: 5–56.

INDEX

184 *Rethinking Security in Post-Cold War Europe*